D1601407

THE UNITED KINGDOM CONFRONTS THE EUROPEAN CONVENTION ON HUMAN RIGHTS

The United Kingdom Confronts the European Convention on Human Rights

Donald W. Jackson

University Press of Florida
Gainesville/Tallahassee/Tampa/Boca Raton
Pensacola/Orlando/Miami/Jacksonville

02 01 00 99 98 97 6 5 4 3 2 1

Library of Congress Cataloging-in-Publication Data
Jackson, Donald Wilson, 1938–
   The United Kingdom confronts the European Convention on Human Rights /
Donald W. Jackson.
     p. cm.
   Includes bibliographical references and index.
   ISBN 0-8130-1487-5 (alk. paper)
   1. Human rights—Great Britain. 2. Human rights—Northern Ireland. 3. Human
rights—Europe. 4. Convention for the Protection of Human Rights and Fundamen-
tal Freedoms (1950). I. Title.
   KJC5132.J32   1997   96-21379
   342.41'085—dc20
   [344.10285]

The University Press of Florida is the scholarly publishing agency for the State
University System of Florida, comprised of Florida A & M University, Florida
Atlantic University, Florida International University, Florida State University,
University of Central Florida, University of Florida, University of North Florida,
University of South Florida, and University of West Florida.

University Press of Florida
15 Northwest 15th Street
Gainesville, FL 32611

To EWJ in his eighty-ninth year

Contents

List of Tables   viii

Preface   ix

1. Studying Human Rights Comparatively   1

2. The European Convention on Human Rights and Its Institutions   11

3. Prevention of Terrorism and the Convention   31

4. Prisoners' Rights and the Convention   64

5. Nationality and the Convention: "Civis Britannicus Sum!"   82

6. Freedom of Expression and the Convention   106

7. The Convention in United Kingdom Courts   126

8. A Charter of Rights for the United Kingdom?   153

Appendix: Selected Provisions from the Convention for the Protection of Human Rights and Fundamental Freedoms   174

Notes   181

References   183

Index   201

TABLES

2.1. Cases brought against state defendants   17

2.2. Claims decided and claims with violations   19

2.3. Claims brought under articles that produced dissents   21

2.4. Judges dissenting in ten or more cases   23

2.5. Participants' votes: cases with at least one dissent   24

7.1. References to the European Convention in English cases   127

8.1. United Kingdom's violations of the European Convention on Human Rights through February 1996   155

PREFACE

This is a study of legal conflicts and transitions. The conflicts have arisen between the United Kingdom (and its parliamentary and common law traditions), on the one hand, and the European Court of Human Rights (and the European Convention on Human Rights and Fundamental Freedoms, which the European Court has interpreted and applied since its beginning in 1959), on the other. The transitions have been within the policies, the common law, the courts, and the ministries of state of the United Kingdom, as they have sought to adapt to the reality of having been found forty-one times (from February 1975 through June 1996) to have violated the European Convention on Human Rights.

For Americans the different ways one can refer to the United Kingdom can be confusing and sometimes misleading. The United Kingdom includes England, Wales, Scotland, and Northern Ireland, but Great Britain includes England, Wales, and Scotland, while excluding Northern Ireland. English common law, which applies per se to England and Wales, does not include Scotland, which has a separate legal system in which Scots law is applied. Most of the conflicts in this book involve the application of English law by English courts, but when issues concerning Northern Ireland are involved, the law of the United Kingdom, as applied to the six counties of Ulster that are part of Northern Ireland (three counties of Ulster are part of the Republic of Ireland), is at stake. The devolution of political power from London to Belfast has varied with the intensity of the conflict between Republicans and Loyalists in Northern Ireland. It is reasonable to assume for purposes of this book that when the European Court of Human Rights finds that the United Kingdom has violated the convention, it will be decisions taken in London, either in Parliament or the ministries of state, that have caused the violation. When that is not the case, the context of the issues should make clear what other authorities are involved. Northern Ireland will be the most obvious exception, but there have also been cases from the Isle of Man and Guernsey, both dependencies of the British crown, that have reached the European Court of Human Rights.

I have tried to make this book accessible to American readers with little previous exposure to the law or politics of the United Kingdom. That sometimes results in my providing explanations or definitions that will be obvious to readers in the United Kingdom. I apologize in advance to such readers, yet I hope that they will find the perspective and substance of the book worthwhile, once the irritation of the obvious is endured.

My overarching purpose is to show how human rights principles, as contained in the European Convention on Human Rights, have brought some measure of accountability to those who exercise power and discretion in the United Kingdom. While assessing the consequences of such accountability is no easy matter, this book broadly concludes that practice of judicial review by the European Court has mostly produced desirable outcomes. Unaccountable power and unreviewable discretion clearly are the archvillains of the book, and they often have had secrecy and excessive deference to authority as their trusted servants in the cases we will study.

Chapters 2 through 6 of this book were presented at various sessions of the Research Committee on Comparative Judicial Studies of the International Political Science Association, including the XVth World Congress of the IPSA in Buenos Aires, 1991; the interim meeting at the Forli Study Center of the University of Bologna, 1992; the interim meeting at St. John's College, Santa Fe, New Mexico, 1993; and the XVIth World Congress of the IPSA in Berlin, 1994. I am indebted to C. Neal Tate of the University of North Texas and to Martin Edelman of the State University of New York at Albany, the former and present convener of the Research Committee, for the exceptional opportunities they have provided for intellectual exchange and support.

Much of the research for this book was done on leave from my university while I lived on Dorset Square in London in the spring of 1994. I am grateful to Texas Christian University for my research leave. My research was also generously supported by funds from the endowment of the Herman Brown Chair of Political Science at Texas Christian University, the position I have held since 1981. I am also thankful to Kevin Boyle and Françoise Hampson of the Human Rights Centre at the University of Essex for their encouragement and intellectual guidance. Professor Hampson gave me the benefit of an exceptionally careful and constructive review of my manuscript. In all, my colleagues in the Political Science Department of Texas Christian University have provided an environment that made this book feasible.

A version of chapter 2 was previously published in the *1993 Windsor Yearbook of Access to Justice*, 13: 217–36, and a shortened version of chapter 3 was published in the *Journal of Terrorism and Political Violence* 6, No. 4: 507–35 (Winter 1994). I am grateful to the editors of those journals for their interest and support.

Finally, the encouragement, constancy, and compassion of my wife and supporter, Joanne Jackson, have kept me going when otherwise I might have thrown in the towel.

1

Studying Human Rights Comparatively

This book will examine in depth certain violations by the United Kingdom of The European Convention for the Protection of Human Rights and Fundamental Freedoms (1950) (hereafter referred to as the ECHR). Unlike the Universal Declaration of Human Rights (1948), the ECHR contains only civil and political rights.[1] It provides ultimately for judicially enforceable human rights obligations through an international treaty, which, at the end of 1995, was adhered to by thirty-one European countries that have "ratified the Convention and fully accepted its control mechanism" (Drzemczewski 1995, 247). The ECHR first went into effect in 1953, but the first judges of the European Court of Human Rights were not appointed until 1959. Fifteen European countries, including the United Kingdom, were then obligated under the ECHR. During the first thirty years (1959–89) of the European Court of Human Rights, the United Kingdom was found to be in violation of the ECHR twenty-three times; measured both by the number of complaints before the Court and by the violations found, it was the most frequent offender. The countries nearest the United Kingdom during the first thirty years were Belgium and Italy, with fourteen and thirteen violations respectively. In the past six years the Court has found eighteen more violations by the United Kingdom. Since 1989, Italy also has enhanced its frequent offender status before the European Court, chiefly through a large number of violations of Article 6.1 involving excessive delay in its judicial system.

From the forty-one violations of the ECHR by the United Kingdom, I have selected four human rights topics covered by decisions of the European Court of Human Rights. The four topics were chosen both because of their policy significance and because the volume of decisions on each topic by the European Court (or the volume of related decisions by U.K. courts) has been sufficient to support an analysis of the development of human rights policy within each topic. The four topics, broadly described, are the prevention of terrorism, the rights of prisoners in penal institutions, immigration and nationality, and freedom of expression. Not surprisingly, the prevention of terrorism has chiefly involved the continuing conflict over Northern Ireland. The rights of prison inmates have implicated the rights of inmates to correspond with their attorneys and to initiate complaints and litigation about their treat-

2 The United Kingdom Confronts the European Convention on Human Rights

ment while in custody. Immigration and nationality issues have involved immigrants to the United Kingdom or persons seeking asylum in the United Kingdom, most often from the West Indies, Africa, or Asia (mainly from the Indian subcontinent). Freedom of expression has primarily concerned press freedom, although radio and television media have also been included. The most notable issues have been the conflict between freedom of the press and the desire to protect the integrity of the judicial process and freedom of the press versus national security or confidentiality interests involving the British intelligence services.

In my view, one of the most interesting aspects of the broad subject of human rights covered in this book involves the tension between the United Kingdom—a liberal state that has long prided itself on the freedoms of its subjects—and an international institution, the newly fledged European Court of Human Rights, sitting at Strasbourg, which has repeatedly found it necessary to hold the United Kingdom in violation of the ECHR. For those whose familiarity with the United Kingdom comes chiefly through history or literature courses—sometimes supplemented by tourism—it may come as a surprise that the United Kingdom has proved to be such a frequent violator of the ECHR. After all, our commonplace knowledge leads us to cite the United Kingdom as the land that gave us Magna Carta, and many Americans would place the United Kingdom at or near the top of any list of freedom-loving countries. This book certainly will not suggest that such traditional generalizations are entirely wrong, but, rather, that they are glib and that they provide quite an incomplete portrait of human rights under English law and practice.

A key insight into the limitations of such generalizations might come through our speculation about what the condition of human rights might be in the United States *without* the Bill of Rights and the post–Civil War amendments to the Constitution of the United States or *without* the federal courts to enforce them. Through their exercise of the power of judicial review, American courts, especially federal courts, can declare the actions of governmental agencies and officials to be inconsistent with the Constitution of the United States and therefore void. We can readily imagine that with no rights document or with no power of judicial review, we would have to rely on our commonly held traditions and ultimately on the self-restraint of our politicians and bureaucrats for the security of our human rights. That would be a frightening prospect indeed, even given our own judicial failures and shortcomings in enforcing human rights. However, that speculative state of affairs is largely the reality of the United Kingdom. It is a country *without* an authoritative domestic rights document and *without* courts that exercise the power of constitutional judicial review, at least as that power is understood in the United

States. As practiced in the United Kingdom, judicial review represents merely the power of U.K. courts to hold that administrative agencies or officers have exceeded or grossly misused the power delegated to them by acts of Parliament (Sunkin 1992).

Perhaps it is more reasonable to rely on the self-restraint of British politicians and bureaucrats than on our own, but that might well seem dubious, even to Americans who sometimes see the United Kingdom through Anglophile lenses, and the very idea would certainly be risible in some circles in the United Kingdom. Instead, the impulse among many thoughtful observers in Britain is to seek a written constitution, or, at the least, a bill of rights. The Charter 88 movement was created in Britain to that end. Writing in 1992, Lord Scarman, one of Britain's "Law Lords" (a member of the House of Lords who sits as a member of a committee of that House, which serves as the highest appellate court in Britain), quoted from the Charter 88 manifesto the following sentence: "No democracy can be considered safe whose freedoms are not encoded in a basic constitution." To this he affirmed that "I hold that view strongly." He then specified "four essential safeguards" that a written constitution ought to provide: the protection of the human rights and fundamental freedoms of everyone within the jurisdiction, the setting of legal limits upon the legislative and executive power of the Crown and Parliament, the protection of regional and local government by the adoption of the principle of subsidiarity, and the establishment of an independent judiciary having the duty and power of protecting the constitution (Scarman 1992, 14–15).

Ronald Dworkin, one of the world's leading contemporary legal philosophers, also favors a bill of rights. He began the first chapter of his pamphlet *A Bill of Rights for Britain* with the heading: "Liberty Is Ill in Britain," and his first paragraph gives this overview (Dworkin 1990, 1):

> GREAT BRITAIN was once a fortress for freedom. It claimed the great philosophers of liberty—Milton and Locke and Paine and Mill. Its legal tradition is irradiated with liberal ideas: that people accused of crime are presumed to be innocent, that no one owns another's conscience, that a man's home is his castle. But now Britain offers less formal legal protection to central freedoms than most of its neighbors in Europe. I do not mean that it has become a police state, of course. Citizens are free openly to criticise the government, and the government does not kidnap or torture or kill its opponents. But liberty is nevertheless under threat by a notable decline in the *culture* of liberty—the community's shared sense that individual privacy and dignity and freedom of speech and conscience are crucially important and that they are worth considerable sacrifices in official convenience or public expense to protect.

The chapters that follow, especially 3–6, will illustrate the tension between "human rights and fundamental freedoms" and the "legislative and executive power of the Crown and Parliament in the United Kingdom." We will see that but for the ECHR—and the institutions that enforce it—British officialdom might be largely unconstrained and unaccountable in many important matters and ways. To the extent that accountability does exist, it is mostly manifested through parliamentary oversight and through a relatively free British press. But in order to serve that purpose both Parliament and the free press require access to accurate and up-to-date information, and such information is often within the exclusive control of officialdom. These chapters will also illustrate that secrecy often is a core value of British officialdom. Indeed, it seems that secrecy in Britain is the most reliable guardian of unaccountable power, but a sometimes complaisant and deferential judiciary helps as well.

Another line of argument about the low level of accountability of officialdom in the United Kingdom can be based on an analysis of the concentration of governmental power within the past 100 years in the portfolios of a few top political leaders and their associated civil servants. In the early years of the nineteenth century—before the Reform Act of 1832—Parliament was dominated by the king and his ministers and the aristocracy. For a brief period between the major reform acts of 1832 and 1867, Parliament had perhaps its golden years with respect to the ability of debates in the House of Commons to influence opinions and outcomes. The power of the king and the aristocrats had been reduced by the enfranchisement of the wealthiest and most influential members of the new industrially based middle class during those years, but Britain was clearly still governed by an elite. After the second Reform Act in 1867, but especially following the enactment of the 1884 Representation of People Act, which extended the franchise sufficiently that Britain could for the first time reasonably be viewed as a popular democracy, modern political parties began to replace the loose alliances and competing factions of aristocrats, wealthy gentlemen, and captains of industry that had previously contended for power in Parliament. Modern political parties were created by the necessity of mobilizing the emergent popular vote. The organizational structures and control mechanisms that evolved within modern parties served chiefly to impose party discipline on those who sought election to Parliament under each party's mantle (Norton 1991, 288–90). And elections conducted amongst mass publics brought increasing attention to the party leader (and therefore the prospective prime minister) as the popular symbol of the party. The chosen party leader and those brought to office (or to the shadow cabinet) through the leader's patronage began to coalesce power and eventually to reduce the individual backbencher in Parliament to a participant in ritual debates, whose outcomes are preordained because the votes of ordinary members are controlled through party discipline as administered by the party whips. To be sure, there still are "free" votes on limited but significant issues—usually ones involving public morality, such as abortion or the death penalty. But whether the reality of parliamentary democracy has ever actually approximated its place in public mythology is a question that I will not seek to answer here. Nonetheless, the power of the public myth is well represented in the words of Enoch Powell (1978, 30), himself a prominent parliamentarian: "The British are a parliamentary nation: internally and externally they are conditioned and defined by that institution and that historical experience. If our values are in danger, and if our freedom and our independence are in danger, it is because Parliament is endangered, and endangered in the only way an institution can be—by inner loss of conviction." A typical contemporary critique of parliamentary government is contained in the observation that "To put it baldly: the Government governs; Parliament is the forum where the exercise of government is publicly displayed and is open to scrutiny and criticism. And the Commons does not control the executive—not in any real sense: rather the executive control the Commons through the exercise of their party majority power" (Ryle 1981, 13).

In simple words: in order to get ahead in British party politics long ago it became necessary to be a good party soldier. Loyalty (and, we trust, sometimes competence as well) was rewarded with advancement. Outright rebellion, or even marching to the beat of one's own drummer, leads—at best—to a permanent seat on the back benches and usually to isolation and political insignificance. Of course, the rebellion of groups or factions is quite another matter, for if enough members choose to rebel on the same issue at the same time, the safety of numbers and the possibility of denying a majority in the House of Commons to the government of the day makes such rebellions possible. But the large point is that usually only the holders of high office, and especially the top leaders of the majority party, possess real power in Parliament. In Bagehot's terms (1867, 61 *et seq.*) the ordinary member of Parliament eventually became a part of the "dignified" aspect of British government along with the queen and the House of Lords. Bagehot's distinction between the "dignified" and the "efficient" parts of the English government was an early example of *realpolitik*. In his pioneering book, *The English Constitution*, he went behind the façade of British politics to describe who actually held and exercised power.

Of course there are exceptions when even an individual member of the Commons may be effective. Sometimes diligent casework on behalf of a constituent may make a difference, and there have been individual parliamentarians, like Enoch Powell, who have been noted for the power of their rhetoric in the House of Commons or for their efficacy in putting difficult questions to the government. Usually, however, real power rests with the leaders of the party.

The top leaders of the majority party in the House of Commons hold high government office. As a minister of state, a high official has direct access to the top level of the British Civil Service—to the senior civil servants who have been assigned to his or her particular ministry. While politicians come and go, the senior civil servants in a ministry are professionals who have continuity—continuing access to the files and to the history and traditions of the ministry. They are the ones who can answer the fundamental questions likely to be put by a new minister confronting a policy decision for the first time: What have *we* done on this before? What are *our* options? The civil servants are the stewards of information and also of secrecy. The veil of secrecy that they drape is such that the policy files of a preceding government are closed to its successors. Only the senior members of the permanent civil service have the continuity for the long view of policy.

For the purposes of this book the home secretary is the best example of a cabinet-level minister with broad discretionary powers. There is no equivalent position in the American government. The home secretary is responsible for all aspects of domestic policy and administration that have not been delegated to a particular ministry. For example, industry, the environment, agriculture, social security, health, education, employment, and transport all currently have specific ministries and a cabinet officer assigned to each of them. The Home Office is a residual ministry for domestic policy in terms of its responsibility, but most important for us is the fact that the Home Office oversees law enforcement in general, the correctional system, and immigration: three of the four policy arenas covered by this book. We should also note that since the United Kingdom is a unitary system, quite unlike the American or Canadian federal systems, in principle all power is held by the central government in London. While Parliament may devolve certain responsibilities to local or regional governments, it may also reclaim those responsibilities at its pleasure. So the home secretary is broadly responsible, for example, for policing throughout England and Wales, although he shares responsibility with the local police authorities and chief constables in the force areas outside London. In London the home secretary shares responsibility for policing with the commissioner of the metropolitan police.

Parliament has conveyed to the home secretary, and to those who exercise power in his name, the discretion to make numerous decisions that routinely affect the liberties of British subjects. Senior civil servants advise the home secretary on the uses of his discretion, but his decisions, and the exercise of his discretion, often are beyond review by U.K. courts. Readers of this book no doubt will be struck at the end by the sources, diverse subjects, and breadth of the home secretary's discretion. His discretion includes, for example, the "royal prerogative" as an independent source of power in connection with the maintenance of the "Queen's peace within the realm" (*R. v. Home Secretary, ex parte Northumbria Police Authority,* Court of Appeal, 1987, 563). And this power is in addition to the statutory powers delegated to the home secretary by Parliament. Judicial review (in the British sense) may allow an examination of whether the home secretary has acted *ultra vires,* that is, without sufficient authority to act on a specific subject having been delegated by Parliament, but except for the most extreme cases, this form of judicial review ordinarily cannot be used to determine whether official discretion was appropriately exercised. For those held in custody the writ of habeas corpus is the traditional means through which one can contest the legality of one's detention, but we will see in the chapters that follow that British courts have been quite reluctant to second-guess the home secretary's uses of discretion even when a writ of habeas corpus is sought. However, as we also shall see in the following chapters, the European Court has been much more willing to apply the ECHR.

How can we evaluate the United Kingdom's human rights record? Is it appropriate to measure the United Kingdom by contrasting it with an ideal pattern of popular democracy, as the Charter 88 proponents seem to suggest? And are there special dangers for an American scholar in evaluating the human rights performance of the United Kingdom? There certainly are enough difficulties in understanding the conflicting powers, factions, and interests engaged in human rights controversies within the United States to daunt most efforts to study human rights comparatively. And it may be inappropriate simply to judge one country by the standards of another. Moreover, Americans should be careful to avoid both judgmentalism and hypocrisy, for the United States itself has had little to brag about during most of its history with respect to human rights. Our long history of officially condoned racial segregation is merely the most obvious example. As the present century comes to an end, we still need reminding that our Supreme Court's close attention to human rights dates at the earliest from about 1931 (when the Supreme Court first applied the "prior restraint" rule in the case of *Near v. Minnesota*), or from 1932 (when the case of *Powell v. Alabama* represented the first step toward federal enforcement of the right to counsel in state criminal proceedings), or from 1938 (when Mr. Justice Stone suggested—in a now famous footnote in the case of *U.S. v. Carolene Products Co.*—the Supreme Court's willingness to become more vigilant over noneconomic personal rights and liberties), or from 1954 (when *Brown v. Board of Education* launched the Court's efforts to end official segregation) or even from 1961 (when in *Mapp v. Ohio* the Supreme

Court opened what was to become the civil liberties decade of the 1960s). Whatever the beginning, for most of our history the Supreme Court has *not* been an especially vigilant guardian of freedom or democracy. For these and other reasons Americans can claim no consistently high moral ground regarding human rights. We can and do use the promises of the U.S. Bill of Rights as the standard for assessing the conduct of American public officials and the content of American public policy. But those standards may be quite inappropriate for others. So if indeed we ought not rely entirely on our own traditions and standards for the assessment of other countries, what other standards for comparison might we use?

Some contemporary analysts argue for the transcendence of human rights over national sovereignty, but others see this as a form of cultural imperialism—if not the imperialism of a single nation, the imperialism of Western political and religious values over other traditions (see Forsythe 1991, ch. 1). In Western political and philosophical discourse, arguments over the source and extent of fundamental human rights are ancient (Renteln 1990, 17), and the conventional wisdom today is they can be resolved only by persuasion, or by force, there being no obvious objective answers. But there is an advantage offered by the perspective of this book. The United Kingdom has been an adherent to the ECHR from its beginning—and for the entirety of the period of the European Court's decisions (since the beginning of the Court in 1959). Since the United Kingdom has agreed to be bound by the ECHR and by the decisions of the European Court, there should be no problem of cultural imperialism in assessing the U.K. by the standards of the ECHR, especially since the U.K. has no authoritative rights document of its own. Of course, others may disagree. Renteln (1990, 10) argues that ratification as a basis for authoritative human rights will not suffice, since those who ratify instruments such as the Universal Declaration of Human Rights or the ECHR may not be representative of a state's population. That, however, is a ubiquitous problem, even of the best representative democracies.

We may also be able to undergird the standards of the ECHR by some universal principles. In his recent book, *The Internationalization of Human Rights,* David Forsythe proposed that we develop a list of such universals by examining contemporary state practices. According to this position, universal, nonderogable rights (those that cannot be suspended even in dire circumstances) such as those in the following list of human rights violations can be found empirically in the virtually universal agreement of nation-states: piracy; slavery, the slave trade, and slavelike practices; genocide; torture; aerial hijacking; and major war crimes (grave breaches of the law of war) (Forsythe 1991, 8). To this list he would also add summary execution and the practices of racism. Nonderogable values "trump" all other legal arguments. A universal prohibition against torture would be one example. A derogable right is one that can be suspended, by following established procedures, during an emergency. In the United States the suspension of the writ of habeas corpus is one example. The right of derogation under Art. 15 of the ECHR was invoked by the United Kingdom in its campaign against terrorism in Northern Ireland, as we shall see in chapter 3.

We should note that of the four human rights topics we will consider in this book, two of them arguably have involved violations of such universals by the United Kingdom. In chapter 3 we will see that the United Kingdom was alleged to have engaged in torture in its interrogation of suspected IRA terrorists and was found to have done so by the European Commission on Human Rights, and in chapter 5 we will see that the immigration policies of the United Kingdom almost certainly have been tainted by racism.

So we have both the ECHR and some possible universal principles to guide our evaluation. However, legal positivists make an important point when arguing that the only demands that truly can be claimed as rights are those that are ultimately enforceable. The ECHR does, at the least, offer the prospect of enforceability. As we shall see in chapter 3, the first U.K. case before the Court— and the U.K.'s first violation—was a prisoners' rights case, *Golder v. United Kingdom* in 1975, so our time span for analysis of enforceable human rights in this book is 1975 through February 1996.

A special problem: Had the ECHR itself been directly binding on all U.K. institutions and officials since its ratification in 1950, this book probably would not have been written. But the United Kingdom has not chosen to adopt the ECHR as part of its domestic law. The United Kingdom takes the position that treaties and domestic law are distinct legal entities, and that treaties do not become directly binding on the domestic legal order unless Parliament passes enabling legislation that specifically makes it so (Bernhardt 1993). The consequence of that position is that usually even a clear violation of the ECHR has no remedy in British courts. There have been a few instances in which British courts have found support for rights in the common law, but usually the only resort has been an application to the European Commission on Human Rights, and, in due course, to the European Court of Human Rights. Decisions of the European Commission and of the European Court of Human Rights are binding on the United Kingdom as international treaty obligations, so the United Kingdom ultimately can be required to conform its policies to the requirements of the ECHR—and to pay damages to an aggrieved applicant—even though no cause of action was available to the applicant under U.K. domestic law. Thus the United Kingdom has often been embarrassed by human rights violations that its own courts could do little or nothing to resolve.

Once we have examined the selected human rights issues and European

Court decisions in chapters 3–6, in chapter 7 we will review the decisions of U.K. domestic courts that have cited the ECHR since its beginning. Our purpose will be to illustrate the evolution of the common law as it adapts to the reality of the ECHR and the prospects for its enforcement by the European Court of Human Rights in Strasbourg. The first English citation[2] was in 1974. Since then, 169 case references by U.K. courts were found and reviewed in preparing chapter 7, but only about sixty-two of those decisions contained some sort of relatively substantial discussion of the ECHR or its applicability in the United Kingdom. The ECHR article most often cited was Art. 10 on freedom of expression (sixteen citations), followed by Art. 8 on privacy rights (twelve citations) and Art. 6 on due process (eleven citations).[3]

In the final chapter we will consider the questions of whether the ECHR ought to be adopted as part of British domestic law and whether the United Kingdom ought to adopt its own domestic bill of rights. There has been a lively debate on these two interrelated questions in Britain, and we will present an overview of the several sides of the debate. My own perspective on these questions is guided by Kenneth Davis's key suggestion in the preface to the 1971 edition of his important book, *Discretionary Justice.* After proposing an imaginary scale—with precise rules at one end and unfettered discretion at the other—Davis argues that:

> I believe that officers and judges do reasonably well at the rules end of the scale, because rules make for evenhandedness, because creation of rules usually is relatively unemotional, and because decision-makers seldom err in the direction of excessive rigidity when individualization is needed. And probably injustice is almost as infrequent toward the middle of the scale, where principles or other guides keep discretion limited or controlled. *I think the greatest and most frequent injustice occurs at the discretion end of the scale, where rules and principles provide little or no guidance, where emotions of deciding officers may affect what they do, where political or other favoritism may influence decisions, and where the imperfections of human nature are often reflected in the choices.* (1971, v; emphasis added)

The book will reveal that largely unfettered and often unreviewable discretion is characteristic of the United Kingdom's system of government. The powers exercised by, or in the name of, the home secretary offer the best examples. Finding the means to make such discretion reviewable and to hold it accountable, whether under a bill of rights written for the United Kingdom or through the extant ECHR, is entirely consistent with Davis's insight.

The next chapter will present some basic but necessary background information on the ECHR and its related institutions and officials.

2

The European Convention on Human Rights and Its Institutions

The purpose of this chapter is to provide a brief introduction to the ECHR and the institutions that were created to implement it. A congress that was held at The Hague in May 1948 (for which Winston Churchill served as the honorary president) led to the creation of the Council of Europe, and the ECHR was the progeny of the Council (Teitgen 1993). Founded in 1949 to achieve greater unity among its members, particularly by "safeguarding and realizing the ideals and principles which are their common heritage," the Council of Europe is much more inclusive (twenty-three members at the end of 1989; thirty-nine members as of February 26, 1996, with applications pending for Belarus, Bosnia-Herzegovina, and Croatia) than the European Union (at present with fifteen members). To be a member of the Council, a member-state must, "accept the principles of the rule of law and the enjoyment by all persons within [its] jurisdiction of human rights and fundamental freedoms" (Hunter 1993; Mahoney and Prebensen 1993, 621–22). Those who work with and study European Union institutions, sometimes seem to ignore the Council of Europe and the institutions it has spawned. Yet it is important to know that in November 1950 the Council of Europe proposed for ratification by its member-states The European Convention for the Protection of Human Rights and Fundamental Freedoms.

The ECHR, which has been amended or supplemented by nine protocols (with Protocols 10 and 11 pending ratification as of this writing), first went into effect in September 1953. Broadly speaking, the ECHR provides international protection for a variety of civil and political rights much like those contained in the U.S. Bill of Rights (1791) or the Canadian Charter of Rights and Freedoms (1982). The work of the European Court of Human Rights has recently begun to draw more attention in North America, as an increasingly important body of precedents has accumulated, but research on the court so far has been published mostly in Europe and much of that is formal doctrinal analysis. European legal scholarship on the ECHR, the Commission, and the Court is indeed vast. Perhaps most notable for both perspective and background are the official publications of the Council of Europe and the European Court of Human Rights itself, especially the annual *Yearbook of the European Convention on Human Rights*. Two articles by Marc-André Eissen (1986; 1989), longtime registrar of the Court, are especially helpful, given the special vantage of the author. Overall, the most important recent contribution to the literature on the Court is the book edited by Macdonald, Matscher, and Petzold (1993). Macdonald and Matscher are current judges of the Court, while Petzold is the deputy registrar.

Member-states are required by international law to honor the decisions of the European Court of Human Rights and eventually to implement those decisions under domestic law and practice.

The ECHR called for the creation of both the European Commission of Human Rights (hereafter the Commission) and the European Court of Human Rights (hereafter the Court), both of which sit in Strasbourg. The first election of commissioners took place in 1954, and the first judges were elected in 1959. The Commission and the Court both are composed of a number of members equal to the number of ratifying state members. Commissioners are elected by a majority of the committee of ministers of the Council of Europe from a list prepared by the bureau of the parliamentary assembly. Each group of representatives of a state member in the parliamentary assembly is entitled to put forward three names for a position on the Commission, two of whom shall be of its nationals (Art. 21),[1] but in practice only the state for which a position is vacant prepares a list of three candidates in order of preference. Commissioners are elected for six years and may be reelected.

Formally, judges of the Court are elected by a majority of the parliamentary assembly of the Council of Europe from a list of persons nominated by members of the Council, each state member again being entitled to nominate three candidates, at least two of whom shall be its nationals (Art. 39). The now customary practice, however, is that only the state member for which a judge is being elected submits nominations.[2] Moreover, the actual practice is that the council of ministers recommends the election of a candidate, and that recommendation is routinely followed by the parliamentary assembly. While nominees and judges usually have been nationals of the nominating state, that is not strictly necessary. For example, in the first election of judges, Ireland included a German law professor amongst its three nominees, and Judge Ronald St. John Macdonald, a Canadian national, was nominated by Liechtenstein and elected to the Court in 1980. No two judges may simultaneously be nationals of the same state (Art. 38). The only criteria for selection are that candidates must be of "high moral character" and either possess the qualifications for high judicial office or be a "jurisconsult" (that is, a person learned in public international law) of recognized competence (Art. 39.3). These criteria are the same as those for the International Court of Justice (Jacobs 1975). Since the beginning, judges of the Court have served only part-time and the Court's sessions are not continuous throughout the year. Given the ever-increasing pressure of the caseload, the judges spent an average of 140 working days in 1991, as contrasted with sixty-three working days in 1985 (Meyer-Ladewig 1993).

After initial staggered terms of three, six, and nine years, judges are now ordinarily elected for a term of nine years, and there is no limit placed on their reelection. For example, René Cassin of France, father of the Universal Declaration of Human Rights and Nobel Peace Prize Laureate, served 21 years from his election in 1959 until his death at age 89 in 1980. However, during his tenure on the Court he actively participated in only a few cases. It was not until the late 1970s that the Court's docket began to grow substantially, hence judges serving in the early years participated in few cases. The president of the Court as of this writing, Judge Ryssdal of Norway, was first elected to the Court in 1972.

Basic Procedures

A brief summary of the procedures under which cases come before the Commission and the Court should be helpful in understanding the work of these institutions. Any state party to the ECHR may submit to the Commission an allegation of a breach by another member. State members can also recognize the competence of the Commission to receive complaints from individuals, groups, or nongovernmental entities (Art. 25), and all contracting state members at the end of 1989 had done so. The opportunity for individual complaints has had the effect of greatly expanding access to the Commission and the Court. Thus, complaints from private parties are now the most common means for alleged violations to come before the Commission. Before complaints are examined on their merits, they are reviewed as to their admissibility under the ECHR, and through 1989 about 90 percent of the complaints were deemed inadmissible (most commonly under Art. 26, which provides that the Commission, and hence the Court, may consider cases only when domestic remedies have been exhausted). The Commission is also prohibited from receiving anonymous complaints, those that are "manifestly ill founded," or those that represent an "abuse of the right to petition" (Art. 27). The Commission is charged to study the allegations, and to pursue a friendly settlement if possible. Failing that, the Commission reports to the committee of ministers, informing the committee whether it has found a breach of the ECHR, and, if so, recommending action. Its recommendations may include referral of the complaint to the Court for decision.

Within three months of the Commission's report, a state party or the Commission may take a case to the Court. The jurisdiction of the Court extends only to cases that are thus referred to it by the Commission or by a state member (Art. 48). If a case is not referred to the Court, the committee of ministers is empowered to decide whether there has been a breach of the ECHR (Art. 32).

While the Court holds public sessions in which evidence, including original materials, may be received and witnesses as to facts may be heard, the Court uses its powers in this area only in exceptional circumstances. Ordinarily the Court relies on the fact-finding of the Commission; however, in the case of *Brozicek v. Italy* (1989) the Court took additional evidence from a witness and consulted a handwriting expert at the request of the Italian government (Rogge 1993, 677). Even though cases must be referred to the Court as prescribed in Art. 48, the actual complainants may now be represented before the Commission and Court through counsel. The president of the Court sits ex officio, but the other members of a panel are drawn by lot. Panels (called chambers) formerly were composed of seven but now have nine members. The judge elected with respect to the state that is the defendant before the Court is assigned as a member of the panel. A chamber may relinquish jurisdiction in favor of a plenary session of the Court in especially important cases. In practice, plenary sessions are convened in about one-third of the cases.

The registrar and his assistants attend both the public and in camera sessions of the Court. They prepare a list of questions to be considered by the Court during in camera deliberations. They also record a confidential summary of those sessions. During the in camera deliberations they may also take the floor to refresh members as to established Court precedents. Once tentative decisions are made, a drafting committee consisting of members of the provisional majority is formed. The registrar and his assistants, after meeting with the provisional majority, prepare the first draft opinion. Given the current volume of the cases, the registrar assigns each case from the beginning either to himself or to a member of his staff (as of my interviews conducted in August 1990 there were twelve attorneys on the staff of the registry). The assigned staff member prepares the first draft of the judgment following the deliberations of the Court. The draft is submitted to the drafting committee after it has been reviewed by the registrar himself. The writing of the judgment then proceeds through a process of revisions, and the drafting committee may meet a second time, or occasionally even a third time. The registrar attends each of these sessions.

Apparently there is ample opportunity for the registry's legal staff to distill the deliberations of the Court and to produce an intelligible draft. It seems that the registrar and his assistants have a much more important role in decisions than would be the case for any nonmember staff in U.S. federal appellate courts. Indeed, there is *no* nonmember position in a U.S. federal appellate court that is comparable to the position of the registrar of the European Court. For example, long-established practice in the Supreme Court of the United States is that nonmembers are not allowed in the Supreme Court's conference room during deliberations, and while law clerks may prepare drafts for their justice after he or she has been assigned the opinion at the Supreme Court's conference, there is no staff member who meets with a working majority of the Supreme Court to formulate an opinion. Moreover, the integral role of the registrar of the Court is no doubt undergirded by the long tenure (twenty-six years as of 1994) of the registrar. In any given session of the Court, he is likely to be the most knowledgeable person with respect to its precedents.

Of course, none of this is to suggest that the members of the Court don't make up their own minds on the issues before them. The frequency of dissents on the Court, as we shall see below, is evidence of the independence of its members.

The Commission began functioning in 1955. The Court's first judges were elected for the fifteen original member-states (Austria, Belgium, Denmark, the Federal Republic of Germany, France, Greece, Iceland, Ireland, Italy, Luxembourg, the Netherlands, Norway, Sweden, Turkey, and the United Kingdom) on January 21, 1959, but the first judgment on the merits of a case was not delivered until July 1, 1961.

Since the Commission's beginning in 1955, its work has become quite substantial, certainly in terms of case volume. By 1982, the Commission had received over 9,000 complaints and found about 200 of them to be admissible. Most of the refusals came under Art. 26 or 27, that is, the failure to exhaust domestic remedies or those that were deemed to represent an "abuse of the right to petition." Also by 1982, about thirty cases had been brought before the Court. But by 1987, the Court had decided more than 100 individual cases. By October 1992, 379 cases had been referred to the Court since its beginning, and sixty-two were still pending. Thus, while it took the Court from 1961 (the year of the first decision on the merits) through the end of 1987 to make a few more than 100 decisions on the merits, the next 200 decisions on the merits took about five more years.

THE PROBLEM OF DELAY AND ACCESS TO JUSTICE

At the beginning of October 1992, nearly 2,500 cases were pending before the Commission, more than 1,500 of which had not yet been reached by the Commission. The current caseload is such that it is common for more than five years to pass between the filing of a complaint with the Commission and the final judgment of the Court, and durations of six or seven years are usual. Most observers have found such delay in access to justice to be quite intolerable (Lalumière 1993), and it is a special irony that the Court has itself so often found violations by state members involving instances of excessive and unreasonable delay in their administration of justice, when its own process has become painfully slow. Such delays before the Commission and the Court clearly have become a significant obstacle to justice, especially given the requirement that domestic remedies must be exhausted before a complaint may be entertained by the Commission.

The responses to the inadequacies of the present system are to be found in Protocol No. 11 to the ECHR, which was signed by twenty-seven of the state members to the ECHR in May 1994. Upon ratification by a sufficient number of state members, a new European Court of Human Rights will replace the current Commission, the Court, and the committee of ministers (in terms of its current responsibilities). The new Court will be a full-time permanent tribunal and the judges will take up residence in Strasbourg. Presumably with a full-time Court, the influence of the professional staff of the current Court may decline. The new Court will consist of a number of judges equal to the number of state members to the ECHR, but it will sit in committees, chambers, and grand chambers. Committees will consist of three judges, chambers of seven judges, and grand chambers of seventeen judges. Committees will screen complaints much as does the present Commission. Chambers ordinarily will render judgment, but the litigants can request that the case be referred to the grand chamber. However, reviews by the grand chamber are to be reserved for especially important cases. All cases between state parties will be before grand chambers. The committee of ministers will continue in its role of supervising the execution of the Court's judgments (Drzemczewski and Meyer-Ladewig 1994).

THE FIRST THIRTY YEARS OF THE COURT, 1959–89

As noted before, through the end of 1989, the Court had announced decisions on the merits in 151 cases, and in 108 of these it found a violation of the ECHR. It is important to remember that the cases before the Court are ones that have already been screened by the Commission; thus, it is not surprising that such a high percentage of violations should be found.

Table 2.1 reveals the state parties that were defendants and the violations found from the Court's first decision on the merits in 1961 through the end of 1989. Given the subject of this book, we should first note, as we did in chapter 1, that from 1959 through the end of 1989, the United Kingdom, the country having no judicially enforceable rights document of its own, headed the list of state defendants, with respect to the number of complaints, those found admissible by the Commission, and the cases in which the United Kingdom was found to be in violation of the ECHR (Brewer-Carías 1989, 51). Françoise

Table 2.1. Cases brought against state defendants, 1959–1989

Countries	Cases brought against	Cases in which violations were found
United Kingdom	37	23
Belgium	22	14
Austria	21	12
Federal Republic of Germany	20	8
Sweden	19	10
Italy	15	13
Netherlands	15	10
Switzerland	14	6
France	9	2
Portugal	6	4
Denmark	5	1
Ireland	4	3
Spain	2	2
Iceland	1	0
Norway	1	0
Total	191[a]	108

a. Of these, 151 cases were decided on the merits. Eight cases were struck from the list, one case was not decided on the merits, and 33 cases (two of which were pending only on Art. 50 determinations) were pending before the Court at the end of 1989.
Source: European Court of Human Rights, Survey of Activities, 1959-89 (Strasbourg: Council of Europe, 1990). The figures for the 108 violations were also independently verified through case coding and content analysis conducted for this study.

Hampson suggests, however, that there are several ways in which violations can be counted, so while the United Kingdom is indeed a frequent violator, she believes that there is little to be gained by creating a pecking order of violators (Hampson 1990).

Since 1989 the United Kingdom has been the state defendant in thirty-six additional reported cases before the European Court and has been found in violation in eighteen of them (through February 1996): Granger (1990, Art. 6.1 and 6.3c violations), Fox, Campbell and Hartley (1990, Art. 5.1 and 5.5 violations), McCallum (1990, Art. 8 violation), Thynne, Wilson and Gunnell (1990, violations of Art. 5.4 and 5.5), The Observer and Guardian (1991, Art. 10 violation), The Sunday Times (No. 2) (1991, Art. 10 violation), Campbell (1992, Art. 8 violation), Darnell (1993, Art. 6.1 violation), Boner (1994, Art. 6.3 violation), Maxwell (1995, Art. 6.3 violation), Welch (1995, Art. 7.1 violation), *McMichael* (1995, violations of Art. 6.1 and 8), *Tolstoy Miloslavsky* (1995, Art. 10 violation), *McCann and Others* (1995, Art. 2 violation), *John Murray* (1996, violation of Art. 6.1 taken with 6.3c), *Hussain* (1996, violation of Art. 5.4), *Goodwin* (1996, violation of Art 10), and *Benham* (1996, violation of Art. 6.1, 6.3).

Remember that since the United Kingdom has not incorporated the ECHR into its domestic law, a human rights claim under the ECHR can be brought to the European Commission and Court, but not to U.K. domestic courts. Had the failure to incorporate the ECHR into domestic law been a contributing factor in the number of violations experienced by the U.K., the Scandinavian adherents to the ECHR ought to be in the company of the U.K. as frequent violators, since they also have not incorporated the ECHR (Hampson 1990, 122). Nonetheless, they are not frequent violators. However, the U.K. is the only adherent to the ECHR that has no inclusive constitutional document.

The provisions most often found to be violated by the United Kingdom through the end of 1989 were—in fourteen cases—Art. 8 (protecting privacy and family life) and—in nine instances—Art. 6 (certain due process requirements). Since the beginning of 1990 through June 1996, there have been three additional violations of various sections of Art. 5, seven violations of Art. 6.1 or 6.3, three additional violations of Art. 8, and four more violations of Art. 10.

It should be noted that in two cases involving the treatment of suspected Irish "terrorists," the United Kingdom served notices of derogation; the first derogation was in *Ireland v. United Kingdom* (1978), but that derogation was no longer in effect when the second case (*Brogan et al.* [1988]) reached the Court. Derogation is a procedure under Art. 15 whereby a state party may withdraw from application of certain provisions of the ECHR in time of "war or other public emergency threatening the life of the nation." The emergency is to be determined by the institutions acting under the ECHR and not by the state party acting alone. Both Ireland and the United Kingdom agreed to the facts of emergency status under Art. 15 in *Ireland v. United Kingdom*. When found to be in violation of the ECHR in the *Brogan* case in 1988, the United Kingdom refused to comply and served another notice of derogation (Hampson 1990, 152). That derogation was sustained by the Court in the case of *Brannigan and McBride v. United Kingdom* (1993).

Table 2.2 reveals that Art. 6.1, invoked in seventy-four claims from 1959 through 1989, was by far the most frequently litigated provision of the ECHR. Essentially, Art. 6.1 contains many of the components of due process, including the right to a prompt, public, fair, and impartial hearing. Apart from the five violations of this provision by the United Kingdom that were reviewed above, of the total of fifty-six violations of this provision, the largest number (twenty) involved the "excessive and unreasonable duration of litigation" in

Table 2.2. Claims decided and claims in which violations were found, 1959–1989

Article	Claims decided	Violations found
6.1	74	56 (22 cases involved delay, excessive delay found in 20 cases)
8	33	22
14	25	4
5.4	17	11
5.1	16	6
5.3	15	10
Protocol 1, Article 1	14	3
13	14	3
6.3	12	10
10	12	3
3	11	3
6 (in general)	10	3
11	9	1
6.2	8	1

Note: Includes provisions adjudicated in more than five cases. Figures may include multiple claims and multiple violations in single cases. These figures do *not* include provisions that the court determined were not necessary to the adjudication of particular cases, even though those provisions were raised by the complainant.

the courts of member-states. Italy, with five violations, was the most frequent offender, followed by Portugal and the Federal Republic of Germany, each with four; Austria, with three; and France, Spain, Switzerland, and the United Kingdom, with one each. It is worth noting that since 1989 Italy has been found to be in violation of this provision in more than fifty additional cases. Thus Italy has become the most frequent violator of the ECHR, due almost entirely to claims involving "excessive and unreasonable delay" under Art. 6.1.

With thirty-three claims and twenty-two violations, Art. 8 provided the next most frequent number of violations and claims, though less than half, in both instances, of those claims involving Art. 6.1. Art. 8 amounts to a right of privacy, by providing for a right to respect for "private and family life, home and correspondence."

Art. 14, with twenty-five claims, contains the ECHR's equivalent of the Equal Protection Clause of the Fourteenth Amendment to the U.S. Constitution. It provides that the rights and freedoms secured by the ECHR shall be free of discrimination based on "sex, race, color, language, religion, political or other opinion, national or social origin, affiliation with a national majority, property, birth or other social status." It is notable that while Art. 14 is often invoked, the Court has rarely found violations under it. Since Art. 14 provides for the application of the rights and freedoms secured by the ECHR without discrimination as to sex, race, and so on, claims under Art. 14 are usually read in conjunction with another provision of the ECHR. Of the four violations of Art. 14 found by the Court through 1989, two of them were in connection with Art. 8 (the right of privacy, and so on). And two of them have been in connection with Art. 1 and 2 of Protocol 1, which provide for the peaceful enjoyment of one's possessions and for the right to education. Sometimes, however, the Court finds a discriminatory outcome under another article and therefore finds it unnecessary to resort to Art. 14 (see, for example, *Airey v. Ireland* [1979]), in which the Court found a discriminatory denial of access to courts due to poverty to be a breach of Art. 6 (without need to resort to Art. 14).

The various paragraphs of Art. 5 specify other components of procedural due process. As table 2.2 shows, if claims involving Art. 5.1 (no deprivation of liberty except in specified instances), Art. 5.3 (right to be brought promptly before a magistrate, prompt trial or bail), and Art. 5.4 (prompt determination of the lawfulness of detention) are added together, they make up forty-eight adjudicated claims and twenty-seven violations through the end of 1989, second only to Art. 6.1. Since Art. 6.1 itself provides for fair, impartial, prompt, and public proceedings, it is clear that the vast majority of the violations (83 of the 136 violations reported in table 2.2) found by the Court during its first 30 years have involved procedural fairness and due process, broadly described. Within that context, excessive and unreasonable delay has been the most frequent problem. To these eighty-three violations, we might also add the three Art. 3 violations, which involve inhuman or degrading treatment or punishment and therefore usually focus on penal systems, rather than on broader substantive freedoms.

In contrast, claims involving substantive freedoms, like the protection of freedom of expression in Art. 10 or the right to respect for private and family life, home, and correspondence in Art. 8, included only twenty-five violations during the first thirty years. Moreover, the protection for freedom of thought, conscience, and religion found in Art. 9 and the protection for freedom of association and assembly in Art. 11 were rarely adjudicated (nine claims in all) and only one violation has been found. That was in the case of *Young, James and Webster v. United Kingdom* (1981), in which a violation of the freedom of association (through the dismissal of nonunion railway employees following a union shop agreement) was found.

Dissent Behavior

A case-by-case tally of the votes of European Court justices on the 151 decisions on the merits made between 1959 and 1989 reveals that the various provisions contained within Art. 5, 6, 8, and 14 have produced the most division amongst members of the Court. This is summarized in table 2.3.

Again, the fair and prompt hearing requirements of Art. 6.1 have been the most prolific, in this instance in producing conflicting judicial views. Twenty cases (27 percent of the seventy-four Art. 6.1 cases) have met the criteria for inclusion in table 2.3. If we add Art. 6 and the various sections of Art. 5 (other components of procedural due process), together they involve thirty-nine (59 percent) of the sixty-six instances of dissents that met the criteria for inclusion in table 2.3.

Art. 8 (respect for private and family life, home, and correspondence) is the next most frequent source of dissent, although it is a minor source compared to Art. 5 and 6 taken together.

The only other division that stands out is produced by Art. 14's antidiscrimination requirements, with four notable divided cases. However, if we look at dissenting judges rather than cases, ten members of the Court have participated in ten or more dissents during their tenure between 1959 and 1989. Table 2.4 presents their dissent behavior divided into two columns.

Table 2.3. Claims brought under articles that produced three or more dissents in plenary decisions or at least two dissents in panel decisions, 1959–1989

Article	Frequency of dissents
6.1	20
8	8
6.3	5
10	5
5.1	4
14	4
5.3	3
Protocol 1, Article 1	3
5.4	2
5.5	2
6 (generally)	2
13	2
3	1
5 (generally)	1
12	1
Protocol 1, Article 3	1

Note: Includes separate opinions on points where the votes of the justices were contrary to the majority.

The first column records dissents in those cases in which a majority of the Court found a violation of the ECHR. The second records dissents when the majority of the Court found no violation. Since violations were found in 108 of the 151 decisions on the merits, it is to be expected that most dissents would appear in the first column. While that is usually the case, there are still some notable observations. Keeping in mind that only ten of the thirty judges who participated in ten or more cases before the Court also meet the criterion of having dissented ten or more times, Judge Matscher of Austria stands out for having dissented *only* when the majority found a violation, while Judge Spielman of Luxembourg dissented *only* when the majority found no violation. These apparently are the two members of the Court best representing decisional extremes. Generally leaning in the same direction as Judge Matscher are Judges Vilhjálmsson of Iceland, Bindschedler-Robert of Switzerland, Gölcüklü of Turkey and Pinheiro Farinha of Portugal. Most conspicuous in joining Judge Spielman at the "other end" of the Court are Judges Cremona of Malta and Pettiti of France.

The relative differences between these judges can best be seen in a two-by-two table.

Judge Bindschedler-Robert of Switzerland and Judge Matscher of Austria served together on the Court between 1977 and 1991. Altogether they participated in forty cases in which at least one dissent was registered by a member of the Court. Table 2.5 reveals that they voted together 75 percent of the time in such cases.

At the other end of the Court, Judges Spielman of Luxembourg and Pettiti of France participated in twenty-nine cases between 1986 and 1989 in which there was at least one dissent. Table 2.5 shows that they voted together 76 percent of the time in divided cases.

In contrast, Judges Spielman and Matscher both participated in twenty-nine cases between 1986 and 1989 in which the Court was divided by at least a single dissent, but they voted together only 24 percent of the time.

Given the total number of cases involving Art. 6.1, it should not be surprising that the dissents that often find Judges Matscher, Bindschedler-Robert, Gölcüklü, and Pinheiro Farinha voting together commonly involve Art. 6.1. They dissent usually when a majority of the Court has found a violation.

A good example of these dissents can be found in the case of *Barberà et al. v. Spain* (1988). That case involved a complaint against Spain, raising several issues under Art. 6.1. These included the transfer of the accused from Barcelona to Madrid only a few hours before his trial began, the replacement of the presiding judge and one of his associates at the last minute and without notice, a trial that lasted only one day, and the admission into evidence of a 1,600-page pretrial dossier, without having its contents read aloud in court or in public (a

Table 2.4. Judges dissenting in ten or more cases, 1959–1989

Judges	Total dissents	Dissents in cases where majority found a violation	Dissents in cases where majority found no violation
Zekia (1961–88) Cyprus	13	6	7
Cremona (1965–) Malta	15	5	10
Vilhjálmsson (1971–) Iceland	23	20	3[a]
Bindschedler-Robert (1975–91) Switzerland	21	16	5
Gölcüklü (1977–) Turkey	16	13	3
Matscher (1977–) Austria	24	24[a]	None
Pinheiro Farinha (1977–) Portugal	22	16	6
Pettiti (1980–) France	13	2	11
Evans (1980–) United Kingdom	14	13	1[a]
Spielman (1986–) Luxembourg	11	None	11

Note: Includes separate opinions on points where the votes of the justices were contrary to the majority.
a. Includes one dissent as to the applicability of an article of the Convention, rather than as a dissent as to a violation.

procedure referred to in Spain as *por reproducida*). The majority (by a vote of ten to eight) found an Art. 6.1 violation through a decision that amounted to a "totality of circumstances" rule, that is, all of the deficiencies of the trial, added together, constituted a violation. Judges Bindschedler-Robert and Matscher were among the dissenters. They found that the defense in the case did not meet its burden of using procedures under Spanish law to challenge these deficiencies, and they explicitly rejected a totality of circumstances rule.

The Sunday Times case (1979) (reviewed in depth in chapter 6) is another interesting example of dissents that included Judges Bindschedler-Robert and Matscher, in this instance along with seven others (the Court found a violation by a vote of eleven to nine). The case was brought against the United Kingdom, which through the decision of the "Law Lords" of its House of Lords had restrained the publication of a newspaper series about "deformed thalidomide children" on the grounds that the publication of the articles would prejudice pending civil suits against the manufacturer of the drug. A bare majority of the Court found this to be a violation of the freedom of expression protected by Art. 10. Judges Bindschedler-Robert, Matscher, and five others, however, found the prohibition of the articles to be necessary to ensure the due administration of justice.

Table 2.5. Participants' votes in cases with at least one dissent, 1959–1989

		Judge Bindschedler-Robert	
		With majority	In dissent
Judge Matscher	With majority	16	4
	In dissent	6	14

		Judge Pettiti	
		With majority	In dissent
Judge Spielman	With majority	16	3
	In dissent	4	6

		Judge Matscher	
		With majority	In dissent
Judge Spielman	With majority	7	12
	In dissent	10	0

Judge Bindschedler-Robert, who was a member of the Court from 1975 to 1991, was both a lawyer/bureaucrat with the Swiss federal government and a professor of public law before joining the Court. Judge Matscher, who has been on the Court since 1977, was experienced as an Austrian diplomat (for seventeen years), university law professor and dean, and rector of Salzburg University (1974–75). Judges Gölcüklü of Turkey and Evans of the United Kingdom, who often voted with Judges Bindschedler-Roberts and Matscher were, respectively, a law professor at the University of Ankara and a career lawyer with the U.K. Foreign Office.

Judges Spielman, Pettiti, and Cremona seem to represent the opposite tendency, that is, they more commonly dissent when the majority of the Court has found no violation. Judge Pettiti of France, who has been on the Court since 1980, comes from a background as *avocat* and human rights activist. Between 1980 and 1989 he dissented thirteen times (15 percent of his total participation), and ten of his dissents were in favor of finding a rights violation. Five of his dissents were in Art. 6.1 cases. Judge Spielman, a member of the Court since 1986, also came to Court from his experience as a legal practitioner, chiefly as a public prosecutor or administrator. He has dissented in eleven (22 percent) of the cases in which he participated on the Court between 1986 and 1989, and *all* of his dissents were in favor of finding a rights violation when the majority had found none. Four of his dissents were in Art. 10 (freedom of expression) cases, and three were in Art. 6.1 cases. Two examples will illustrate Spielman's and Pettiti's decisional tendencies.

In the 1988 case of *Schenk v. Switzerland*, the complaint was that Switzerland allowed the use as evidence in a criminal trial of an unlawfully obtained recording of a telephone conversation. The majority (by a vote of thirteen to four) applied the rough equivalent of a harmless error rule, finding that the trial as a whole was nonetheless a fair one and that there was other evidence sufficient to sustain the conviction. Judges Spielman and Pettiti were among the dissenters. They would have applied a strict exclusionary rule, holding that no court can, "without detriment to the proper administration of justice," allow the introduction of evidence that has been obtained by unfair, or—above all—by unlawful means.

The judgment in *Nielsen v. Denmark* (1988) is the second example of a case in which both Judges Pettiti and Spielman dissented, in this instance along with five others (the vote was nine to seven against finding a violation). This case involved a complaint against Denmark in which a twelve-year-old child, who, while not mentally ill, was hospitalized in the psychiatric ward of a state hospital for more than five months on the application of his mother. Nine members of the Court held that the custodial rights of the mother prevailed so that the protection offered by Art. 5.1 (the right to liberty and security of the person) did not apply. Judges Pettiti and Spielman held that the length of the committal and the fact that the child was indeed not mentally ill, both of which were tolerated by Denmark, involved the state in a violation of Art. 5.1. Even though they are frequently joined by others in dissent, judging from their aggregate dissent behavior, Judges Pettiti and Spielman are the two members of the Court most likely to find human rights violations over a variety of complaints. This conclusion is tentative, however, for it is valid only for judges who participated in ten or more cases and who dissented ten or more times.

The point of examining dissent behavior is to illustrate that, just as is the case with justices of the U.S. Supreme Court, there are some clear patterns reflected in judges' votes on the European Court of Human Rights. Those patterns are bound to reflect—to some degree—different priorities, values, and life experiences.

Background Characteristics of Judges of the Court

Next we will examine the life experiences of the fifty-seven judges who served as members of the Court between 1959 and 1989. Raimo Pekkanen of Finland was elected to the Court on September 25, 1989, but he participated in no judgments before the end of the year. The position of the judge elected with respect to Cyprus was vacant at the end of 1989.

The average age of judges (who participated in decisions through the end of 1989) as of their first election was sixty-two years. The average age at election has been statistically constant since the beginning in 1959, so sixty-two represents a typical age at the time of election today as well. The average age at death or retirement of the first fifteen members of the Court was seventy-five. Seven of the fifteen initial members remained on the Court past their eightieth year. The average tenure in office of the fifteen judges chosen in the first election (1959) was thirteen years. The average age at retirement of those selected since the first election has been seventy-one years. The average age of the members of the Court at the end of 1989 was sixty-seven years. Rolv Ryssdal of Norway, now eighty-one and the current president of the Court, has been a member of the Court since 1973 and its president since 1985. Elizabeth Palm of Sweden was fifty-three and the youngest member of the Court when she was elected in 1989.

All of the initial members of the Court were males, and only three of the fifty-eight judges who served through the end of 1989 have been women. Two of them, Judge Denise Bindschedler-Robert of Switzerland and Judge Elisabeth Palm of Sweden, were members of the Court at the end of 1989. Judge Inger Helga Pederson of Denmark, elected in 1971, was the first woman on the Court.

Of the fifteen judges elected at the first election in 1989, ten (66 percent) had principal careers as law professors (or as *jurisconsults* as Art. 39 describes them). Several of the original judges were especially distinguished figures in international law. Lord McNair of the United Kingdom served as a member and president of the International Court of Justice at the Hague prior to his election to the Court. René Cassin of France was a recipient of the Nobel Peace Prize by virtue of his work on the Universal Declaration of Human Rights. Judge Mosler of Germany was the longtime professor and director of the Max Planck Institute of Public International and Foreign Law at Heidelberg University. Rolv Ryssdal of Norway, the current president of the Court, is a former chief justice of his country.

An interesting even if somewhat arcane fact is that six of the original fifteen judges of the Court included their membership on the Permanent Court of Arbitration at The Hague in their résumés. That "court" was created by the Hague Peace Conference in 1899; however, it is not a court at all but, rather, a panel of individuals who are appointed by the states that are parties to The Hague Convention. Each state is required to designate four members of the panel. The panelists are available for service as arbitrators of international disputes. However, in the first forty years of its existence, only nineteen arbitration panels were convened, so that during those forty years only twenty-eight of the 500 members named to the Permanent Court of Arbitration actually served. Thus, its principal continuing purpose has been that it nominates candidates for membership on the International Court of Justice (Hudson 1944, 159; Jancovic 1983, 328).

We can see from the backgrounds of the judges of the European Court of Human Rights that the Permanent Court of Arbitration has also been an important source of members for the European Court. Since the adherents to the ECHR are supposed to maintain four members continuously on the panel of the Permanent Court of Arbitration, it is likely that nominating states simply had a short list of distinguished *jurisconsults* who were available for service on the European Court at the first election in 1959.

As noted previously, ten of the fifteen original judges had principal prior careers as professors of international law. Of the more recent members of the Court, fewer have had principal prior careers as academicians, even though several have held adjunct appointments. Seven of the members of the Court at the end of 1989 had principal prior careers as judges. Six had principal prior careers as attorneys in public service.

These career backgrounds can be compared with Jan ten Kate's (1989) study of the Dutch Supreme Court, in which he reported that the number of career judges appointed to that court had declined and their places had been occupied by attorneys and by professors of law. Citing Hondius (1988), Jan ten Kate noted that his findings about the Dutch Supreme Court are quite different from the German *Bundesgerichtshof* or the French *Cour de cassation,* for which members are recruited from the professional judiciary of their respective countries. It is interesting that while service on the ordinary judiciary in France (apart from the administrative courts) is largely a separate profession, whose members are educated at the *École Nationale de la Magistrature* (Abraham 1993), none of the Frenchmen who served on the European Court of Human Rights through 1989 had been a career judge. René Cassin was first a professor, then a prominent figure at the United Nations (if he was the "father" of the Universal Declaration of Human Rights, Eleanor Roosevelt was the "mother"), and also vice president of the French *Conseil d'État*. His successor, Pierre-Henri Teitgen, was first a professor, then a leader of the Resistance, another prominent participant in adoption of the Universal Declaration of Human Rights, a member of the French National Assembly, and minister of state in various administrations. Louis-Edmund Pettiti, the current member for France, was chiefly a practicing *avocat* prior to his appointment.

The Politics of Human Rights Adjudication

Of course, the European Court of Human Rights is an unusual entity relative to the ordinary domestic courts of European states. Leaving aside the various extant national constitutional courts, most European domestic courts do not routinely deal with broad questions of public law or human rights but, rather, with the detailed application of private law, whether derived from a code or from common law precedents. Where, as in France, separate administrative courts exist, they do address questions of public right and power, but the *droit administratif* is itself a separate and highly specialized body of law. To be sure, in the United Kingdom common law judges are increasingly called upon to exercise "judicial review" over administrative agencies (Sunkin 1992, 1993). Nonetheless, public international law and its related international agencies represent still another specialized field. It follows naturally that those professionally experienced in international law will be the key movers in the creation of rights documents like the ECHR and its consequent institutions. However, once established, the rights enforceable through such institutions may substantively have little to do with the traditional body of public international law. Of course, how the rulings of the Commission, the Court, and the council of ministers are enforced is an important matter of international law and relationships, but the judges of the European Court of Human Rights have little, if anything, to do with enforcement. If this line of reasoning is correct, it is fair to ask: What is the most appropriate background and training for membership on a court charged with the protection of human rights? Just as it has never been obvious what sort of training and experience are most suitable for membership on the Supreme Court of the United States relative to other U.S.

courts, the European Court of Human Rights may be *sui generis* amongst European courts. Probably the closest equivalents are the several national constitutional courts of European countries and, supranationally, the Court of Justice of the European Community.

Alec Stone's (1992) book on the *Conseil constitutionnel* suggests the sometimes partisan, but always highly political and policy-laden nature of constitutional adjudication in France. That is hardly a surprising conclusion for students who follow the U.S. Supreme Court, but in France judicial politics tends to be hidden behind a façade of professional legalism. Such a façade is not unusual in Europe, nor indeed in the United Kingdom. But while the ideological and political backgrounds of nominees to the U.S. Supreme Court are closely scrutinized by the media and by the Senate, judges of the European Court of Human Rights, who make decisions comparable to justices of the U.S. Supreme Court, are, relatively speaking, likely to be anonymous and faceless officials to most members of the European general public. Yet the work they do in assessing human rights in various domestic contexts is political as well as legal.

INTERPRETATIONS AND DECISION MAKING

It seems that judges of the European Court of Human Rights approach their work with the understanding that they are supposed to use the customary rules of interpretation that apply to international agreements. Thus, the ECHR is to be interpreted in good faith and in accordance with the ordinary meaning of words in their context, having due regard for a provision's object and purpose. According to Sir Vincent Evans, a former member of the Court of United Kingdom, the Court has adopted a dynamic or "evolutive" style of interpretation, rather than a static one. Several jurists and scholars have independently confirmed this suggestion (Macdonald, Matscher, and Petzold, 1993). An evolutive style of interpretation means that the provisions of the ECHR ought to be interpreted in light of current conditions and circumstances. According to Judge Evans, "the time is gone" when the members of the Court simply sought to apply the "original intent" of the framers and negotiators of the ECHR. Instead, the principle of effectiveness is inherent in the approach of the Court. The ECHR was not written to establish rights that are "theoretical or illusory." Thus the Court has adopted a liberal approach to interpretation, and according to Judge Evans, there is little chance of its turning back.

In the recent volume (1993) of which he was coeditor, Judge Matscher (as we saw in table 2.4 above, the judge most likely to dissent when a majority of the Court has found a violation of the ECHR) has written an article on interpreting the ECHR. He also speaks of an evolutive or dynamic method of interpretation, as contrasted with a static or historical method. One element in this is the conscious effort to give effective protection (*effet utile*) (1993, 67) to the rights recognized by the ECHR. He suggests, "This means that the concepts used in the Convention are to be understood in the context of the democratic society of today, and not in that of forty years ago when the Convention was drafted" (1993, 68). He also writes of an "autonomous interpretation," one that transcends a meaning peculiar to a particular member-state and seeks a general definition and understanding (1993, 70). However, he cautions that the Court may have reached the limits of judicial discretion, and that "At times they have perhaps even crossed the boundary and entered territory which is no longer that of treaty interpretation but is actually legal policy-making" (1993, 70). His concerns are no doubt reflected in his dissent behavior shown in table 2.4. Yet, whether the act of judging human rights under the ECHR *can be* primarily a matter of "treaty interpretation" is, at least, an open question.

Nadine Strossen has suggested that the Court has recognized important privacy rights under Art. 8 that go well beyond those sustained by the U.S. Supreme Court in recent years (1990, 872). She especially noted the 1981 *Dudgeon* case for its nullification of Northern Ireland's statute that criminalized homosexual relations between consenting adult males as contrasted with the 1986 decision of the U.S. Supreme Court in *Bowers v. Hardwick*. Her more general point is that, after a slow and cautious beginning, the European Court of Human Rights has aggressively embraced a broad interpretation of rights, while the U.S. Supreme Court has been narrowing its comparable interpretations. Either way judicial construction may go—liberal or conservative or broad or narrow—the political aspect of the work of both courts is inevitable, just as is its importance.

3

Prevention of Terrorism and the Convention

This chapter will examine several cases before the European Court of Human Rights that have judged the efforts of the United Kingdom to control terrorism in Northern Ireland within the constraints of the ECHR. The earliest cases came to naught. Known collectively as the *Northern Ireland Cases*, they were filed in 1968 on behalf of certain individuals and of the Northern Ireland Civil Rights Association and alleged a shopping list of violations of the ECHR. They eventually were struck from the list of cases pending before the Commission for failure of the complainants to diligently prosecute their complaints (Boyle et al. 1975, 156). In May 1972, applications were filed on behalf of *Donnelly and Others*, complaining of torture and of inhuman and degrading treatment under Art. 3. The applications were declared admissible by the Commission in April 1973 but the Commission's report was not made until December 1975, by which time agreed compensation had been reached on several of the claims. The Commission then withdrew its finding of admissibility (Boyle et al. 1975, 157).

Six key decisions of the European Court will be reviewed in depth in this chapter, but the background to those decisions is quite complex. We will close with two recently announced decisions of the European Court. *McCann and Others v. United Kingdom* (decided on September 27, 1995) held the United Kingdom to have violated Art. 2 (the right to life) in the killing by forces of the Special Air Service (SAS) in Gibraltar of three members of a team of suspected IRA terrorists (*Statewatch* 1995c, 18–20). In the case of *John Murray v. United Kingdom* (decided on February 8, 1996) the European Court found an inference drawn against the defendant by an experienced judge (under the provisions of the Criminal Evidence [Northern Ireland] Order 1988) from his refusal to respond to police questions and to testify in his own behalf before a "Diplock Court" was not a violation of Murray's rights under Art. 6.1 and 6.2. However, the court did find a violation of Art. 6.1, taken with Art. 6.3c, regarding Murray's lack of access to a lawyer during the first forty-eight hours of his police detention.

THE KEY DECISION: *Ireland v. United Kingdom* (1978)

On December 16, 1971, the Republic of Ireland filed an application with the European Commission on Human Rights alleging that the emergency procedures applied against suspected terrorists in Northern Ireland violated several provisions of the ECHR. The parties, statutes, and events at issue in this case are complex and may be difficult to follow. At the least, a brief overview of Northern Ireland's history of conflict during the last thirty years or so, and of the emergency legislation that has been applied there, is essential to understanding the European Court's ruling. But even accomplishing that is problematic because of the dearth of disinterested observers. The "facts" that are reported here have been compared in several sources.

Background

The Irish Republican Army (IRA) was a key player in the Dublin Easter Rising of 1916. Reactions to that rising, and to the execution of some of its leaders by the British government, led proximately to the establishment of the Irish Free State in 1922. Six counties of Ulster, with their Protestant majorities, have remained ever since "Northern Ireland," ruled as part of the United Kingdom, either directly from London or from a "devolved" government in Belfast. Since the Easter Rising, the IRA has engaged in many campaigns with various purposes. The most recent campaign immediately preceding the present conflict (which began in the late 1960s) was the IRA Border Campaign of 1959–62, which being mostly ignored by local people, was judged a failure by those of both friendly and hostile views. Indeed it probably reduced the IRA, for a while, to a paper tiger. Thus, the IRA itself probably was *not* a major threat when the most recent "Troubles" in Northern Ireland began in the late 1960s (Bell 1993, 129; Clutterbuck 1977, 64).

The events leading up to the most recent conflict began relatively quietly with various nonviolent campaigns for civil rights for Catholics, such as those of the Homeless Citizens League of 1963 or the Campaign for Social Justice of 1964. Observers of Northern Ireland agree that Catholics as a group in Northern Ireland were then still a poor and disadvantaged minority. (When the words "Catholic" or "Protestant" are used in this chapter, they are used in their "tribal" or categorical sense. In Northern Ireland these terms may have little to do with theology, but much to do with bigotry.) In the views of their advocates, the Catholics clearly were disadvantaged and discriminated against, especially in terms of housing and employment, and the government that ruled over them from Belfast was seen as a sometimes gerrymandered Protestant government with an almost entirely Protestant police force. The amount of discrimination (as contrasted with economic disadvantage) suffered in Catholic areas is, not surprisingly, the subject of dispute. The Cameron Commission Report (1969) was taken as documenting widespread discrimination against Catholics. However, others argue that Catholics in Northern Ireland were not the objects of discrimination disproportionate to their numbers (Ewing 1976).

A former researcher for the Conservative Central Office, Ewing relies especially on Richard Rose's empirical study of housing (1971), which, as she reports, failed to reveal systematic discrimination against Catholics. A recent appraisal of the relative positions of Catholics and Protestants in Northern Ireland can be found in Boyle and Hadden's *Northern Ireland: The Choice* (1994).

The Northern Ireland Civil Rights Association (NICRA) was formed in January 1967. Its strategy and tactics were like those of the 1960s civil rights movement against racial discrimination in the United States. However, even simple statements like that in the previous sentence depend on one's sources and on the points of view they reflect. For example, former U.K. Army officer Richard Clutterbuck writes that by 1972 NICRA was run by the "official" Marxist wing of the IRA. Moreover, he states that NICRA was "conceived" by the "Trotskyist element of the IRA as a suitable front organization to attract a wide spectrum of popular sentiment in the North" (1973, 60–61). On the other hand, former civil rights activist Michael Farrell describes NICRA as a "sober, moderate body" (1976, 245). Its appeal, which sought to transcend left-right ideology, was to all those who had suffered discrimination at the hands of the Protestant majority, including its devolved Protestant-led government and its paramilitary police force, the Royal Ulster Constabulary (RUC), supplemented by the Protestant "B Special Constables" (Bell 1993, 94).

Meanwhile a small but aggressively hostile Protestant movement was growing after the emergence of the Reverend Ian Paisley as a Protestant leader in the election of 1964. In 1966, a group calling itself the Ulster Volunteer Forces "declared war" on the IRA and its allies (*Ireland v. United Kingdom*, ser. A, 12).[1] The Ulster Defense Association, eventually the most prominent "Loyalist" or Protestant paramilitary organization, first appeared in the spring of 1972 (*Ireland v. United Kingdom*, ser. A, 20).

The IRA itself split into the "Official" and "Provisional" wings in 1969–70, after the Easter riots of 1969. The Officials sought to emphasize class conflict rather than the traditional Republican agenda, which simply pitted Catholics against Protestants. They publicly rejected the use of violence except "defensively" and were therefore accused of failing sufficiently to defend Catholics against their enemies, while the "Provos" ("Provos" is the slang for "Provisional," taken from the Provisional government established in Dublin during the Easter Rising of 1916) ostensibly continued to embrace and to use political violence. For example, the Official IRA bomb attack in England at Aldershot in February 1972 was, according to the account of the Official IRA, a reprisal for the killing of thirteen Catholic demonstrators by soldiers of Britain's Parachute Regiment in Derry (Londonderry) on "Bloody Sunday" (January 30, 1972) (Bell 1993, 288). Whatever the purpose of the Aldershot bombing, the results were that a Catholic priest, five women, and an elderly gardener were killed (Clutterbuck 1973, 59). The even more indiscriminate bombings by the Provisional IRA that have become familiar in recent years began later.

Beginning in Belfast, but spreading quickly to Londonderry in August 1969, a nasty confrontation developed between the RUC and Protestant demonstrators on one side and the Catholic residents of Derry's Bogside on the other. Eventually British armored cars and CS gas were pitted against a hail of Republican cobblestones and Molotov cocktails. When the RUC reached the limits of its resources, the British Army was sent into Northern Ireland at the request of the Northern Ireland prime minister to James Callaghan, British (Labour Party) home secretary. At best, the Army's purpose was to keep the hostile forces apart and, if possible, to maintain order (Yonah and O'Day 1986, 57). But these events signaled a continuing violent conflict in Northern Ireland with a sufficient number of willing Catholic (including a revitalized IRA) and Protestant (including Loyalist paramilitary forces) participants to keep it going, with varying intensity, until recently.

On August 9, 1971, the government of Northern Ireland led by Prime Minister Brian Faulkner began to use the powers of detention and internment already available to it under the Civil Authorities (Special Powers) Act (Northern Ireland) 1922. In invoking emergency powers, Faulkner said, "Every means has been tried to make terrorists amenable to the law. Nor have such methods been without success, because substantial numbers of the most prominent leaders of the IRA are now serving ordinary prison sentences. But the terrorist campaign continues at an unacceptable level, and I have had to conclude that the ordinary law cannot deal comprehensively or quickly enough with such ruthless violence" (*Compton Report* 1971, iv). Section 2(4) of the 1922 Special Powers Act contained the following broad and ominous language: "If any person does an act of such a nature as to be calculated to be prejudicial to the preservation of the peace or maintenance of order in Northern Ireland and not specifically provided for in the regulations, he shall be deemed to be guilty of an offence against the regulations." Had this provision, much like the "guilt by analogy" of the former Stalinist penal code in the Soviet Union, been enforced and eventually contested before the European Court of Human Rights, it might well have been found to be a violation of Art. 7 of the ECHR, which provides that no one shall be guilty of an offense that did not constitute a criminal offense under national law when it was committed.

The timing and extent of the various emergency regulations involved in this case can be complicated and confusing. Thus, in arguing its case against the U.K., Ireland proposed to the European Commission on Human Rights that events be divided into three phases for purposes of presentation, which the Commission accepted and which are used here (*Ireland v. United Kingdom*, ser. B, 41).

Phase I: August 9, 1971, to November 7, 1972

The first day of this period was the beginning of detention and internment, while the end was the first day of emergency powers under the Detention of Terrorist Order, which stemmed from the resumption of direct British rule in March 1972. Emergency measures during Phase I were exercised under the Civil Authorities (Special Powers) Act (Northern Ireland) 1922. These included the following powers (*Ireland v. United Kingdom*, ser. B, 42–45):

(1) *Arrest and detention for interrogation:* During Phase I under Regulation 10 any officer of the Royal Ulster Constabulary could authorize arrest and detention of any person for the purpose of interrogation without warrant for not more than forty-eight hours. According to Ireland's complaint, such arrest and detention might involve no commission of crime, no suspicion of a specific crime, and no requirement that any particular criteria for arrest be satisfied.

(2) *Arrest and remand in custody:* Under Regulation 11(1) any constable or member of the United Kingdom forces might arrest on suspicion without warrant anyone for having acted, or being about to act, in a manner prejudicial to the peace or maintenance of order—or any person suspected of having committed an offense. Individuals so arrested could be held in custody without trial for any period of time. Allegedly the only limitation was that the person making the arrest must have genuinely suspected the arrested person of something, even though that suspicion might have been objectively unreasonable. The United Kingdom claimed that this power in practice was "responsibly exercised" and for only seventy-two hours.

(3) *Detention:* Under Regulation 11(2) the minister of state for home affairs (Northern Ireland), and later (after March 1972) the British secretary of state for Northern Ireland, could serve a detention order on a suspect in custody and that person could be detained for an indefinite period.

(4) *Internment:* Under Regulation 12(1) an individual could be interned on the recommendation of a police officer or of the advisory committee created under the Special Powers Act, if the authorizing authority believed internment was expedient in the interests of the preservation of peace and the maintenance of order. Internment could be for any period of time, but was reviewable by the advisory committee. The advi-

sory committee was first chaired by a Northern Ireland county court judge, and later by a deputy judge of the crown court in Oxfordshire. However, the advisory committee had no power to order the release of an internee. An internee had no right to appear himself or to be represented by counsel before the committee, no power to test or examine the grounds for internment, and no right to examine or to call witnesses before the committee.

According to Ireland's complaint, internees had no effective access to court, the writ of habeas corpus being available chiefly to correct technical errors of officers in failing to comply with the letter of the regulations. The only other ground for challenge under habeas corpus was to prove that the relevant official(s) acted without bona fides, which would have required proof of what was in their minds. For example, if an official genuinely suspected a person, that was sufficient grounds for arrest, however unfounded his suspicion might be.

Ireland's strongest case was against the procedures and practices during Phase 1. The United Kingdom conceded that such practices should be exercised only in "conditions of gravest emergency" (*Ireland v. United Kingdom*, ser. A, 79). The 1972 report of the Diplock Commission had indeed explored "the minimal conditions for due process of law in Northern Ireland," but it found that the potential for intimidation of witnesses and juries was such that normal process was not possible. One assumption of the Diplock Report (1972, 9) was "that witnesses to a crime will be able to give evidence in a court of law without risk to their lives, their families or their property. Unless the State can ensure their safety, then it would be unreasonable to expect them to testify voluntarily and morally wrong to compel them to do so." The recommendations of the Diplock Commission contributed to the provisions of the Emergency Powers Act, 1973. Most notably the controversial "Diplock Courts" were created as one consequence of the Diplock Commission's report. These special courts allowed the trial of criminal cases for certain scheduled offenses before a judge, thereby abrogating any right to a jury trial (Diplock Report 1972).

The United Kingdom also argued that many of the provisions employed in 1971–72 had been superseded by subsequent provisions and that the European Commission had no need to express any legal judgment on them.

Seven hundred and seventy detention orders and 525 internment orders were issued in 1971. By November 10, 1971, 980 persons had been arrested. Reports of ill treatment followed soon after the first arrests on August 9, 1971 (*Ireland v. United Kingdom*, ser. A, 25).

Operation Demetrius, August 9, 1971

"Operation Demetrius" was the large and concerted operation against several hundred persons suspected of terrorism launched at dawn on August 9, 1971, the first day of the declaration of emergency powers. Security forces began with a list of 452 suspects. Some say it was a flawed list. The principal historian of the subject, J. Bowyer Bell (1993, 216), wrote, "The list had been stitched up from old lists, fallout from the dry-run raids of the army, and a hit list of critics, some from the civil rights people, some from old grievances, some simply handy radicals. The 450 names represented not the core of the gunmen but the dregs of bad intelligence." Three hundred and fifty-four persons were arrested on that day, 104 of whom were released within forty-eight hours. Sometime thereafter but still in August 1971, twelve suspects, and in October two more, were taken to an unknown center for interrogation. Meanwhile Belfast was burning and the IRA was still active. Indeed on Friday, August 13, the Provisional IRA held a press conference in Belfast in which it was reported that only two Provos had been wounded and only thirty had been interned (Bell 1993, 223).

The Five Techniques

Twelve suspects were subjected to what was known as in-depth interrogation or the "five techniques": hooding, wall-standing, subjection to noise, relative deprivation of food and water, and sleep deprivation. Hooding consisted of covering the head with a black hood, except when being interrogated or when held in a room alone. Wall-standing involved the suspect's standing with his legs spread apart and feet back causing him to stand on his toes, with the weight of the body supported mostly by his fingers against the wall, except when occasionally allowed to lower his hands to restore circulation. Subjection to noise involved continuous exposure to a buzzing monotonous noise at a volume calculated to isolate the suspect from communication with others. Food and water deprivation amounted (by the most favorable account) to one round of bread and one pint of water in six-hour intervals. Sleep deprivation was practiced prior to interrogation. It was often related to wall-standing. If a suspect collapsed or fell asleep while standing, he was raised to his feet and the wall-standing posture was renewed and enforced.

   The European Commission on Human Rights heard 100 witnesses regarding interrogations. The "illustrative cases" it reviewed in its report involved allegations of abusive conduct that sometimes far exceeded even the five techniques. The Commission noted from the Compton and Parker Committee reports conducted by the United Kingdom that the longest period of wall-standing was for forty-three and one-half hours, and there were six instances of twenty hours or more (*Ireland v. United Kingdom*, ser. B, 268). The Compton inquiry, chaired by Sir Edmund Compton, was appointed on August 31, 1971, to investigate allegations of brutality and ill treatment. The *Compton Report* noted eleven cases of the five techniques in its first report and three more in its supplemental report. A committee chaired by Lord Parker (1972) examined the use of the five techniques and a majority of the committee found them to be justified under the circumstances. Lord Gardiner alone found them unjustified.

The United Kingdom admitted that the five techniques had been used for one week in August and another in October 1971 (*Ireland v. United Kingdom,* ser. B, 289). The European Commission noted that the five techniques had never been written in army manuals, but had been transmitted orally for emergency use in "colonial-type" situations at the English Intelligence Centre (*Ireland v. United Kingdom,* ser. B, 268; ser. A, 41). According to the United Kingdom, they eventually were abandoned and were expressly prohibited in an army manual of August 1972. Indeed, Prime Minister Edward Heath himself announced to the House of Commons on March 2, 1972, that the five techniques would no longer be used (*Ireland v. United Kingdom,* ser. B, 399). The United Kingdom also gave the European Court its "unqualified undertaking that the five techniques would not be reintroduced" (*Ireland v. United Kingdom,* ser. A, 43).

The United Kingdom gave three reasons for these emergency measures: the widespread intimidation of witnesses, the need to apprehend those responsible for directing and planning terrorist acts, and the ease of terrorist escape across the border. Of these, the extent of intimidation of witnesses was most insistently disputed by Ireland and the United Kingdom (*Ireland v. United Kingdom,* ser. B, 86–87).

On three occasions (for purposes of the complaints involved in *Ireland v. United Kingdom,* the last one being on August 25, 1971) the United Kingdom had notified the secretary general of the Council of Europe that these security measures were taken under Art. 15 in derogation of its obligations under the ECHR. Sec. 15.1 of the ECHR provides that "in time of war or other public emergency a High Contracting Party may take measures derogating from its obligations under the Convention to the extent *strictly required by the exigencies of the situation*" (emphasis added). Ireland complained that the measures taken were "far greater and more extensive than the measures which would be strictly required by the exigencies of the situation and were inconsistent with the United Kingdom's obligations under international law." The alleged violations of Art. 3, 5, and 6 drew the greatest attention of the Commission, as we shall see below. Ireland also complained that certain deaths, particularly those occurring on "Bloody Sunday" (January 30, 1972) in Londonderry, violated the U.K.'s obligation under Art. 1 "to secure to everyone within its jurisdiction the rights protected by the Convention," the Art. 2 provision against unlawful deprivation of life, and Art. 14's provision against discrimination based on political opinion (read with Art. 5 and 6 in this instance). The Commission found the complaints under Art. 3, 5, 6, and 14 to be admissible. However, it found no discrimination under Art. 14.

Phase II: November 7, 1972, to August 8, 1973

The first day of the period marked the beginning exercise of emergency measures under the Detention of Terrorists Order, while the end is the beginning of measures under the Northern Ireland (Emergency Provisions) Act 1973. On March 30, 1972, the U.K. Parliament passed the Northern Ireland (Temporary Provisions) Act 1972, which suspended self-government in Northern Ireland. The Detention of Terrorists Order was made under that Act. The powers of arrest and detention were not much changed by this order except that anyone suspected of terrorism could be held without trial only for a period of twenty-eight days, unless his case was reviewed by a commissioner, who could determine whether he ought to be held further without trial for an indefinite period, or be set free. The commissioner's proceedings were closed, but the prisoner and his counsel could be (but need not be) admitted. Still, they had no right to examine witnesses or to present their own witnesses. An appellate tribunal was established, but the tribunal ordinarily decided on the record rather than receive fresh evidence (*Ireland v. United Kingdom*, ser. B, 59–62).

Phase III: August 8, 1973, to August 7, 1975

The first date of this period is the beginning of the Emergency Provisions (Northern Ireland) Act 1973 (hereafter called the Emergency Provisions Act). The Emergency Provisions Act in effect repealed the Detention of Terrorists Order, but established its own procedures. These were similar to those immediately preceding, and Ireland's complaints were largely as before. On the last date of Phase III, Parliament passed the Northern Ireland (Emergency Provisions) Amendment 1975. This act took into account recommendations for civil liberties and human rights presented by the Gardiner Commission to Parliament in January 1975. It was not at issue in *Ireland v. United Kingdom*. The provisions most recently in force are the Northern Ireland (Emergency Provisions) Act 1991 and (for the rest of the United Kingdom) the Prevention of Terrorism (Temporary Provisions) Act 1989.

The Complaints Brought by Ireland against the United Kingdom

Beginning with Phase I, Ireland maintained that the steps taken by the United Kingdom under the Civil Authorities (Special Powers) Act 1922 violated a number of provisions of the ECHR, especially the five techniques, which were alleged to violate the provision in Art. 3 against torture and cruel and inhuman treatment or punishment.

The provisions of Art. 4 that prohibit slavery, servitude, and forced or compulsory labor were alleged to be violated by the emergency detention and internment powers exercised by the United Kingdom.

Art. 5.1 of the ECHR guarantees the right to liberty and security of the person, subject to six exceptions: lawful detention of a person after conviction by a court; arrest for noncompliance or in enforcement of a court order; arrest for appearance in court; detention of minors under court orders; arrest due to infectious disease, unsound mind, drug addiction or vagrancy; and arrest due to unlawful entry into the country or for purposes of deportation or extradition. Paragraphs 5.2–5.5 provide for due process safeguards such as the right to be informed of the reason for an arrest, the right to be taken promptly before a magistrate, the right to have the lawfulness of one's detention determined by a court, and the right to compensation for unlawful arrest or detention. Art. 6.1 establishes due process in criminal cases, the particular safeguards of which are detailed in paragraphs 6.2 and in 6.3 (a)–(e). All of these requirements were alleged to have been violated by the United Kingdom.

Finally, Ireland argued that the emergency provisions had been employed by the United Kingdom in a discriminatory manner in violation of Art. 14 (read with Art. 5 and 6) in that they involved discrimination against Irish Republican political opinion.

The United Kingdom's Responses to These Charges

The United Kingdom relied chiefly on the evolution of policy during the three periods we have reviewed. Phase I, admittedly with the most problematic practices, had been replaced with procedures providing some procedural safeguards, and the five techniques had been abandoned. The U.K. was also able to present to the Commission the reports of the various commissions of inquiry that it itself had instituted, including the *Compton Report* in November 1971, the *Parker Report* in January 1972, the *Diplock Report* in December 1972, and the *Gardiner Report* in January 1975. The U.K. argued that the evolution of policy was always toward less stringent measures with greater safeguards. All of the steps taken had, in its account, been strictly required by the emergency it confronted in Northern Ireland, and since the earlier measures were no longer the current practice, the U.K. urged that the Commission need not rule on them at all. Its final argument was that it had sent timely notices of derogation to the secretary general of the Council of Europe whenever it felt it necessary to deviate from the requirements of the ECHR.

The Ruling of the Commission

The Commission began by finding that the broad undertaking of Art. 1 to secure to everyone within a nation's jurisdiction the rights and freedoms safeguarded by the ECHR could not be the subject of a separate breach.

Article 3: Certainly the key decision of the Commission was that it felt bound to express its judgment on the five techniques, even though they had been abandoned by the United Kingdom. The Commission unanimously found these techniques, designed to produce "disorientation" or "sensory deprivation," to be a "modern system of torture" and thus a practice of inhuman treatment and torture under Art. 3; "the five techniques applied together were designed to put severe mental and physical stress, causing severe suffering, on a person in order to obtain interrogation from him" (*Ireland v. United Kingdom*, ser. B, 410–11). The protection provided by Art. 3 was *not* susceptible to derogation under Art. 15.2. This was especially important, given the Commission's conclusions regarding derogation of obligations under Art. 5, as we shall see.

Article 5: The issue under Art. 5 was not whether its provisions had been breached. Even the United Kingdom agreed that they had. The question was whether the U.K. was justified by emergency conditions in its derogation under Art. 15.1 and whether the measures taken by it were strictly necessary. Since the decision of the European Court of Human Rights also treats these questions, we need only note here that the Commission found unanimously that the United Kingdom's derogation was sufficient under Art. 15, both as to the emergency that caused it and as to the necessity of the steps taken (*Ireland v. United Kingdom*, ser. B, 126).

Article 14: After an extensive review of the facts,[2] the Commission found no discrimination. The Court itself had much to say on this question as well.

The Judgment of the European Court of Human Rights

The British government was quite unhappy with the Republic of Ireland's decision to refer its complaint to the European Court of Human Rights (Guelke 1988, 166). This was indeed the first interstate case brought before the Court, and despite the "unqualified undertaking" of the United Kingdom that the five techniques would not be reintroduced, the European Court of Human Rights agreed with the Commission that it was bound to rule on those techniques under Art. 3. The Court particularly noted that it had more than an adjudicative function; it was also its purpose "to elucidate, safeguard and develop the rules instituted by the Convention" (*Ireland v. United Kingdom*, ser. A, 62).

Cruel, inhuman, and degrading treatment: On the merits of the case the Court found the five techniques to be inhuman because they were premeditated and caused, at the least, intense physical and mental suffering. The techniques were degrading "since they were such as to arouse in their victims feelings of fear, anguish and inferiority capable of humiliating and debasing them and possibly breaking their physical or moral resistance" (*Ireland v.*

United Kingdom, ser. A, 66). But then the Court gratuitously distinguished between torture on the one hand and cruel, inhuman, or degrading treatment on the other. Torture, the Court said, was an aggravated and deliberate form of inhuman treatment. "Although the five techniques, as applied in combination, undoubtedly amounted to inhuman and degrading treatment, although their object was the extraction of confessions, the naming of others and/or information and although they were used systematically, they did not occasion suffering of the particular intensity and cruelty implied by the word torture as so understood" (*Ireland v. United Kingdom,* ser. A, 67).

The Court did not offer to disclose exactly how to measure the intensity and cruelty of suffering experienced, but it did find the use of the five techniques on fourteen internees to be cruel, inhuman, and degrading, even if this did not amount to torture. It also found that one other internee (T6 in the record) had individually suffered cruel treatment: "T6 had not been allowed time to drink the water, which sometimes was spilt, deliberately. When examined by a doctor, he had bruises on his right shoulder and legs, a black eye, and contusions on his chest and arms" (*Ireland v. United Kingdom,* ser. B, 290). Cruel and inhuman treatment had also been practiced in the Palace Barracks, Hollywood.

Violations of Article 5 and derogation under Article 15: Once again the question was not whether violations of Art. 5 had occurred, but whether the derogation by the United Kingdom was proper. The derogation covered the issues of arrest for interrogation, arrest and detention without sufficient cause, and detention and internment, often on "good faith" suspicion alone; in all of these instances, review was available only by executive officers or by special committees or tribunals created for the emergency itself. Judicial review through habeas corpus was available only to the limited extent accorded under the common law. And whatever the violations may have been, there was little doubt about the seriousness of the emergency the security forces confronted.

The United Kingdom reported to the Commission that in the first half of 1971 there had been 245 bomb explosions and eight civilians, seventy soldiers, and two members of the Royal Ulster Constabulary shot dead. In July 1971 alone there were eighty-six explosions and two soldiers killed. A major riot occurred on August 5, and on August 9, 1971, internment began. From August 1971 to March 30, 1972 (when the U.K. assumed direct rule) there were reported 1,130 explosions, 2,000 shootings, and 158 civilians, fifty-eight soldiers, and seventeen policemen shot dead (*Ireland v. United Kingdom,* ser. B, 76–78).

To these facts the Court applied an interesting "evolutionary" understanding of justice, finding that whatever the early days may have brought, the course of legislation and practice was always "in the direction of increasing respect for individual liberty." To be sure, their point that it may not be possible "to accomplish everything at once" (from the very beginning of a public emergency) is unexceptionable, but the authority to arrest, detain, and intern remained—at least on paper—much the same as at the beginning. Moreover, the review procedures introduced in 1972 and after, as well as the protection afforded by habeas corpus, may have been largely illusory, as we shall see in the section on Discretion and Emergency Powers under the Common Law below. Nonetheless, the Court noted the various efforts of the United Kingdom to examine and moderate its own practices and held that "Art. 15 must leave a place for progressive adaptations" (*Ireland v. United Kingdom*, ser. A, 83). To that must be added the discretion, called the "margin of appreciation," accorded the United Kingdom under Art. 15. The "margin of appreciation" involves that latitude accorded a country in achieving legitimate objectives, such as national security, in a manner consistent with necessity in a democratic society (Merrills 1993, 199–202).

Taken together, these factors led the Court to the conclusion that the United Kingdom had not taken steps beyond those that were "strictly required" by the emergency itself. Moreover, it had not disregarded any "other obligations under international law" (*Ireland v. United Kingdom*, ser. A: 84–85). One observer concluded that the European Court's analysis of the "strict necessity" of these emergency measures was "neither rigorous nor convincing" (Hartman 1981, 33). The judgments of the Court often consist of serial statements or conclusions and reveal very little of the reasoning that may have led to the Court's conclusions.

Discrimination under Article 14: From the onset of emergency powers on August 9, 1971, up to February 5, 1973, those powers were used exclusively against those suspected of IRA or other Republican terrorism. After February 5, 1973, emergency powers were used against Loyalist terrorists as well, but instances involving the IRA were far greater in number. The Court found several reasons for rejecting Ireland's complaint that the United Kingdom had engaged in discriminatory enforcement. At the outset they found "profound differences" between Loyalist and Republican terrorism. They found the IRA to be both a more frequent threat and a larger and "more structured" foe. The Court said that through its use of intimidation the IRA was more capable of acting with impunity, while it was easier to bring routine criminal charges against Loyalists. Even after it had assumed direct rule in March 1972, the Court was prepared to concede to the United Kingdom the right to proceed first or predominantly against its most formidable foe. Eventually in February 1973, the United Kingdom moved against the Loyalists as well, even though the preponderance of actions continued to be taken against the IRA because their actions continued to be more frequent and less susceptible to conventional legal processes. All these findings led the Court to the conclusion that there had been no discrimination under Art. 14 (taken with Art. 5).

So in the end, given the effect of derogation, the United Kingdom was found guilty only of violations of Art. 3, but of cruel and inhuman treatment rather than torture. The dissent of the judge then sitting on the European Court of Human Rights from the United Kingdom is interesting for rejecting even that outcome.

Judge Fitzmaurice's dissent: The dissent begins with Judge Sir Gerald Fitzmaurice's careful effort to dissociate himself from minimizing or "playing down" the five techniques, while still questioning the evidence on the nature of these practices. For example, note the following: "there still remains an element of considerable uncertainty on a number of points of obvious importance when it comes to assessing the degree of overall severity entailed by their use—e.g. the length and frequency of the periods of hooding and deprivation of sleep, food and water, the quality of the subjection to noise (something which affects some people very badly, others hardly at all), the real length of the maximum continuous period of wall-standing involved, and to some extent the exact posture, in which quite slight variations could make a considerable difference to its bearability" (*Ireland v. United Kingdom*, ser. A, 121). His major concern was with the proper definition of the terms "cruel," "inhuman," and "degrading." He agreed that the five techniques involved "harsh treatment," "ill treatment," or "maltreatment," but "inhuman treatment" was, he suggested, of a whole different order. He also rejected the commonplace meanings of the words cruel, inhuman, and degrading. These, he argued, are often used rhetorically. If such words are used to describe the five techniques, he asked, what words would be used to describe something even worse? "[W]hat language should be used to describe kicking a man in the groin, or placing him in a blacked-out cell in the company of a bevy of starving rats?" If everything that is physically or mentally injurious to human beings is deemed inhuman, he argued, then the word would become meaningless (*Ireland v. United Kingdom*, ser. A, 121–22).

Of course, he has a point, but the key difficulty may be that he expects too much precision of language. The majority found the practices to be cruel, degrading, and inhuman. Fitzmaurice did not. Can their differences be objectively measured? Or can we only use imprecise words to *describe* our conclusions? Judges and lawyers easily play just this sort of language game when seeking to give the illusion of precision, for example, in assessing the severity of the public emergency. When *exactly* does an emergency justify a derogation under Art. 15? It takes some detachment to apprehend the inevitable imprecision and probable futility of some language games. Thus as Humpty

Dumpty said to Alice, "When I use a word it means just what I choose it to mean, neither more nor less." But Alice disagreed. "The question is whether you can make words mean so many different things." This Humpty Dumpty trumped by replying, "The question is which is to be master—that's all" (Carroll, *Through the Looking Glass*). In the balance of this paper we will several times encounter other language games, but sometimes the verbal distinctions may make more sense analytically, for example, when working out the distinction between the subjective and objective reasonableness of suspicions.

DISCRETION AND EMERGENCY POWERS UNDER THE COMMON LAW

The following pages recount events that probably are little known in the United States; they are even less well known than the background events in Northern Ireland reviewed above. Nonetheless, they certainly may enlighten our understanding of the United Kingdom's use of emergency powers.

During World War II, almost 2,000 persons were interned in Britain without formal charges and without trial. To be sure, most of them were enemy aliens, but some of them were British citizens. All of them were held under Regulation 18B of the Defence Regulations. Brian Simpson's excellent book, *In the Highest Degree Odious* (1992) is the best source on this subject. Most of what is written here is drawn from it. My purpose here is only to relate enough background to help understand the relevant common law cases. Simpson's book is highly recommended for its detailed treatment of this subject.

The Emergency Powers (Defence) Act 1939 provided for regulations that would allow the home secretary to detain persons in the interests of "public safety or the defence of the realm." Regulation 18B, as first issued in September 1939 and as amended in November 1939, provided for such detention. The amendment required the home secretary to have *reasonable cause* to believe that a person was of hostile origins, or had hostile associations, or to have been concerned in acts prejudicial to the public safety or the defense of the realm. If the home secretary was reasonably satisfied, he could issue a detention order against any such person (Simpson 1992, 424). Regulation 18B provided for review by an advisory committee, which could review a detainee's complaints. The advisory committee could recommend, but not direct, that a detainee be released. We should note that detention under 18B is practically the same as internment under Regulation 12(1) of the Civil Authorities (Special Powers) Act 1922, as it was enforced in Northern Ireland in 1971.

It should also be stressed that detention in Britain during World War II was not an innovation, but it is interesting that the nineteenth-century precedents—all of them—stemmed from the efforts of Britain to rule Ireland. Simpson cites the Habeas Corpus Suspension Acts, last used in Ireland in 1866–67, the

Protection of Life and Property (Ireland) Act 1871, and the 1881 Act for the Better Protection of Person and Property in Ireland (Simpson 1992, 2–5).

World War I brought detention to Britain itself, when the Defence of the Realm Act led in 1915 to Regulation 14B, which endured until 1923, and which was the immediate precedent for 18B during World War II. The Restoration of Order in Ireland Act 1920 continued detention in Ireland after the Easter Rising, and, as we have seen, the Special Powers Act of 1922 was still in effect in Northern Ireland when arrest for interrogation, detention, and internment began on August 9, 1971.

The Greene and Liversidge Cases

Two World War II detainees appealed their detention all the way to the House of Lords. Ben Greene was a British subject born in Brazil, but his mother was born a German national. He was both a longtime member of the Labour movement and a Quaker pacifist. His commitment to pacifism may have been so strong that he became vulnerable to German propaganda regarding both the causes of the war and Britain's participation in it. He certainly had contacts with fascists and with admirers of Hitler, and he apparently believed that the war with Britain had not been Hitler's fault. Greene was detained for "hostile associations" in May 1940.

Robert W. Liversidge was a native born British citizen, whose parents were Jewish immigrants from Russia. He had been involved in a variety of questionable business dealings during his early adult years, and had acquired a false name (Liversidge) and a Canadian passport in that name. During the late 1930s he became associated with some shady right-wing businessmen in London, had some German business contacts, and also had several acquaintances in British intelligence. He was, however, commissioned as a pilot officer in the RAF in late 1939, and served successfully as an intelligence officer. Indeed, he was serving at Fighter Command headquarters when he was arrested in May 1940. The reasons for his arrest are unclear. An acquaintance of Liversidge was investigated for his part in a wartime racket, and this brought attention to Liversidge as well. Investigation of his background revealed that he had used several identities and that he was commissioned and serving under a false name. He was also serving where he had access to state secrets. One possibility is that he may have known that the British had broken German codes and were able to monitor the Luftwaffe's flight plans (Simpson 1992, 333–39). In any event, he was detained for his "hostile associations."

Liversidge's suit was against the home secretary for false imprisonment, while Greene brought a writ of habeas corpus to question the legality of his detention.

Greene v. Secretary of State for Home Affairs (1941): What might have become a complicated factual dispute on the grounds for Greene's detention became simple with their lordships giving the home secretary what amounted to absolute and final discretion on questions of detention. Greene had been given six paragraphs of particulars regarding his activities, which were alleged to represent acts prejudicial to the public safety and defense of the realm, although the detention order had only cited hostile associations. Either way, the House of Lords viewed the matter as over once the home secretary produced the detention order and represented to the court that he had in good faith ordered Greene's detention. It was up to Greene to produce evidence that the home secretary acted without bona fides. This was virtually impossible, for the necessary condition for detention was subjective, not objective. The courts could only make sure that the steps required by the regulation had been followed in good order.

Liversidge v. Anderson (1941): Liversidge had sued for false imprisonment, to which the home secretary responded with the detention order issued under 18B as grounds for detention. Then Liversidge applied for particulars as to the grounds for his imprisonment. His application was rejected by a King's Bench judge and that ruling was upheld by the Court of Appeal, which, however, granted leave to appeal to the House of Lords. The question was a simple one: who had the burden of proving or disproving the justification for the detention?

Liversidge argued that the general rule was that whenever legislation interferes with the liberty of a subject, the legislation ought to be construed in favor of the subject and against the Crown, but most of the Law Lords would have none of that. The general rule, Viscount Maugham wrote, had no relevance when dealing with a public danger when the safety of the state is involved. On a similar point, Clinton Rossiter (1948, 158, footnote 22) cited Sir Frederick Pollock's letter of May 14, 1917, to Oliver Wendell Holmes, "It is my private opinion that in time of war there is no such thing as the liberty of the subject." The words "reasonable cause" should be construed to mean only that the home secretary must act on what he in good faith thought to be good cause. No objectively determinable reasonable cause was intended by legislation clearly designed for an emergency. And here is the coup de grâce, "To my mind this is so clearly a matter for executive discretion and nothing else that I cannot believe that those responsible for the Order in Council could have contemplated for a moment the possibility of the action of the Secretary of State being subject to the discussion, criticism and control of a judge in a court of law" (*Liversidge*, 345–46).

The only reservations were contained in Lord Atkin's dissent. In his view the natural construction of the words "reasonable cause" meant an objective condition, which must "in case of dispute be cognizable by a court of law"

(*Liversidge*, 356). To rule otherwise is, in effect, to put the matter beyond judicial review. Atkin suggested that Viscount Maugham had put it well when he wrote, "The only safeguards, if they be safeguards, is that detention `appears to the Secretary of State to be expedient in the interests of public safety or the defence of the realm,' and that he himself is subject to the control of Parliament" (*Liversidge*, 345). So in the end detainees could only take their objections to the advisory committee or seek the intervention of the home secretary himself.

Lord Atkin's dissent contained some harsh words about his fellow judges. In addition to characterizing them with his famous use of the Humpty Dumpty quote from *Through the Looking Glass*, cited above, he expressed the following concern: "I view with apprehension the attitude of judges who, on a mere question of construction, when face to face with claims involving the liberty of the subject, show themselves more executive minded than the executive" (*Liversidge*, 361).

Two articles on the *Liversidge* case are especially interesting. The first recounts the recriminations between Lord Atkin and his peers for the words used in his *Liversidge* dissent (Heuston 1970). The second suggests that while Atkin may have been correct in his interpretation of the language used in the amended version of 18B, the framers of that regulation probably did *not* intend to create the basis for judicial review (Heuston 1971).

Some knowledge of the history of wartime detention in Britain and of the reluctance of common law courts to exercise judicial review in such cases should help place the European Court's ruling on derogation in *Ireland v. United Kingdom* in perspective. A state of emergency has existed in Northern Ireland since its beginning in 1922. During its entire history, statutes have provided emergency powers that have always included arrest and detention, without the safeguards otherwise provided by law (Human Rights Watch 1991, 1). And, as far as British law itself is concerned, common law judges have mostly kept their hands off. This deference to the executive was reinforced by the conclusion of the European Court of Human Rights that an appropriate sense of deference to a nation's own assessment of its state of emergency—coupled with a margin of appreciation—required it to sustain the United Kingdom's derogation. That result governed complaints about emergency powers until ten years later, when the Court's next opportunity arose to apply the ECHR.

Brogan and Others v. United Kingdom (1988)

Brogan and three others were arrested under section 12 of the Prevention of Terrorism (Temporary Provision) Act 1984. That act, the first version of which came into effect in November 1974, proscribed the IRA and in section 12(1) provided that a constable may arrest with warning any person whom he has reasonable grounds for suspecting to be a terrorist. Section 12(4) provides for 48 hours initial detention and section 12(5) provides that detention may be extended for five more days by the home secretary. Section 14(1) defines terrorism as "the use of violence for political ends." Brogan and the other three detainees complained that their detention violated Art. 5.3 because they were not taken promptly before a magistrate.

The European Commission of Human Rights found in favor of Brogan (five days, eleven hours' detention) and Coyle (six days and sixteen hours) on the ground that their length of detention without judicial review violated Art. 5.3. The other two were detained for slightly shorter periods, and their complaints were rejected.

The United Kingdom had withdrawn its derogation under Art. 15 on August 22, 1984, and had represented to the Council of Europe that "the provisions of the Convention are being fully executed" (*Brogan and Others v. United Kingdom*, ser. A, 27–28).

During 1987, extensions for detention beyond 48 hours had been granted for 365 detainees. Eighty-three suspects were detained for more than five days, and of these, thirty-nine were eventually charged with serious terrorist offenses.

The Case of *Brogan and Others* before the European Court

Article 5.3: Art. 5.3 provides that everyone lawfully arrested or detained "shall be brought *promptly* before a judge or other officer authorized by law to exercise judicial power, and shall be entitled to trial within a reasonable time or to release pending trial" (emphasis added). In *Brogan* the Court used an interesting method for determining the meaning of the word *promptly* in this context. The ECHR's two official languages are English and French, and in the French text the word for *promptly* is *aussitôt*, which literally means *immediately*. Of course, none of the four suspects was brought immediately before a judge, thus the Court through its interpretation easily found a breach of Art. 5.3 with respect to all of them. The judge for the United Kingdom again dissented, and protested that the Court needed to strike a fair balance between the requirements of Art. 5.3 and the need of "protecting human rights against the continuing inhumanity of terrorism in Northern Ireland" (*Brogan and Others v. United Kingdom*, ser. A, 46).

Article 5.4: Art. 5.4 provides that anyone deprived of his liberty "shall be entitled to take proceedings by which the lawfulness of his detention shall be decided speedily by a court." The European Court found that there was no violation of Art. 5.4 because an effective remedy through habeas corpus was available to detainees. Given what we have already seen about habeas corpus review in World War II detention cases, it is important to see whether the scope of review may have changed since the *Liversidge* and *Greene* cases of 1941. Among other precedents, the European Court cited the Northern Ireland case of *Ex parte Lynch* (1980).

Ex parte Lynch was a habeas corpus case with facts much like *Brogan*. Lynch was arrested on May 27, 1980, under section 11 of the Northern Ireland (Emergency Provisions) Act 1978 on suspicion of being a terrorist and held until May 30. He was rearrested on June 2 under section 12(1)(b) of the Prevention of Terrorism (Temporary Provisions) Act 1976, and his detention was extended until June 9, but on June 3, his counsel had applied for a writ of habeas corpus. The hearing on the writ was held on June 5. The constable's affidavit in response to the writ was quoted by the Court and included the following:

> 2. On the basis of my existing knowledge and the information given to me at the said briefing I suspected that the said Martin Henry Lynch had been concerned in the commission, preparation or instigation of acts of terrorism.

> 4. I ... arrested the said Martin Henry Lynch informing him that I was arresting him under section 12 of the Prevention of Terrorism (Temporary Provisions) Act 1976 as I suspected him of being involved in terrorist activities and I brought him to Castlereagh Police Office. (*Lynch,* 128)

Counsel for Lynch maintained that the affidavit disclosed neither the acts of terrorism of which Lynch was suspected nor the sources of information and belief as to the facts that led to the arrest. His second point was material as to the scope of review under habeas corpus. Lynch's counsel sought to review the reasonableness of the constable's suspicion; thus some disclosure of the facts on which his suspicion was based was crucial. The Court said, however, that Lynch's counsel sought the "sources of the information and belief on which his suspicion was founded," while the affidavit disclosed the "sources and grounds of his reasonable suspicion" (*Lynch,* 131).

Neither of those statements rings quite true. It is certainly *possible* to seek the nature of the information on which suspicion was founded without seeking the sources of such information, and it is not likely that any British court would require the disclosure of confidential sources at this stage of a case of suspected terrorism. There is a possibility, of course, that the disclosure of certain information would lead to the identity of a source, but were that the case, it certainly would be appropriate for the judge either to proceed *in camera* or to refuse disclosure of the information on those grounds.

It is also not quite right to say that the affidavit in *Lynch* disclosed the *grounds* of the constable's reasonable suspicion. The two paragraphs of the affidavit quoted consist of conclusions or assertions rather than grounds or reasons. According to the Court, all that is required is that the constable state under oath (based on knowledge and information) that he did suspect Lynch. The Court's conclusion was, "In our view it would be perverse, on the affidavit evidence which is available, to deny the reasonableness of the *arresting constable's* suspicion" (*Lynch,* 131, emphasis added). The key point is that since Brogan was arrested under section 12 of the Prevention of Terrorism Act 1984, which had the same language as in the second Lynch arrest, the scope of review that he might have obtained in a British court would have been the same.

The ruling in *Lynch* was also highlighted by the House of Lords in 1984 in *McKee v. Chief Constable for Northern Ireland.* There Lord Roskill spoke for a unanimous bench when he ruled that section 11 of the Northern Ireland (Emergency Provisions) Act 1978, which did not include the word *reasonable* before the word *suspicion,* allowed a constable to arrest McKee on his subjective suspicion, with no requirement that the objective reasonableness of the suspicion be proven to a court. We should note that in *McKee* a constable made the arrest on the instructions of his superior officers. This, Lord Roskill said, ought to protect the constable who "may well not be entitled to question those instructions or to ask on what information they are founded" (*McKee,* 4). In a suit for unlawful arrest and imprisonment, it is not clear why the *superior's* suspicion cannot be subjected to a test of objective reasonableness. The House of Lords, however, did not entertain that possibility. So much for the scope of judicial review offered under habeas corpus.

The European Court of Human Rights acknowledged that Art. 5.4 requires that "the applicants should have had available to them a remedy allowing the competent court to examine not only compliance with the procedural requirement set out in section 12 of the 1984 Act but also *the reasonableness of the suspicion grounding the arrest*" (*Brogan and Others v. United Kingdom,* ser. A, 25, 34–35, emphasis added). Yet it found that the sort of review affirmed by the *Lynch* judgment satisfied the requirement of Art. 5.4 (*Brogan and Others v. United Kingdom,* ser. A, 34–35). So at the end it was only the length of detention without judicial intervention that the European Court found to be a violation in the *Brogan* case.

The next day (November 30, 1988) *The Times* headlined its report of the *Brogan* judgment "European Court ruling a setback to security." On December 21, the home secretary informed the House of Commons that Britain would declare a derogation under Art. 15 because of the *Brogan* ruling. He also advised the House that the derogation would provide time for the government to consider the possibility of introducing a "judicial element" into the period of holding terrorists for questioning. He noted that some countries hold suspects for months, but do not violate the ECHR because of their use of examining magistrates (*The Times,* December 7, 23, 1988).

Two years later the United Kingdom was once more before the European Court, again on a question involving the prevention of terrorism, but this time directly on the question of subjective versus objective suspicion.

Fox, Campbell & Hartley v. United Kingdom (1990)

On February 5, 1986, Bernard Fox and Maire Campbell, who were husband and wife, though separated, were stopped by police in Belfast and taken to an RUC station. They were arrested under section 11(1) of the Northern Ireland (Emergency Provisions) Act 1978 and informed that they were being arrested because they were suspected of being terrorists. Fox was held for forty-four hours and Campbell a few minutes more. Both were released on February 7. Both had initiated habeas corpus proceedings on February 7, but they were released before their applications could be heard. Both had previous convictions for terrorist-related offenses and were questioned about specific and recent terrorist activities.

Hartley was arrested at his home in the presence of his parents on August 18, 1986. He also was arrested under section 11(1) and advised that he was suspected of being a terrorist. He was questioned about his suspected participation in a kidnapping but was released on August 19 after thirty hours of detention. He brought no action before a domestic court.

The complaints of Fox, Campbell, and Hartley to the European Commission were several; the Commission found violations of Art. 5.1, 5.2, and 5.5. Only the issues under 5.1 are critical to the present review.

Section 11(1), under which the three were arrested, provides that a constable may arrest without warrant any person whom he suspects of being a terrorist. Section 11(3) provides for detention for not more than seventy-two hours, unless extended. Section 31(1) defines a "terrorist" as "a person who is, or has been concerned in the commission or attempted commission of any act of terrorism or in directing, organizing or training persons for the purposes of terrorism." "Terrorism" is "the use of violence for political ends and includes any use of violence for the purpose of putting the public or any section of the public in fear." Section 21 proscribes terrorist organizations, including the IRA.

The European Court again recited a litany of horrors in Northern Ireland—2,750 killed in the past twenty years, including 800 members of the security forces, and 31,900 maimed or injured—thus showing its appreciation for the continuing emergency confronted by the United Kingdom. Yet that appreciation was not decisive in this instance.

Sir George Baker had been asked to head an examination of the provisions of the Northern Ireland (Emergency Provisions) Act 1978, and he had reported in 1984 on the distinction between subjective and objective suspicion. He suggested that the suspicion required of a constable under 11(1) is indeed subjective. "If his suspicion is an honest genuine suspicion that the person being arrested is a terrorist, a court cannot enquire further into the exercise of the power. But where the requirement is reasonable suspicion it is for the court to judge the reasonableness of the suspicion. It is an objective standard" (*Fox, Campbell & Hartley v. United Kingdom*, ser. A, 12).

In addition to the *Baker Report*, the European Court cited *McKee v. Chief Constable* as precedent for requiring under section 11(1) merely the subjective standard in which bona fides is the only question. At this point the European Court noted that Section 11(1) of the 1978 Act had been replaced by Section 6 of the Northern Ireland (Emergency Provisions) Act 1987, which came into effect on June 15, 1987. The new section requires reasonable suspicion, and thus the *Fox, Campbell & Hartley* judgment will not require the derogation that the *Brogan* case required (Warbrick 1990, 548).

In ruling four to three that Art. 5.1 requires a judicially reviewable objective standard, the majority of the European Court noted the problems of confidentiality and disclosure in cases of terrorism, but added, "the exigencies of dealing with terrorist crime cannot justify stretching the notions of 'reasonableness' to the point where the essence of the safeguard secured by Article 5 § 1 c is impaired" (*Fox, Campbell & Hartley v. United Kingdom*, ser. A, 16–17).

But, in its eagerness to recognize the need to protect confidential sources, all that the majority required was that the United Kingdom furnish "at least some facts or information capable of satisfying the Court that the arrested person was reasonably suspected of having committed the alleged offense" (*Fox, Campbell & Hartley v. United Kingdom*, ser. A, 18). The facts that Fox and Campbell had previous terrorist convictions and that they were questioned about specific terrorist acts, however, were not sufficient, in the view of the European Court, to satisfy the objective test.

Sir Vincent Evans, the judge of United Kingdom nationality then serving on the European Court, was joined by two others in dissent. While they did not reject the requirement of objective reasonableness, they would have inferred reasonable suspicion from previous convictions and from the totality of facts and circumstances. Their genuine suspicion "must have had some basis in information received by them, albeit from sources which the government maintain they are unable to disclose for security reasons" (*Fox, Campbell & Hartley v. United Kingdom*, ser. A, 24).

Together, the cases of *Brogan* and *Fox, Campbell & Hartley* require an objectively reviewable standard of reasonableness for arrests *and* the prompt review of arrests by a magistrate. As noted above, the Northern Ireland (Emergency Provisions) Act 1987 added the word *reasonable* before the word *suspicion*, so the violation of the *Fox, Campbell and Hartley* case should now be met by statute, at least as to violations arising after the effective date of the 1987 statute (and subject, of course, to the vagaries of judicial review by British judges). However, the implications of the *Fox, Campbell and Hartley* judgment for incidents occurring *before the effective date of the 1987 statute* have had a denouement in the case of *Margaret Murray v. United Kingdom*, which will be reviewed below, after we take up the case of *Brannigan and McBride*. As we have seen, the *Brogan* judgment was the subject of derogation in 1988 by the United Kingdom, the derogation recently being upheld by the European Court in *Brannigan and McBride v. United Kingdom*.

Brannigan and McBride v. the United Kingdom (1993)

Brannigan and McBride were arrested during January 1989. Brannigan was held altogether for more than six days; McBride was held for more than four days. McBride was killed before the European Court could rule on his case. He was one of three people killed at a Sinn Féin center by an RUC officer, who killed himself as well a few hours after the murders (*Statewatch*, 1993). Both were eventually seen by doctors and by their solicitors, but neither was taken before a magistrate for a hearing.

On December 23, 1988, the United Kingdom had informed the secretary general of the Council of Europe of its derogation pursuant to the ruling in the *Brogan* case; thus the issue before the Court in *Brannigan and McBride* was the validity of that derogation. The argument on behalf of the detainees was that given the "quasi-permanent" nature of the state of emergency in Northern Ireland, the margin of appreciation accorded the United Kingdom should be restricted, especially given the Court's ruling in *Brogan* that judicial review was one of the fundamental requirements of a democratic society. The view that the margin of appreciation ought to contract with the duration of the emergency was made also in written submissions by various human rights groups, which suggested that the terms of any derogation ought to be subjected to "strict scrutiny" (*Brannigan and McBride v. United Kingdom*, 569).[3] However, the Court declined the suggestion that the standard of review should be narrowed, the majority declaring instead that a *wide* margin of appreciation ought to prevail (*Brannigan and McBride v. United Kingdom*, 574).

That by itself was probably enough to determine the outcome, but the majority went on to note the insistence of the United Kingdom that judicial participation in the decision to extend detention would have two inevitable consequences: the possible disclosure to the detainee and his counsel of highly confidential information and the possible intrusion on the independence of the judiciary through its participation in the detention process. Taking account of the size and vulnerability of the judiciary in Northern Ireland to terrorist attacks, the majority (twenty-two to four) found that the margin of appreciation had not been exceeded (*Brannigan and McBride v. United Kingdom*, 576). The majority also repeated its problematic previous rulings that the availability of the writ of habeas corpus provided a safeguard under British law.

The four dissents are interesting because they suggest that some judges were growing tired of the persistent state of emergency and consequent derogations in Northern Ireland. Judge Pettiti of France complained that a derogation should not constitute "a *carte blanche* accorded the State for an unlimited duration." He particularly refused to concede that the independence of a judge might be undermined by participating in the decision whether or not to extend a period of detention. Nor was he impressed with the safeguard offered by the writ of habeas corpus, based on the experience with that writ in Northern Ireland since 1974. Finally, he held that "incommunicado detention" was in violation of the standards of international law (*Brannigan and McBride v. United Kingdom*, 583–84).

Judge Walsh of Ireland was also unimpressed by the United Kingdom's concerns about judicial participation. At the experiential level he noted that "rarely, if ever does a court in the United Kingdom press for such [confidential] sources and a police claim of privilege against disclosure is invariably upheld." He also spurned the suggestion that the writ of habeas corpus was available as a safeguard in detention cases, for the simple reason that detention for seven days was perfectly legal under ordinary British law coupled with the fact that the ECHR has not been adopted as part of U.K. domestic law (*Brannigan and McBride v. United Kingdom*, 584–88).

The dissenting opinions of Judges De Meyer and Makarczyk and the concurring opinions of Judges Russo and Martens together suggest that the duration of the derogations by the United Kingdom and the "width" of the margin of appreciation granted the United Kingdom were becoming problematic, but not, of course, for the great majority of the Court (*Brannigan and McBride v. United Kingdom*, 589–93).

Margaret Murray v. United Kingdom (1994)

This case involved an application of the rule in *Fox, Campbell and Hartley* (1990) since it encompassed an incident that occurred in 1982, *prior to the* effective date of the Northern Ireland (Emergency Provisions) Act 1987.[4] We noted in discussing the decision in *Fox, Campbell and Hartley* above that section 11(1) of the 1987 act had added the word "reasonable" before the word "suspicion," thus meeting the requirement of that decision. But since the incident in the *Murray* case had occurred in 1982, the European Court was forced to apply the *Fox, Campbell and Hartley* rule. Thus, it was necessary for the

Court to determine whether Margaret Murray's arrest by the British army was in fact based on "reasonable" suspicion. While the European Commission had found a violation of Mrs. Murray's rights under Art. 5.1c, consistent with the *Fox* ruling the Court found *no* violation (by a vote of fourteen to four). Probably the key to the Court's ruling was its willingness to accept the U.K.'s representation that there existed "strong and specific grounds, founded on information from a reliable but secret source" (*Margaret Murray v. United Kingdom*, 224).[5] Still, the European Court did not yield entirely to the claim of secrecy; it also relied on its review of the evidence produced in the U.K.'s domestic courts regarding Mrs. Murray's allegations. Overall, however, the Court was much more deferential than the Commission had been, and it concluded that the arrest was based on reasonable suspicion under the totality of the circumstances.

The next case we will consider produced a quite different result.

McCann and Others v. United Kingdom (1995)

A recent and important decision on the United Kingdom's efforts to deal with terrorism was delivered by the European Court on September 27, 1995, more than seven years after Mairead Farrell, Danny McCann, and Sean Savage were shot and killed by the Special Air Service in the streets of Gibraltar. While concluding that there was insufficient proof to substantiate the premeditation of these killings, the Court found that the SAS's training and methods in the use of firearms "lacked the degree of caution in the use of firearms to be expected from law enforcement personnel in a democratic society, even when dealing with terrorist subjects" (*McCann and Others v. United Kingdom*, 282; *Statewatch* 1995c, 18).[6] Thus, the Court ruled by a narrow margin (ten to nine) that the killings were in violation of Art. 2's protection of the right to life.

According to the account of the *McCann* decision published in *Statewatch*, the background to the shootings recited in the Court's judgment was quite different than the various accounts of the incident reported by the British government. British security personnel had known about a pending IRA operation in Gibraltar for some time, including the "target, the day and the personnel involved." The suspects were under surveillance by MI5 both in Spain and Gibraltar. The guidelines for the use of deadly force by the SAS provided that "You and your men may fire without warning if the giving of a warning or any delay in firing could lead to death or injury to you or them or any other person, or if the giving of a warning is impracticable." The three suspects could have been arrested as they entered Gibraltar. In the event, they were shot within Gibraltar while unarmed, and no explosives were found in their vehicle. The autopsies indicated that "Farrell had been shot three times in the back, from a distance of three feet. She had five wounds to the head and neck.

McCann had been shot twice in the back and three times in the head. Savage was 'riddled with bullets'. . . . He had been hit by sixteen bullets and had seven wounds in the head and neck, five on the front chest, five on the back, one on each shoulder, three on the abdomen, two in the left leg, two in the right arm and two on the left hand." The official pathologist "agreed it would be reasonable to suppose that the bullets were fired into Savage's head as he lay on the ground" (*Statewatch* 1995c, 19–20).

The U.K. government's first accounts of the Gibraltar killings suggested a whitewash, backed up by a stone wall, and followed by a tactical retreat as contradictory evidence was presented. Early on it was claimed that the IRA suspects were armed and that they had exchanged shots with the SAS. That was not true. It was then asserted that they had been shot only after having planted a car bomb. That too was untrue, although it was true that planting such a bomb was their intention. The government also suggested that the killings had been by the Gibraltar police rather than the SAS, which again was untrue. Eventually the British government was forced to admit that the suspects had been unarmed and that they had no explosives in their possession. The last line of the government's defense was to rely on the security forces' reasonable supposition that the vehicle driven by the suspects did contain a large bomb and that the suspects' furtive movements when challenged suggested either their reaching for weapons or their attempt to detonate the bomb by radio signal.

Many contradictions of the official version of events emerged through a Thames Television program, "Death on the Rock," and through a BBC *Spotlight* program, which was broadcast in Northern Ireland. These programs were shown despite the intervention of Foreign Secretary Sir Geoffrey Howe, who had personally attempted to block their showing.

Deputy Prime Minister Michael Heseltine expressed the government's response to the European Court's ruling. He "suggested the ruling would encourage a 'terrorist mentality,' that the decision was 'incredible' and that the government intended to ignore the ruling and do nothing about it" (*Statewatch* 1995c, 20). Another suggestion coming from the United Kingdom has been that the right of individual petition to the European Court ought to be withdrawn (*European Human Rights Law Review* 1995, 97).

John Murray v. United Kingdom (1996)

The most recent decision of the European Court of Human Rights regarding the United Kingdom's effort to deal with terrorism in Northern Ireland involved a limitation on the right to remain silent and the temporary suspension of the right of access to legal counsel. The Court held by a vote of fourteen to five that there had been no violation of Art. 6.1 or 6.2 of the ECHR by virtue of a judge being allowed to draw adverse inferences from an accused's silence during police interrogation and at trial pursuant to Art. 4 and 6 of the Criminal Evidence (Northern Ireland) Order 1988. The key to the Court's judgment was that it could envision particular circumstances, such as those here, under which a judge could reasonably exercise "ordinary commonsense" in drawing appropriate inferences of guilt from the accused's silence. However, the Court did find a violation (by a vote of twelve to seven) in the denial of access by the accused to a lawyer during the first forty-eight hours of his detention by police. Section 15 of the Northern Ireland (Emergency Provisions) Act 1987 allowed a senior police officer to delay compliance with the rights of access to a lawyer for a maximum of forty-eight hours on the grounds that access to an attorney may lead to interference with the gathering of information about the commission, preparation, or instigation of acts of terrorism or may make it more difficult to prevent an act of terrorism or to secure the apprehension, prosecution, or conviction of any person with respect to an act of terrorism. While the Court accepted that such restrictions on access to a lawyer could represent a "lawful exercise of the power to restrict access," given the circumstances in Northern Ireland, it found that even a lawful restriction on access was capable of depriving an accused of fair procedure in certain circumstances. In the absence of counsel the accused was forced to choose, on his own, between possibly damaging his case by the adverse inferences that might be drawn from his silence and possibly irretrievably prejudicing his defense by breaking his silence. Thus to deny the accused the advice of a lawyer was found to be incompatible with the right to fair procedures under Art. 6 (*John Murray v. United Kingdom,* 48). It should be noted, however, that the sanction applied to the United Kingdom was modest. The Court found that the determination of a violation of Art. 6, coupled with a partial award of costs and expenses, was "just satisfaction" for the violation suffered by Murray.

Conclusions

To review briefly: In the first case we reviewed, *Ireland v. United Kingdom,* Ireland's complaint against the United Kingdom was filed before the Commission on December 16, 1971. Neither the *Compton Report* (August 1971, before the filing) nor the *Parker Report* (March 1972, after the filing) condemned the five techniques of interrogation, but the dissenting member of the Parker Committee (Lord Gardiner) did. On March 5, 1972, Prime Minister Edward Heath accepted Lord Gardiner's view and announced to the Commons that the five techniques of deep interrogation would no longer be practiced. In an army manual published in August 1972, the U.K. government prohibited the use of the five techniques.

While the sequence of these events alone is no proof of causation, it is reasonable to suggest that the complaint then pending before the European Commission may have contributed to the U.K.'s change of policy. To be sure, there was a great deal of publicity about the use of emergency powers in Northern Ireland—much of it hostile—so the complaint before the Commission was only one factor among many. In any event, the Commission found the United Kingdom guilty of practices that amounted to torture, and while the Court found that the five techniques represented cruel treatment rather than torture, the United Kingdom was found guilty of a nonderogable violation of Art. 3.

Through other committee reports, through the cumulative pressure of publicity and politics, and perhaps also through its own efforts to defend its good intentions against the pending complaint by Ireland, the U.K. government also modified its emergency practices to provide some self-imposed limits and safeguards. These steps proved sufficient to convince both the European Commission and Court that the government's derogations were within the boundaries of strict necessity and the margin of appreciation allowed by Art. 15. Nevertheless, the presence of the Commission and the Court probably helped press constraints on the government and its security forces. These might not have come from the U.K. government acting entirely on its own, that is, if the World War II cases on internment are indicative.

It is also important to remember the recent beginnings of the ECHR and its institutions. The ECHR went into effect in 1953, the first judges of the European Court of Human Rights were elected in 1959, and by 1982 only about thirty cases had been brought before the Court. One scholar has commented that "the political foundations of the Convention are such that the Commission is wary of examining Art. 15 in an exacting and thorough manner" (O'Boyle 1977, 183). That would be neither surprising nor exceptional. At a comparable point in its history the U.S. Supreme Court had not accomplished much beyond the establishment of the power of judicial review, and that was done by Chief Justice John Marshall, mostly by clever misdirection.

The direct ruling in the *Brogan* case probably contributed much less than *Ireland v. U.K.* because of its more narrow holding and its successful derogation which, unlike *Ireland v. U.K.*, entirely covered the violation. Still, despite the persistent efforts of the U.K. officials to find a way around derogation by agreeing to some form of judicial review, they failed, and through their derogation were forced to admit their failure.

Their failure may have been due in part to their "habits of thought and preferred way of governing" (Churchill and Young 1991, 346). This would not be surprising if their habits and preferences of governing indeed were those of what has sometimes been called an "elected dictatorship," which (at least in this instance) means a powerful government habituated to secrecy, anxious or fearful about openness, and unaccustomed to externally imposed constitutional constraints (save for the hypothetical supremacy of Parliament). British officials responsible for public security mostly seem to have been unruffled by external constitutional or legal constraints, for the complementary reasons that *usually there were none*—and that complaisant and deferential judges were reluctant to enforce them *when there were*. This has been especially true with regard to the Irish Troubles, but the World War II cases reveal how assertions of national security claims in the U.K. have otherwise secured a strong stockade against judicial intruders.

Overall, the European Court has been fairly deferential to British claims of exigency. In upholding derogations in *Brogan* and in *Brannigan and McBride,* the Court's majority readily conceded the dire difficulties posed by the Northern Ireland conflict, and while the ruling in *Fox, Campbell and Hartley* appeared more assertive in requiring objective reasonableness, the ruling in the case of *Margaret Murray* was once again highly deferential to the claims of exigency.

We should note briefly that it is not only the European Court of Human Rights that has been cast in the role of reviewing British efforts to control terrorism. In a November 1995 decision, the European Court of Justice held that the home secretary's power under the Prevention of Terrorism Act to exclude persons from Britain, without reference of the case to a "competent authority," was in violation of a 1964 EEC directive on freedom of movement within the European Union (*Statewatch*, 1995d, 12).

While it is too early to assess the consequences of the European Court's ruling concerning the Gibraltar killings, the U.K. government's early responses to the ruling do not indicate that the United Kingdom has learned the lessons that the European Court tentatively and deferentially has attempted to teach. It is indeed puzzling to witness how punctilious the British legal establishment can be about substantive and procedural rules within its own domain and how difficult it seems to have been to mobilize the law to protect with equal concern the rights of those who may be involved in the continuing Troubles over Northern Ireland. For example, at a lecture given through Gresham's College in January 1994, Sir David Calcutt spoke for an hour about the scrupulous procedural care he had taken in conducting an inquiry (at the request of the Foreign and Commonwealth Office) into the causes of a hospital fire in the Falkland Islands. Having spent the afternoon before the lecture reading about Operation Demetrius in Northern Ireland (August 9, 1971), I was struck by the incongruity, which the recent ruling on the Gibraltar killings certainly heightens.

With respect to the erosion of the right to silence condoned by the case of *John Murray v. United Kingdom,* it is interesting to note that the provision for allowing inferences to be drawn from the silence of the accused under the

Criminal Evidence (Northern Ireland) Order 1988 became the law throughout the United Kingdom through the Criminal Justice and Public Order Act 1994. It is easy enough to understand the fears induced both by acts of political terrorism and by crimes of violence in general, but the readiness of the current U.K. government to erode the longstanding safeguards provided through the right of silence is nonetheless both alarming and puzzling to those of us who claim protection under a bill of rights that is more than two hundred years old.

But beyond puzzlement there is paradox. The United Kingdom played a part in drafting the ECHR, and on March 8, 1951, it was the first country to deposit its instrument of ratification (Marston 1993). An article in *The Times* of May 26, 1992, reported that the Queen had said in her speech before the European Parliament that the ECHR was "the Council of Europe's greatest single achievement." It has long been commonplace for British government leaders to acknowledge and congratulate themselves on their national history of personal freedom. So it is easy to imagine that those who helped negotiate the ECHR could have thought that a human rights convention was mostly meant for other countries, who, they were certain, needed it far more than did the United Kingdom. One simple example: In a letter of May 31, 1947, quoted in a recent article (Marston 1993, 797), Hector McNeil, the parliamentary under secretary of state for foreign affairs, wrote about the formulation of the Universal Declaration of Human Rights, "In view of the extremely good record of this country in the matter of human rights we have thought it desirable that we should put in some suggestions of our own for a draft and we have given the United Nations to understand that we shall be doing this."

Yet even at the negotiations leading to the ECHR there was another side. An abstract rights document might be a good idea, but an international court with compulsory jurisdiction—and with the right of individual petition—was quite another. Jowett, the Lord Chancellor in 1950, strongly opposed both, and Kenneth Younger, then minister of state in the Foreign Office, circulated a memorandum to the Cabinet on July 25, 1950, that suggested the potential difficulty of common law courts reaching one decision under domestic law only to find "that in the end legislation would be necessary in order to bring the law into agreement with His Majesty's Government's obligations under the Convention" (Marston 1993, 812). Concern was also voiced over the possible application of the ECHR to the colonies, especially if individual right of petition were allowed. In the end the final draft of the ECHR reserved the choice for each of its state members to accept the right of individual petition, and ratification of the ECHR was seen by the government of the day as a matter of political necessity. A Colonial Office draft circular of January 1951 estimated that any conflicts between the ECHR and British law "were minor and technical and unlikely to give rise to a complaint to the European Commission of Human Rights." (Marston 1993, 824). Yet, as it turned out, the United Kingdom accepted the right of individual petition in January 1966 and it was found to be the most frequent violator of the ECHR during the first thirty years of the European Court's history (1959–89).

One of the contributions of the United Kingdom's having been found several times to be in violation of the ECHR over its efforts to deal with terrorism in Northern Ireland has been to help move the country toward incorporation of the ECHR in U.K. domestic law. Indeed, as we have seen, the United Kingdom is unique among the original members of the Council of Europe in having no written constitution *and* in having failed to incorporate the ECHR into its domestic law. As early as 1977, after the European Commission had returned its report, but before the European Court had given judgment in *Ireland v. United Kingdom,* the U.K.'s Standing Advisory Commission on Human Rights had recommended incorporation of the ECHR in its report on "The Protection of Human Rights by Law in Northern Ireland." More recently, in May 1990, *The Times* quoted Lord Hutchinson's dismay expressed before the House of Lords that "the long trek to a foreign jurisdiction to find the sustenance of justice must surely be a matter of shame to this government" (*The Times,* May 24, 1990).

As of mid-1996, the fragile truce between the Republicans and Unionists in Northern Ireland first declared in 1994 has broken down, due, in large measure, to the renewal of IRA bombings in England (regardless of the degree to which this renewal may have been provoked by the intransigence of the British government). Even more ominous is the fact that the recent riots arising out of "triumphal" marches by "Orangemen" through Catholic neighborhoods in Northern Ireland have rivaled the riots of the early seventies in numbers of participants. It is too soon to tell whether the peace process has been irreparably damaged, but despite the fact that the peace talks that began in June 1996 have not yet been called off, the present prospects for peace seem dim. A return both to violence and to the U.K. government's previous responses to violence may be at hand. As recently as 1993, *The Times* called for the renewal of internment. "After two generations of violence the IRA has closed its ears to the outside world, loyalist terror has reared its head and millions live in fear. In such a climate, talk of bringing terrorists `in from the cold' is not only misguided; it obscures what needs to be done. We believe the endemic terrorism that afflicts Ireland and Britain alike demands selective internment, applied even-handedly to all terrorist groups, republican or loyalist" (March 28, 1993).

Note that the 1993 editorial in *The Times* did not mention that the United

Kingdom had been held in violation of the ECHR or that it had been required to invoke derogation in the context of the decisions of the European Court of Human Rights that we have reviewed. Yet the response of the U.K. government to the Gibraltar killings suggests that we have not seen the last of the conflicts between the U.K.'s "prevention of terrorism" and its adherence to the European Convention on Human Rights.

4

Prisoners' Rights and the Convention

This chapter will review a striking line of prisoners' rights cases from the United Kingdom before the European Commission and Court of Human Rights, beginning in 1969 with the first application to the European Commission and concluding with a 1992 judgment of the European Court. This twenty-three-year period encompasses a plethora of complaints filed before the European Commission by U.K. prisoners. Why do these represent such an unusual line of cases? Because they demonstrate the exceptionally dogged insistence of U.K. prison and Home Office officials—laymen and lawyers alike—to have their own way in running their prisons *versus* the equally persistent efforts of the European Commission and Court of Human Rights, whose mutual purpose was the enforcement of the ECHR. The efforts of Commission and Court finally helped bring some small measure of accountability to British prisons—critical observers of British prisons might say that these European institutions also contributed to the "pursuit of decency" within the "bricks of shame" of British prisons. The two quoted phrases are from Vivien Stern's *Bricks of Shame: Britain's Prisons* (1993) and Andrew Rutherford's *Criminal Justice and the Pursuit of Decency* (1993). Rutherford, a former deputy governor in the British Prison Service and longtime chairman of the Howard League for Prison Reform, and Stern, director of the National Association for the Care and Resettlement of Offenders (NACRO), are both prominent critics of British criminal justice whose perspectives have contributed to this chapter.

THEORETICAL POSSIBILITIES

Building on Herbert Packer's (1968) now familiar distinction between the "Crime Control" and the "Due Process" models of the American criminal justice system, Andrew Rutherford's recent book proposes that three competing credos are evident amongst criminal justice practitioners. *Credo One* consists of a system of beliefs and values that strongly condemns criminal offenders, holds that they ought to be dispatched to prison as quickly and with as few procedural obstructions as possible, and relishes the notion that once in prison they ought to be kept there for a long time and treated in a highly punitive and degrading manner. *Credo Two* is preeminently a set of beliefs and values congruent with large bureaucracy. This credo proposes that prisoners ought to be dealt with as smoothly and efficiently as possible. As always, efficiency is defined by the savings of time and resources, and routinized behavior is often the result. Thus, when engaged in competing for and utilizing scarce resources, this credo usually prefers convenience for the system over costly and time-consuming demands of inmates. For example, Prowse (1992, 124) quotes Lord Denning in *Becker v. Home Office* (1972, 682): "If the courts were to entertain actions by disgruntled prisoners, the governor's life would be made intolerable. The discipline of prisons would be undermined. The Prison Rules are regulatory directions only. Even if they are not observed, they do not give rise to a cause of action." Credo Two favors the pragmatic and expedient over the moral claims for vengeance of Credo One, and also over the claims of individual humanity of the third.

Credo Three is skeptical about the utility of prison and about the length of sentences, concerned about the social causes of crime, empathetic with both victims and offenders, committed to the rule of law, and insistent on openness and accountability (Rutherford 1993, chap. 1).

Probably no one is capable of adhering consistently to the claims of a single credo—certainly not over an entire career in a justice system, but individuals and institutions do have central tendencies. Without saying more at this point, let me simply propose that we keep the three credos in mind when we read the review of the prisoners' cases that follows—and see which seems the best fit.

U.K. Prison Cases before the European Commission and Court

The cases reviewed here cover a variety of prison issues, but the one thing they have in common is that they were all brought against the United Kingdom by prisoners' applications to the European Commission of Human Rights. The cases are arranged in chronological order, rather than in order of importance of individual cases. Here chronological order is important, for it illustrates the principal point of this chapter, which is to portray the resistance to change by those responsible for British prisons, and the consequent protracted, difficult, and recurring confrontations between the British Prison Service (and British courts) and the European Court and Commission over prisoners' rights.

Knechtl v. United Kingdom (1970)

On May 16, 1969, an application was made to the European Commission on Human Rights on behalf of Gyula Knechtl, an action that eventually produced, for the first time, some modest redress for a U.K. prisoner under the ECHR. Knechtl was a refugee from the Hungarian uprising of 1956 who had lived in England since 1957. In May 1964, he was convicted of robbery with violence and received a sentence of nine years imprisonment.

In December 1967, while serving his sentence, his left leg was amputated below the knee. His leg had been X-rayed in Pankhurst Prison in November 1964, and he continued to complain about the leg and to receive assorted medical treatments, either in prison or hospital, through June 1967, when he first petitioned the home secretary, complaining that he had not received adequate medical treatment. He continued to receive a variety of treatments through the December 1967 amputation.

In January 1968, Knechtl petitioned the home secretary for legal aid in order to "bring charges" against the Home Office. The home secretary responded a week later denying the petition but offering to reconsider if Knechtl would specify the charges he wished to bring. In March, Knechtl again petitioned, this time saying that he wished to bring charges against the Home Office for gross negligence. On May 7, the home secretary asked for particulars, and a week later Knechtl answered, asking again for legal aid and legal advice concerning his disablement. His request was denied on July 5.

Somehow Knechtl must have found a solicitor, for in January 1969 he wrote the home secretary advising that he wished to bring charges against the Home Office for gross negligence "through which I lost a leg or part of a leg," and that *his solicitor* had advised that he needed to ask leave of the home secretary to file suit. That request was denied on May 4, 1969, and Knechtl's application to the European Commission was made on May 16. Between June 1969 and May 1970, Knechtl's case was reviewed by the parliamentary commissioner. Knechtl had also written to Quintin Hogg, his former M.P., who had submitted Knechtl's correspondence to the parliamentary commissioner (in effect an ombudsman). The parliamentary commissioner responded on May 26, 1970, that he had found no evidence of maladministration (1970 *Yearbook of the European Convention on Human Rights*, 730–63).

The government's submission revealed the state of U.K. law at that time, which was that Rule 33 of the Prison Rules 1964 gave the home secretary essentially unfettered discretion to impose restrictions on the communications between a prisoner and anyone else, while Rule 34(8) provided that a prisoner "shall not communicate with any person in connection with any legal or other business," except with leave of the home secretary. The government advised, however, that "it was not the practice of the home secretary to refuse leave to communicate with a solicitor if the complaint seemed to reveal a reasonable cause of action."

In the view of the home secretary, Knechtl had simply failed to furnish particulars, and the process to secure leave from the home secretary was still open to him. In that sense he had not exhausted his remedies under domestic law. Of course, a statute of limitations loomed in the background. The statute would have run out only a short time after the date of Knechtl's expected release from prison. By letter of October 1, 1970, the U.K. government gave its undertaking that it would not plead the statute, were a suit to be filed by Knechtl within six months of his actual release from prison (1970 *Yearbook of the European Convention on Human Rights*, 740).

Knechtl's position was that once he had informed the home secretary that he wished to bring suit against the Home Office for gross negligence relating to the loss of his leg while in custody, sufficient information had been provided, yet he had still been denied. As far as he could tell, the home secretary's decision had been final.

Application of Art. 6.1

Art. 6.1 provides in part that in determination of "his civil rights" everyone is entitled to a "fair and public hearing within a reasonable time by an independent and impartial tribunal established by law." The U.K. took the position that Art. 6.1 did not guarantee access to the courts in civil cases, but only to procedural due process once there. The distinction between the right of access and the right to a fair hearing, was, it said, well known to international lawyers. Moreover, restrictions on those held in physical confinement in prisons were a "necessary consequence of the inherent characteristics of confinement." Restrictions were both necessary and justifiable to protect against "frivolous or vexatious litigation," and unrestricted access to the outside for purposes of pursuing litigation could easily be used "for a criminal or other improper purpose" (1970 *Yearbook*, 750). Thus, if Knechtl had been willing to submit the particulars to show that his purpose was reasonable, the process of seeking leave of the home secretary should have been sufficient to safeguard his rights.

Knechtl's response was that if Art. 6.1 guaranteed access to courts, then the right to communicate with a solicitor was a necessary condition for that right, especially given that he was required to apply for legal aid. Legal aid would have been granted only after review by a panel of lawyers, and it was also the case that British courts routinely struck pleadings that revealed no reasonable cause of action, so the safeguards thought by the home secretary to be necessary within the prison system were, according to Knechtl, provided outside that system.

The Commission's Decision of Admissibility

In deciding whether Knechtl's complaint was admissible, the Commission was not required to rule on the merits of issues raised under Art. 6 and 8. Thus, on December 16, 1970, the Commission found that the application was not manifestly ill founded and that the question raised under Art. 6.1 was an important one, "whose determination should depend upon an examination of the merits." Only the question of the right of access to the courts under Art. 6.1 was deemed admissible, since that was the main issue on which other issues would depend.

Knechtl's application was finally resolved by a friendly settlement, producing a change in policy that allowed access to a solicitor in cases of possible medical malpractice (Churchill and Young 1991, 301). In light of this settlement, what is the point of elaborating Knechtl's application? There are two reasons. The first is to illustrate the state of the law and the discretionary authority claimed by the home secretary at the point of Knechtl's application to the European Commission. The second is that the concession made by friendly settlement represented the first European-induced constraint on the exercise of executive power over U.K. prisoners. But others were soon to follow.

The Golder Case (1975)

An application to the European Commission on behalf of Sidney Golder was first submitted in 1969. The early days of Golder's case were much the same as Knechtl's. Golder's case was the first time that the United Kingdom was a state defendant before the European Court of Human Rights. Golder had been convicted of robbery with violence in 1969 and sentenced to fifteen years in prison. A prison disturbance had occurred on October 24, 1969, in a recreation area, where Golder happened to be. The day following the disturbance, a prison officer identified Golder as having been involved and accused him of "swinging vicious blows at me." On the next day Golder and other suspected troublemakers were segregated from other prisoners. He was interviewed about the incident on October 28 and 30 and denied being involved. On October 25, the same day he was identified by the officer, and again on November 1, Golder attempted to write his M.P. On November 4, he wrote to a chief constable. All three letters were about the disturbance of October 24, and all three were stopped by the prison governor because Golder had not raised his concerns through "authorized channels."

On November 4, the officer who originally had identified Golder retracted his statement and a few days later another prison officer reported that he had seen Golder on the day of the incident and that he had not been a part of the riot. Golder was then returned to his regular cell, but on November 10 an entry was made in the prison records listing those against whom charges might be preferred, including Golder. In Golder's personal record a notation eventually was entered: "charges not proceeded with."

All of the negative references in Golder's file were expunged while his case was pending before the Commission in 1971, but before that, on March 20, 1970, Golder petitioned the home secretary complaining that he had been prejudiced by the notations in the records, and expressing the concern that this might have prevented him from being recommended for parole. He requested permission to consult a solicitor with a view to bringing a writ for libel—or, if the home secretary preferred—for an independent examination of his records by a magistrate. The home secretary rejected Golder's petition in April 1970, holding that his prospective action for libel had little likelihood of success.

As we saw in the *Knechtl* case, the prison rules gave the home secretary discretion over a prisoner's correspondence, including his correspondence with a solicitor. Golder's amended application to the Commission was made on March 30, 1971, and the Commission found that it raised admissible issues under Art. 6.1 and 8.

The Commission reported that Art. 6.1 guarantees a right of access to the courts (unanimously) and that Art. 8 was breached as well (by a vote of seven to two).

Right to Contact a Solicitor under Art. 6.1 and 8

The limited right to contact a solicitor for the purpose of a medical malpractice claim, which had been conceded by settlement in *Knechtl*'s case, did not apply to Golder's facts. The Court's ruling on Golder's claim under Art. 6.1 was that the home secretary had in fact prevented him from commencing a civil action for libel. Recognizing this, the Court said that "it follows that the right of access constitutes an element which is inherent in the rights stated by Art. 6 §1 . . . read in its context and having regard to the object and purpose of the Convention" (*Golder v. United Kingdom*, ser. A, 18).

Was the home secretary's rejection of Golder's petition nonetheless a justifiable limitation on his rights? The Court held it was not. Perhaps its most important reason was that the home secretary officially had an interest in the prospective suit, since it would be brought against officers or agencies under his direction. The Court found it understandable that Golder might want the independent opinion of a solicitor on the merits of his suit. So the Court found a breach of Art. 6.1 by a vote of nine to three. The Court also found Art. 8 to have been violated (unanimously) and added to the "insult" by holding that the home secretary's interference with Golder's correspondence was "not necessary in a democratic society" (*Golder v. United Kingdom*, ser. A, 22).

A dispassionate observer might conclude that *Knechtl* and *Golder* together ought to have ensured a prisoner's right to contact a solicitor in the United Kingdom, but that would be wrong. We have yet to encounter the "prior ventilation" rule.

The Requirements of "Prior Ventilation"

A polemical booklet written by Stan Cohen and Laurie Taylor and published by the National Council on Civil Liberties and Radical Alternatives to Prison

(RAP) in 1978 describes the Home Office's subtle and cynical response to *Golder*. A few months after the ruling in the *Golder* case the home secretary announced that the prison rules would be changed. A Circular Instruction 45/75 (August 6, 1975) that contained the following explanation of the *Golder* ruling was sent to prison governors: "The effect of this ruling is that no obstacles must be put in the way of inmates wishing to bring legal proceedings in any civil matter, or seeking the advice of a solicitor about instituting such proceedings and if so advised in instructing a solicitor to institute and conduct the proceedings" (Cohen and Taylor 1978, 42).

However, instead of petitioning the home secretary for leave, what now was required was that a prisoner make written application to the prison governor for facilities to seek legal advice. The governor would grant the request *unless* the inmate's complaint was against the Home Office on a matter arising from his imprisonment. In that event, facilities were *not* to be granted "until the inmate has ventilated his complaints through the normal existing internal channels" (Cohen and Taylor 1978, 43). This became known as the "prior ventilation" rule. Of course, the normal existing internal channels were those within the management and control of prison authorities, but that was not the only problem. Cohen and Taylor stressed (1978, 43) that prison circular instructions were secret, which meant that inmates would have no way of knowing that a letter was stopped under the prior ventilation rule unless someone in a position of authority were to disclose it. And if the prior ventilation rule were followed, that procedure might take up to one year. It did not take long for the prior ventilation rule to be challenged.

Reed v. United Kingdom (1981)

The Circular Instruction of August 1975 that provided for the prior ventilation rule was challenged in an application on behalf of John Michael Reed on February 4, 1976. Reed was serving a life sentence in Hull prison. Like Sidney Golder, he complained that he was prevented from contacting a solicitor, without first obtaining the leave of the home secretary, about an alleged libel by a prison officer, which had caused him to be the subject of disciplinary proceedings on January 15, 1976. After his application to the European Commission, he was allowed to consult his solicitor about that application, but his solicitor was still barred from advising him on the domestic law of libel. On advice of his solicitor, he submitted a written complaint to the governor, and in March 1976 he was at last granted permission to seek advice on domestic law.

Then other issues intervened. Following a riot in Hull prison in late summer 1976, Reed claimed that he had been assaulted by prison officers because of his suspected participation in the riot. He petitioned the home secretary in September 1976 for leave to contact a solicitor about that assault, but because of the prior ventilation rule he was not allowed to seek outside legal advice until September 1978—two years later.

All these events concerning Reed led to a settlement in December 1981 in which the United Kingdom agreed to abandon the prior ventilation rule and to replace it with a "simultaneous ventilation" rule (*Reed v. United Kingdom,* ser. A, 9). The simultaneous ventilation rule required that a complaint be made through prison channels as well as being pursued through outside legal channels, but the outside steps did not await the completion of the internal proceedings. Essentially, nothing changed except that the prisoner was no longer required to await the outcome of the internal proceedings before being granted leave to seek outside legal advice. So in effect the prior ventilation rule lasted from August 1975 until December 1981. Or so it seemed.

The *Golder* ruling, having been eviscerated by bureaucratic artifice in 1975, thus apparently was revived by the *Reed* settlement in 1981. No doubt it was an accident, rather than a symbol of declining value of U.K. prison rules, that the next prison issue came in the *Silver* case.

Case of Silver and Others v. United Kingdom (1983)

Reuben Silver and six others complained in their application to the European Commission on Human Rights about the stopping of sixty-two letters written by them between January 1972 and May 1976. Silver died while his application was pending, but his representative chose to pursue his claim. The sixty-two letters were sent to or received from a variety of persons including family members, members of Parliament, journalists, and solicitors. They also covered a variety of topics, but only Silver complained that he had been denied access to the courts in violation of Art. 6.1. The principal complaints of the other six were that the stopping violated their right to respect for their correspondence under Art. 8 and, under Art. 13, the absence of an effective domestic remedy for that violation.

A number of the letters were stopped by prison authorities on the grounds that they were not sent to relatives or to established friends. Several of them were stopped because they involved legal or business matters and the prisoners had not sought leave to send them. Several were stopped because they violated a prohibition against representations in connection with a prisoner's trial, conviction, or sentence. A few were stopped because they sought by indirection to have the recipient do what the inmate could not do directly (for example, contacting a solicitor without leave). One violated a prohibition against discussing the offenses of other inmates. One was stopped for holding prison authorities up to contempt. Several were stopped because they contained threats of violence and vile language. Several violated the prohibition against sending material intended for publication. A number of the letters contained "unventilated complaints about prison treatment" and were sent to legal advisers or to members of Parliament. Some were stopped simply because of a prohibition in general correspondence against complaints about prison treatment. It is evident that the multiplicity of reasons for stopping letters must have required the expenditure of a lot of staff time—and with focused attention to the detailed reading of the letters.

In November 1972, Silver had petitioned the home secretary for permission to seek legal advice concerning his alleged negligent treatment in prison; included were statements about medical and dental treatment. Permission was refused in April 1973. That was after the *Knechtl* settlement of his medical malpractice case, but before the ruling in the *Golder* case, protecting access to a solicitor in general. In July 1973, he submitted another petition and requested leave to seek legal advice about his dental treatment. Prison authorities claimed that this second petition was granted in October, but Silver claimed he had never been told that. These events occurred before the prior ventilation rule (August 1975), but the actual judgment of the European Court was delivered in March 1983, well after the simultaneous ventilation rule had been substituted. The prison orders regarding the censorship or stopping of correspondence also were substantially revised while Silver's case was pending before the European Court, but the Court had to rule on the law and practice as it had been applied to these seven prisoners.

The refusal of Silver's petition for leave to consult a solicitor was simply held a violation of Art. 6.1, consistent with the *Golder* decision. The results concerning the stopping of letters were more complicated.

Interference with Correspondence

The possible reasons for stopping letters had not been explained to prisoners, despite their presence in prison orders, and these secret rules were held by the Court to be unforeseeable and thus "not in accordance with law" (*Silver v. United Kingdom*, ser. A, 250–51). Standing Order 5, issued by the home secretary, contained detailed provisions, but these had neither been published nor made available to prisoners (Churchill and Young 1991, 305). Most of the restrictions on correspondence—as applied by prison authorities—were unanimously determined by the court *not* to be "necessary in a democratic society." The final tally was that the stopping of fifty-seven of the sixty-two letters was found *not* to have been necessary. Each violation of Art. 8 was also a violation of Art. 13. Since these violations were not contrary to British domestic law, inmates had no domestic remedy, but were able only to apply to the European Commission (*Silver v. United Kingdom*, ser. A, 254 *et seq.*). After the *Silver* case, the Home Office agreed to publish standing orders, as they are revised. Circular instructions, however, continued to be restricted even to the attorney acting on behalf of inmates (Prowse et al. 1992, 123). Following the *Silver* judgment, a detached observer might well conclude that the right of inmates to consult solicitors and to correspond with outsiders had at last been broadly secured against arbitrary interference, but once again that conclusion would be mistaken.

Case of Campbell and Fell v. United Kingdom (1984)

Campbell and Fell were convicted of several serious offenses in November 1973. Sean Campbell was a citizen of the U.K., born in Northern Ireland but a longtime resident of England. Father Patrick Fell, a Catholic priest, was born and lived in England. During their confinement they were put in special security placements because the offenses for which they were convicted were believed to be IRA connected. In September 1976, there was a disturbance at Albany Prison on the Isle of Wight at the instance of six inmates, allegedly including Campbell and Fell. When prison officers dealt with the disturbance, injuries were sustained on both sides, including Campbell and Fell. Campbell's injuries included a broken arm, two broken fingers, a broken leg, broken ribs, and a punctured lung (Prowse et al. 1992, 123). Both Campbell and Fell were charged with disciplinary violations, found guilty, and lost substantial periods of earned remission from their sentences.

Prison Disciplinary Proceedings

Questions were raised by Campbell under Art. 6 concerning the disciplinary proceedings through which he had lost 570 days of previously earned remission. He raised a variety of objections, including the lack of independence and impartiality of the prison's Board of Visitors as the tribunal designated to hear serious disciplinary cases, the closed hearing conducted by the board, and the overall absence of fairness in the proceedings. All these were rejected by the Court, but it did find two violations. One was that the Board of Visitors did not publicly pronounce its decisions and the second was that under the established practices at that time Campbell was not entitled either to seek legal assistance prior to the hearing or to have legal representation at the hearing. Both of these were found to be violations of Art. 6.1, since the seriousness of the consequences for Campbell (570 days' additional imprisonment) in effect made the proceedings before the Board of Visitors a serious criminal matter. Note that in *R. v. Home Secretary, ex parte Tarrant* (1983) the Queen's Bench held that while prisoners were not entitled as a matter of right to legal representation before disciplinary hearings, a Board of Visitors had discretion to grant such representation. The Court there also suggested that in serious disciplinary cases the Board would be well advised to exercise its discretion so as to permit representation.

Prior Ventilation Revisited

In the autumn of 1976, three years after the disturbance, Campbell and Fell asked the home secretary for leave to consult a solicitor regarding the injuries they had received in the incident. Their request was refused under the then extant prior ventilation rule. The internal investigations of their complaints were not completed until February 1977, for Father Fell, and December 1977, for Campbell. The investigation found against Father Fell, but the home secretary suggested that he would be allowed to consult a solicitor if he still wished to do so. The sequence of events with Campbell is more complicated, but eventually he too was allowed to confer with a solicitor. Both prisoners brought proceedings against prison officers, the deputy governor, and the Home Office for assault, and both applied to the European Commission. But, meanwhile, another issue had arisen.

In March 1977, the Albany Prison authorities advised Father Fell's firm of solicitors that any conferences held between Father Fell and his solicitor would have to take place within the sight and hearing of a prison officer. Rule 37(2) provided that when an interview with a solicitor is not about a suit to which the inmate is a party, it is subject to the leave of the home secretary and is to be conducted in sight and hearing of a prison officer. Fell's solicitors replied that they would not accept this condition and would instead take the matter to "the European Court of Human Rights."

As we have noted, by the time Campbell and Fell's applications were before the Court, the prior ventilation rule had been replaced by the U.K. with simultaneous ventilation. However, the Court again felt bound to rule on their application as Campbell and Fell themselves had experienced the rules. The prior ventilation rule was therefore again ruled to violate both Art. 6.1 and 8 (*Campbell and Fell v. United Kingdom*, ser. A, 47 et seq.). The rule requiring conferences between Father Fell and his solicitor to be held in the sight and hearing of a prison officer had also been changed by the time the European Court ruled (the revision required that they be held in the sight, but not in the hearing, of a prison officer). The Court found that the rule violated Art. 6.1 (*Campbell and Fell v. United Kingdom*, ser. A, 49) as it had been applied to Father Fell. Other restrictions on their correspondence were also held to violate Art. 8, but the correspondence rules had already been revised in light of the decision in the case of *Silver and Others*. Next to go was the requirement of simultaneous ventilation.

We should note that in *T v. United Kingdom* (1986) the Commission found that a prisoner who had been segregated under prison rule 43 because of his refusal to wear prison clothing and who spent up to twenty-three and a half hours daily in his cell was entitled to special consideration. Thus, the Commission found several violations of Art. 10.1, which protects the right to freedom of expression, subject to restrictions that are necessary in a democratic society under Art. 10.2. The violations included the denial of access to writing materials for certain prolonged periods, the blanket prohibition against the prisoner's sending his "academic writing" to addresses outside the prison, and restrictions on his access to newspapers.

Case of Byrne and Others v. United Kingdom (1987)

Simultaneous ventilation eventually was admitted by the U.K. to violate the ECHR, chiefly because it had already been ruled to be contrary to the common law. Indeed, the common law ruling was mentioned in the resolution of the committee of ministers in *Byrne and Others*. In *R. v. Home Secretary, ex parte Anderson* (1983) the Queen's Bench ruled that the prison rule that required that a complaint about prison treatment be made through internal proceedings before leave would be granted to seek outside legal advice was *ultra vires* since the Prison Act of 1952 contained no provision on which such a rule could have been based. The Queen's Bench decision specifically mentioned the *Golder* (1983, 781) and *Silver* (1983, 782) cases, and the *Golder* case was cited as a reason for narrowly construing the Prison Act.

A brief aside: It may prove difficult to keep track of the several rulings on prior and simultaneous ventilation that are close to one another in time. The settlement in *Reed v. United Kingdom,* in which the U.K. agreed to withdraw the prior ventilation rule and substitute simultaneous ventilation, was reached in December 1981. The Queen's Bench decision in *R. v. Home Secretary, ex parte Anderson* holding simultaneous ventilation to be *ultra vires* was made in December 1983, some six months before the European Court's judgment in *Campbell and Fell* in June 1984. The European Commission's report in *Byrne and Others* was adopted in December 1985, but the resolution of the committee of ministers in that case was not adopted until March 1987. This confusion of facts, dates, and rules is primarily due to the slow progress of cases before the European Commission and Court in general, and also to the differential progress of particular cases, from prison incidents to initial applications to the Commission to resolutions of the committee of ministers or to final judgments of the European Court.

You may find the next applicants familiar. The four inmate applicants in *Byrne and Others* were incarcerated at Albany Prison on the Isle of Wight. They were four of the six inmates who were involved in the Albany Prison disturbance of September 1976. The other two were Campbell and Fell, whom we have already met. The solicitors who sought to visit the four applicants in 1976 and 1977 again encountered the prior ventilation rule as well as the requirement that conferences be held in the sight and hearing of prison officers. To these complaints the Commission simply applied the judgment in *Campbell and Fell*, which had already held both practices to violate Art. 6. By the time the Commission's report was before the committee of ministers, however, the United Kingdom advised that committee of the Queen's Bench decision in *R. v. Home Secretary, ex parte Anderson*. Thus, the March 1987 decision of the committee of ministers acknowledged the U.K.'s concession that the rules of prior ventilation and simultaneous ventilation were both unlawful. Dare we now hope that we have heard the last of them? To be sure, we have not finished with rules about prisoners' correspondence.

Case of Farrant v. United Kingdom (1987)

Actually the *Farrant* case involved a narrow point that had not previously been covered. David Farrant, an inmate at Blundeston Prison, complained that eighteen of his letters had been stopped by prison authorities. Several of them were stopped because they dealt with Farrant's efforts to bring a private criminal prosecution against two police officers. Others were stopped due to the "unofficial organisations" rule. This was a prohibition against writing to private interest or lobbying groups regarding prisoner complaints. And three were stopped because of the prior ventilation rule, since all sixteen letters had been written in 1975 and 1976, before it was abandoned.

The "unofficial organisations" rule was treated much like the correspondence rules in *Silver v. United Kingdom*. It was an overly broad blanket prohibition and the U.K. had offered no specific reasons for its application to Farrant's letters to a prisoners' rights organization. The Commission found this stopping to be a violation of Art. 8.

The Commission also ruled against the prohibition of letters seeking to institute a private criminal prosecution. But this prohibition had, like the simultaneous ventilation rule in *Byrne*, already been encountered in British courts, two years before the Commission's report. In *Raymond v. Honey* (1983) the House of Lords had already applied a common law rule against denying access to courts to an instance similar to Farrant's. When Farrant's case came before the committee of ministers, the United Kingdom cited *Raymond v. Honey* and agreed that this restriction had been eliminated. Otherwise, the outcomes in *Farrant* simply supplemented the Court's ruling about correspondence in the *Silver* case.

We have progressed to the point where there ought to be few issues left to examine regarding prisoners' correspondence, which is true with regard to cases with broad policy implications. Thus, in the case of *Boyle and Rice v. United Kingdom* (1988) another shopping list of prisoners' grievances was reviewed, which included miscellaneous restrictions on correspondence, but the only violation found was in a single instance, in which even the government of the United Kingdom agreed that a mistake had been made in stopping a personal letter—and it did not offer to justify it. In *Grace v. United Kingdom* (1989) a general restriction against prisoners seeking and corresponding with pen pals was found by the Commission not to be necessary in a democratic society and, believe it or not, the simultaneous ventilation rule appeared again. It was formally found by the Commission to violate Art. 8 (*Grace v. United Kingdom*, 40–41). Other restrictions were, however, found to be reasonable in *Grace*, including a rule against using the pretext of letters on legal matters (which were not limited as to number) to circumvent prison limits on personal letters, a rule prohibiting letters that contain "obscure or coded messages" that are not "readily intelligible or decipherable," and a rule allowing correspondence between inmates, but subject to their being stopped by prison authorities for specifically prescribed reasons. In *Costello v. United Kingdom* (1985) the Commission had previously found that a general prohibition on correspondence between inmates was overly broad and not justifiable in a democratic society. This brings us to the two most recent European cases on prisoners' rights.

Case of McCallum v. the United Kingdom (1990)

The *McCallum* case did for Scottish prisons what *Silver* had already done for English prisons. Scottish prisons were governed by the Prisons (Scotland) Act 1952, which in section 35(1) authorized rules, the first version of which was the Prison (Scotland) Rules 1952. There is very little new in the Court's judgment, which is best evident by its length (three pages) in which it simply ratified the Commission's longer report. The Commission had found seven separate violations of Art. 8 with respect to the stopping of letters. The approach of the Commission and the particulars of the violations were similar to those in the *Silver* case. We should note that courts in Scotland have been at least as skeptical about the impact of the ECHR as English courts (see *Moore v. Secretary of State for Scotland*, 1985).

Case of Campbell v. United Kingdom (1992)

This last case represents another step forward by the European Court. Thomas Campbell was convicted of murder in 1984 and was serving a life term in Scotland. At certain times in his imprisonment he was a category A inmate (the highest degree of security risk). From the beginning of his sentence he was represented by a solicitor. From 1985 forward his correspondence with his solicitor was opened and screened by prison authorities. Campbell complained about the screening of his letters but was told that all correspondence would be screened except letters sent directly to the European Commission on Human Rights. Campbell's complaint on the screening of his correspondence with his solicitor was filed with the Commission in January 1986, and in its report of July 1990 the Commission ruled that the opening of his correspondence with his solicitor was a violation of Art. 8.

The United Kingdom argued that screening such letters was necessary to determine whether they contained "prohibited material," but the Court's view was that the lawyer-client relationship was privileged and ought to prevail. This indeed had been the implication of its holding in *Campbell and Fell* that conferences between client and solicitor might be held in the sight, but *not* in the hearing, of a prison officer. The Court had also held recently in *S v. Switzerland* (1991) that the attorney-client relationship required privacy of communication. The screening of letters was, however, subject to a few provisos (*Campbell v. United Kingdom* ser. A, 19):

> Prison authorities may open a letter from a lawyer to a prisoner when they have reasonable cause to believe that it contains an illicit enclosure which the normal means of detection have failed to disclose. The letter should, however, be opened and should not be read. Suitable guarantees preventing the reading of the letter should be provided, e.g., opening the letter in the presence of the prisoner. The reading of a prisoner's mail to and from a lawyer, on the other hand, should only be permitted in exceptional circumstances when the authorities have reasonable cause to believe that the privilege is being abused in that the contents of the letters endanger prison security or the safety of others or are otherwise of a criminal nature.

Sir John Freeland, the judge of U.K. nationality then sitting on the Court, dissented. The prison rules differentiated between correspondence between inmate and solicitor regarding pending or contemplated legal actions and general correspondence with a solicitor. Judge Freeland was willing to concede the protection of privileged communication in the former but not in the latter. Note that in *McComb v. United Kingdom* (1986), the U.K. had advised the Commission that it was prepared to refrain from opening correspondence between a prisoner and a solicitor regarding a matter to which the prisoner was already a party. It was not clear whether that position took into account the words of Lord Denning in *Guilfoyle v. Home Office* (1980), in which he suggested that correspondence regarding a prisoner's application to the European Commission could not be in connection with legal proceedings to which the prisoner was a party because the proceedings before the Commission were *not* legal proceedings. Lord Denning said, "It is right and proper that the governor should be able to read and examine any letter between Guilfoyle and his solicitor relating to a petition to the European Commission (*Guilfoyle v. Home Office*, 947). However, Judge Freeland suggested in his dissent that since conferences between solicitor and client then could be held in the sight but not in the hearing of a prison officer, privacy was already secured to an inmate in "an effective and practical manner" (*Campbell v. United Kingdom*, ser. A, 31).

CONCLUSION: A CONFRONTATION BETWEEN CREDOS?

Before attempting to generalize from these cases, let me add a few observations about British prisons from other sources. Cohen and Taylor's sometimes polemical but always precise and specific critique of British prisons includes the following:

> Among all government departments, the Home Office is notorious for its resistance to outside enquiry. . . . The almost pathological secrecy which surrounds the Prison Department, though is perhaps best illustrated in the way it insulates itself from its own secrets. It's old news to deplore the fact those large scale enquiries about disturbances in English Prisons over the last decade . . . have not been released to the public. . . . What is less known, is that the findings of these enquiries remain largely secret even to those running the system, such as prison governors.
>
> . . . The system is run like a military operation: to keep the secret from the enemy (prisoners, the public) everyone in the hierarchy is only told what he needs to know for his part in the master plan (Cohen and Taylor 1978, 15–16).

And one more illustration from the same source: "the Prison Department produces a large number of *Standing Orders*. These in turn are amended and elaborated in a further series of regular *Circular Instructions* and similar documents. In one version of these documents . . . the section dealing merely with the question of communications, contains some *five hundred* separate rules about how the relevant Prison Rules should be interpreted and applied" (Cohen and Taylor 1978, 20; emphasis added).

Surely that is an example of bureaucracy unabated and resistant to change. Another contemporary advocate of prison reform repeats an anecdote to suggest a simple alternative:

> David Wickham, young assistant governor, wrote of his experiences during the industrial action of 1980 when he worked in a temporary prison staffed mainly by people from the army. What struck him was the quality of what he called "staff-inmate relationships" which were better than he had seen elsewhere in his career. The reason for this was neither dif-

ficult nor expensive. It was, he says, very simple. The military staff dealing with the prisoners addressed them as "Mister." (Stern 1993, 47)

And why such a passion for secrecy? Secrecy, Stern suggests, has two justifications. The first is the "public's wish *not* to know, not to have even to think
about people who it is felt have by their own actions, put themselves beyond
the reach of legitimate concern" (emphasis added). The second reason is less a
reason than a description. It is the same "obsession with secrecy that is deeply
embedded in the culture of prison administration" that Cohen and Taylor described above (Stern 1993, 3).

Those who have written about the U.K. prisoners' rights case agree that,
for whatever reasons, the Home Office was forced to change, always reluctantly, and whenever possible by framing changes in policy as narrowly as
possible (Hampson 1990; Churchill and Young 1991). One observer puts this
down to pragmatism as the prevailing ideology of the Home Office (Zellick
1979, 115). Sometime between the *Golder* decision in 1975 and the *Silver* decision in 1983, it should have become evident—even to prison authorities—
that substantial changes were inevitable. Yet nine years passed between the
decision in *Golder* and the Home Office's acceptance that prison officials should
not be capable of impeding access to courts (Stern 1993, 106). To be fair, the
Home Office must have sensed the direction of change and, to some degree,
attempted to respond to it. In most of the post-*Golder* cases, by the time a
prisoner's case was before the European Commission or Court for determination, the rules that had been applied to the applicant prisoner had already been
changed. Why then was it necessary for the U.K. to continue for so long to
contest these applications before the Commission or Court? Perhaps because
the changes they had made were usually incremental and did not confront the
fundamental issue, which seemed in a narrower sense to be control versus
accountability, but in a broader sense it was indeed a contest among the three
credos that we met at the beginning of this chapter.

In Vivien Stern's words, the third credo, that is, "'the justice model' in its
most humane version, lays stress on a prisoner's right to be well-treated, kept
in hygienic conditions and given the freedom to accept or reject the education,
training and counseling opportunities available. It also calls for much more
clarity about prisoners' rights and machinery through which such rights can
be maintained" (1993, 49).

The series of cases we have reviewed illustrate quite well what Rutherford
meant by the first and second credos. Whether motivated by moral outrage
and vengeance or simply secluded by a short-sighted view of bureaucratic convenience (we probably should also add by a heavy measure of inertia), those
who were responsible for the U.K.'s policy in these cases have given us a para-

digm of dogged but fruitless resistance. Vivien Stern (in 1993 still optimistic about the future) has said it well: "It is in the interests of the Home Office to do away with this secret use of absolute power. It may buy some short-term control but in the longer term the major element of a just and human prison system, fairness, is missing. A sense of injustice is fostered by such measures that leads in the end to the loss of control" (1993, 235).

In the end the motives for significant change came within the United Kingdom as well as from Strasbourg. The prison riots at Strangeways Prison in Manchester in April 1990 led to copycat riots in other prisons. In April 1990, Strangeways was certified for 970 inmates, but on the first day of the riot held 1,647. With crowding came the problem of keeping inmates locked in their cells for most of the day, the daily "slopping out" of cells with no toilet facilities, the weekly showers and weekly change of clothes, and inevitably, the poor quality of the food (*Woolf Report* 1991, 48–50).

Following the April 1990 riots, Lord Justice Woolf was asked to conduct an inquiry. His February 1991 report summarized a major lesson learned from his inquiry as the "importance of security, control and justice to a stable prison system." The following section is headed by the conclusion that "The disturbances demonstrate a need to pay more attention to justice within prisons" (226). Once again the third credo.

In October 1993, Lord Woolf publicly spoke out against the Conservative Government's prison policy, which had called for locking away more offenders for longer periods of time. A week later Lord Woolf was joined by seven senior judges headed by Lord Ackner (a law lord) and by Lord Justice Farquharson, a senior member of the Court of Criminal Appeals. The result was a front page headline in *The Observer* of October 17, "Top Judges: Jail not the answer." Lord Ackner was quoted as saying, "The Government's intention to be tougher on crime seems to me to be largely an irrelevance. Judges will do what they have been doing recently: use prison only as a last resort, and then impose the shortest sentence possible because prison doesn't work."

5

Nationality and the Convention: "Civis Britannicus Sum!"

This chapter is another that begins with a substantive theme, British nationality and immigration policy, but becomes in the end an essay about officialdom and administrative discretion. In the instance of nationality and immigration, the chief uses of discretion have come in the last half of this century, and, as we have seen before, discretion has been placed in the home secretary and those who act under his authority.

In 1954 the U.K. minister for colonial affairs said, "[W]e still take pride in the fact that a man can say *Civis Britannicus sum* [I am a British citizen] whatever his colour may be, and we take pride in the fact that he wants and can come to the Mother Country" (Bevan 1986, 76). That is no longer the case, and the changes since 1954 have made the difference.

BACKGROUND

The prevailing British imperial view favored the free movement of capital and labor within the British Empire. Indeed, it was not until the Aliens Act 1905 that any serious effort was made to control immigration, and that was not to be applied to subjects of the empire. There was earlier legislation, but it was relatively limited in scope. Dummett and Nicol's study of British nationality and immigration (1990, 11–12) reports what few of us today realize: that pervasive control over national borders is largely a phenomenon of the twentieth century. Before this century it was often possible to travel extensively without a passport and to take employment where one could find it.

The Aliens Act 1905 followed a royal commission report in 1903, which conceded that while they had "no accurate guide as to the number of alien immigrants in this country," their entry into Britain had led to a variety of complaints about the societal impact of free entry and abode. The commission "concluded that fears about alien immigration were largely ill-founded" (Dummett and Nicol 1990, 102). Alien immigrants at that time were mostly Jews from Eastern Europe, and the (now all too familiar) complaints against them included their tendency to congregate in certain districts and their reluctance to assimilate (Bevan 1986, 69). In fact, the Aliens Act 1905 applied only to aliens who arrived in steerage, specifically exempting "cabin passengers" who generally were better off. Poor immigrants, however, were examined as to their ability to support themselves and for the possession of marketable skills. The means to support oneself was evidenced by £5 for each applicant and £2 for each dependent. Persons with a serious illness or infirmity, "lunatics," and felons were subject to exclusion. However, political crimes were not disqualifying, political asylum holding an important place in British tradition (Bevan 1986, 66–72).

The Aliens Restriction Act 1914, intended for the emergency of the Great War, gave the home secretary largely uncontrolled discretion (as we have seen, the like of which he held under a number of other statutes) to regulate aliens, and despite the Armistice of 1918 the emergency powers were extended into peacetime by the Aliens Restrictions (Amendment) Act 1919 (Bevan 1986, 72–74). The 1920 Aliens Order made under the 1919 Amendment gave the home secretary the power to deport any alien whose presence in the kingdom was not "conducive to the public good" (Gordon 1985, 9). It is especially interesting that both the first Official Secrets Act and the beginnings of counterintelligence in what eventually came to be MI5 were due to fears of German espionage in the years leading up to the Great War (Dummett and Nicol 1990, 105–6). Officialdom, it seems, often conceives its natural children—secrecy and suspicion—in trying times and nurtures them in peacetime. As Dummett and Nicol point out (1990, 148–49), while discretion over aliens and immigration rests nominally in the person of the home secretary, in reality discretion is exercised by civil servants in the Home Office, as we have seen, a ministry particularly known for its conservatism, its secrecy, and its suspicion of outsiders.

However, the imperial view favoring free movement of subjects of the empire (as contrasted with aliens) was carried forward into the commonwealth and was set out as a principle in the British Nationality Acts of 1914 and 1948. Subject to a few minimal exceptions, Section 4 of the 1948 Act provided that every person born within the United Kingdom-and-Colonies shall be a citizen of the United Kingdom-and-Colonies by birth. Free mobility remained the defining principle as to subjects of the empire, and then the commonwealth, until the Commonwealth Immigrants Act 1962, which controlled the immigration of all holders of commonwealth passports except (1) those born in the U.K., (2) those holding U.K. passports issued by the U.K. government, and (3) those included on the passport of a person covered by (1) or (2). Those seeking entry to fill a specific job and those who possessed certain skills deemed in short supply might also be allowed entry by work voucher. The rest might be considered for entry, under quotas, in order of application, with preference being given those with war service (Layton-Henry 1992, 72–75).

The second Commonwealth Immigrants Act (1968) was passed chiefly to prevent the free immigration of East African Asians to the U.K. (Gordon 1985, 16). The 1968 Act went through Parliament in five days. One reason for the haste was to frustrate the efforts of Asian Kenyans who might flood charter flights to London once the prospect of restrictive legislation was clear (Dummett and Nicol 1990, 198–205). The 1968 Act provided that *all* holders of U.K. passports would be subject to immigration controls unless they or at least one parent or grandparent had been born, adopted, or naturalized in the U.K., or registered as a citizen of the U.K. (Layton-Henry 1992, 79). That policy continued until the Immigration Act 1971, in which a Labour government, responding to rising public anxiety about immigration and to the political fallout it produced, for the first time introduced the concept of *patriality.*

The most notable rhetoric in the cause of restricting immigration was Enoch Powell's "river of blood" speech of April 20, 1968, in which he opposed the Race Relations Bill 1968:

> Here is the means of showing that the immigrant communities can organize to consolidate their members to agitate and campaign against their fellow citizens, and to overawe and dominate the rest with legal weapons which the ignorant and the ill-informed have provided. As I look ahead I am filled with foreboding. Like the Roman, I seem to see "the River Tiber foaming with much blood!" That tragic and intractable phenomenon which we watch with horror on the other side of the Atlantic but which there is interwoven with the history and existence of the States itself, is coming upon us here by our own volition and for our own neglect. (Layton-Henry 1992, 80–81)

Powell's rhetoric, and the political activities of others who were quick to exploit such fears, shook both the Labour and Conservative parties so that neither acted thereafter as reliable protectors of the rights of citizens of the United Kingdom-and-Colonies. Both parties were intimidated by popular perceptions, despite the fact that it was repeatedly demonstrated that, except for the five-year period 1958–63, emigration from Britain exceeded immigration (Castles and Kosack 1985, 31).

Indeed, the 1971 Act was expanded on by a Conservative government in 1981. The key distinction became that between *patrials* and *nonpatrials.* In *R v. Home Secretary ex parte Phansopkar and Others* (1975, 502), Lord Denning described this distinction:

> In 1971 the Parliament of the United Kingdom invented a new word. It made a new man. It called him a "patrial." Not a patriot but a patrial.

Parliament made him one of us; and made us one of them. We are all
now patrials. We are no longer in the eye of the law, Englishmen, Scots-
men or Welshmen. We are just patrials. Parliament gave this new man a
fine set of clothes. It invested him with a new right. It called it the "right
of abode in the United Kingdom." It is the most precious right that anyone can have. At least I so regard it. It is declared in simple but expressive
words. Every patrial "shall be free to live in, and to come and go into and
from the United Kingdom without let or hindrance."

The two classes of *patrials* and *nonpatrials* in both the 1971 and 1981 acts
largely happen to coincide with the division of the commonwealth into the
old and new. The old commonwealth (chiefly Australia, Canada, and New
Zealand—and for a while South Africa and Rhodesia) was predominantly white.
The new commonwealth (most of the rest of the former empire) was mainly
nonwhite.

Under the British Nationality Act 1981, which came into force on January
1, 1983, the following had the right of entry and abode in the U.K. and became
British citizens:

I. Those with rights of abode *before* the British Nationality Act 1981
came into effect, as follows:

A. All who had citizenship of the United Kingdom-and-Colonies by virtue of having been (1) born, (2) adopted, (3) naturalized, or (except in
the case of women married to a citizen before the passing of the 1971
Act) (4) registered, in some part of the U.K. or islands.

B. Those whose (1) parent was a citizen of the United Kingdom-and-Colonies with a right of abode when the child was born or adopted, or (2)
whose grandparent had citizenship of the United Kingdom-and-Colonies at the time when the parent was born or adopted.

C. Citizens of the United Kingdom-and-Colonies who had at any time
been settled in the U.K., and had at the time been ordinarily resident
there as a citizen for the previous five years or more.

D. Commonwealth citizens born to or legally adopted by a parent who at
the time of birth or adoption had citizenship of the United Kingdom-
and-Colonies by reason of having been born in the U.K.

E. Certain women (a) by virtue of being a Commonwealth citizen and
either being or having been the wife of a citizen of the United King-

dom-and-Colonies or a Commonwealth citizen who, during marriage, had a right of abode under the rules above, or (b) would have had but for dying before the British Nationality Act of 1948 commenced.

II. People who are, or have been born to or adopted by, or are descended from, British citizens, or have become naturalized or have registered as British citizens, on or after January 1, 1983.

Each of the categories above describes those who are *patrials* and who (coincidentally) are predominantly white. The provisions of the 1971 Immigration Act and the 1981 British Nationality Act (and, to a large degree, the 1968 Commonwealth Immigrants Act) employ what is commonly known in law as a "grandfather clause." In U.S. constitutional law grandfather clauses were employed in the post-Reconstruction period (after 1876) when the southern states, formerly of the Confederacy, sought to exclude illiterate freedmen from the franchise, without, however, also excluding illiterate whites. The simple solution was to exempt from literacy tests those whose fathers or grandfathers had been qualified voters, for example, as of January 1, 1866, or before, while requiring proof of literacy of those recently freed slaves who offered themselves as voters. In time, this ruse proved too patently discriminatory even for a Supreme Court that otherwise was not particularly inclined at the time to challenge racism and was declared unconstitutional in *Guinn v. U.S.* (1915). Of course, it was not until the 1940s, some thirty years later, that the U.S. Supreme Court began to challenge *de jure* segregation in the South. Below in this chapter we will see the fate of grandfather clauses both under English law and under the ECHR.

East African Asians v. United Kingdom (1973)

The text of the Commission's report in this case has only recently been made public (in March 1994) despite the fact that the report was made in December 1973. The reason for the delay is that both parties must agree to publication and the British government did not consent until February 1994. No doubt the fact that the Commission found the United Kingdom had practiced racial discrimination sufficient to constitute degrading treatment under Art. 3 of the ECHR contributed to the government's reticence.

Applications were made in the *East African Asians* case to the European Commission on Human Rights on behalf of 25 *nonpatrial* citizens of the United Kingdom-and-Colonies (CUKC) and six British Protected Persons (BPP), the first of these categories having first been defined by the 1948 British Nationality Act and the second being aliens under the protection of the British sovereign, but recognized as BPPs in the 1948 act. The applicants complained that they had been the subjects of racial discrimination by virtue of the refusal of the United Kingdom to recognize their citizenship or protected status and grant them abode in Britain.

CUKCs had the right of abode within the United Kingdom under the 1948 Nationality Act by virtue of birth within the United Kingdom or within British colonies or territories, provided that they held, or were entitled to, passports issued by the United Kingdom. Legislation enacted in 1968 had revoked that right of abode for certain CUKCs.

When Kenya gained its independence in 1963, those born in Kenya, or with at least one parent born there, could claim Kenyan citizenship. Others with close ties to Kenya might register for Kenyan citizenship within a two-year period. Those who did not claim Kenyan citizenship might have had some other nationality, or might have had the status of CUKCs.

Within the first few years of Kenyan independence, the Kenyan government began to discriminate against Asians who had not taken out Kenyan citizenship. Under the 1962 Commonwealth Immigration Act, those who were CUKCs were entitled, on the independence of Kenya, to U.K. passports and thus were free to emigrate to Britain (Fransman 1989, 114). However, the Commonwealth Immigrants Act 1968 amended the previous Act so that the right of abode was limited to citizens who were actually born, adopted, registered, or naturalized in the United Kingdom, or who had such a parent or grandparent (Fransman 1989, 115). As we have seen, the amendment was designed to limit the entry into the U.K. of Asians from East Africa. Dummett and Nicol (1990, 202) report a particularly apt remark of barrister Anthony Lester on the 1968 Act: "In passing it, a group of citizens temporarily in office have deprived another group of citizens of a fundamental right of citizenship, the right to enter and live in the only country in which they were legally entitled to do so."

The East African Asians in effect became stateless persons. Dummett and Nicol (1990, 203) offer a vivid description of the consequences:

Effectively they were without a citizenship. This became painfully clear as they tried to migrate to, or through, other countries: nowhere could they easily establish admission, even temporarily, since their passports did not show them to be "returnable" anywhere. Those who arrived in the United Kingdom without quota vouchers were refused admission even though there was no other country bound to admit them. They were shuttled back and forth, refused entry in the countries to which the British immigration authorities tried to send them, and sent back again to Britain, where they were refused and put on planes again. Eventually, some of these unfortunates were admitted to Britain and promptly placed in prison. In the long run they had to be released and allowed to remain, but the policy of "shuttlecocking" and subsequent imprisonment was deliberately used to discourage others from coming.

The difficulty with complaining to the European Commission was that the original text of the ECHR contains no specific restrictions on the power of a member-state to legislate regarding either immigration or the right to abode. Art. 3.2 of the Fourth Protocol to the ECHR does provide, however, that "no one shall be denied the right to enter the territory of a State of which he is a national." But the United Kingdom had not ratified this protocol, and there was no constitutional instrument that secured the status of U.K. citizenship against subsequent legislation passed by Parliament. And so the only alternative open was to find some implication of right suggested by the text of the ECHR.

The first issue taken up by the Commission in the *East African Asians* case was whether the refusal of the U.K. to admit the applicants violated their rights under Art. 3.

Article 3

The complaint under Art. 3 was limited to citizens, who arguably had been reduced to second-class status. Art. 3 provides that "no one shall be subjected to inhuman or degrading treatment or punishment," so the argument ran that racial discrimination itself could constitute "degrading treatment" by creating two classes of citizens, primarily along racial lines. The Commission cited precedent (para. 195) that had established degrading treatment as that which "grossly humiliates" one before others, and suggested also that reducing someone to the "status of a second class citizen" might also be degrading (para. 205). They had no difficulty in concluding that racially discriminatory treatment in the abstract might be degrading, but they then had to decide whether the policy of the U.K. was discriminatory in fact and degrading in this context.

Concluding that the policy was racially motivated was the easy part, for even the U.K. government conceded (para. 200) that the Commonwealth Immigrants Act 1968 had a racial motive. The U.K. asserted, however, that its racial motive was benign; according to the home secretary of the day the restrictions on further immigration were "the best way to achieve the idea of a multi-racial society." But the Commission noted that the Commonwealth Immigrants Act 1968 had been preceded by the British Nationality Act 1964, which "facilitated the resumption of citizenship" in the U.K. by "white settlers" in Uganda and Kenya, but not by East African Asians (para. 202). Also, by the time the applications of the East African Asians reached the Commission, the Immigration Act of 1971 had replaced the Commonwealth Immigration Act of 1968, and the 1971 Act, as we saw above, introduced the concept of *patrial* citizens and granted them the right of abode. This usually did not include Asians, but since they continued to be citizens, even under the 1971 Act, they were reduced to "the status of second-class citizens." Thus, the Commission concluded that U.K. policy was racially discriminatory and that it "constitutes an interference with their human dignity which . . . amounted to 'degrading treatment' in the sense of Art. 3 of the Convention" (para. 208). The Commission's conclusion, however, was not applied to the six applicants who had only the status of British Protected Persons, rather than citizenship.

Art. 8 and 14

We should note in passing that the Commission also found that U.K. immigration policy dating from the 1962 Commonwealth Immigrants Act had exempted from immigration control the *wife* of a Commonwealth citizen who had right of settlement in the U.K., but did not accord the same right to the *husband* of a Commonwealth citizen similarly situated. This the Commission found to be an unjustified interference with the right to respect for family life protected by Art. 8 of the ECHR and discriminatory on the ground of sex under Art. 14 (para. 232). This issue was the central point of the case of *Abdulaziz, Cabales and Balkandali* (1985) before the European Court of Human Rights, which we will analyze below. But before doing that, we should see what happened next in the *East African Asians* case.

The Commission's decision of December 13, 1973, found a violation of Art. 3 by vote of eight to three and of Art. 8 and 14, taken together, by vote of nine to two. Ordinarily the next step would be either to refer the case to the European Court for a judicial decision, or to the council of ministers for resolution. But in May 1975, the United Kingdom advised the council of ministers that it had taken steps to facilitate the entry into the U.K. of CUKCs from East Africa and that all of the thirty-one applicants in the instant case were then settled in the U.K. Entry quotas had also been increased from 1,500 to 5,000 (by 1975) and husbands had been permitted to join their wives in the U.K. Hence, no further action was taken by the council of ministers (*East African Asians v. United Kingdom*, Committee of Ministers, 1977). So the first case involving U.K. nationality and immigration policy was not decided by the European Court of Human Rights until 1985.

Case of Abdulaziz, Cabales and Balkandali v. United Kingdom (1985)

Mrs. Nargis Abdulaziz, Mrs. Arcely Cabales, and Mrs. Sohair Balkandali filed applications in 1980 and 1981 with the European Commission on Human

Rights because their husbands were denied permission to reside with them in the United Kingdom. This they alleged to be in violation of Art. 3 (inhuman or degrading treatment), 8 (respect for family life), 14 (taken with Art. 3 and 8, on grounds of racial and sex discrimination) and 13 (in that no effective remedy for these violations existed under U.K. domestic law).

The immigration rules that applied to the three applicants are difficult to follow at best, but tracing their various revisions from year to year indeed becomes tortuous. Under the 1980 Rules when a *nonpatrial* husband or fiancé sought to join his wife or fiancée in the U.K., he might do so *unless* their marriage or intended marriage was "non-qualifying," but only if his wife or fiancée was a CUKC (a citizen of the United Kingdom-and-Colonies, that is, the status conferred by the British Nationality Act 1948 to those born either in the U.K. or one of the British colonies, dependencies, or dominions) who had been born in the U.K.—or one of her parents had been born in the U.K. A marriage or intended marriage was nonqualifying when it was entered into for the purpose of achieving settlement in the U.K., when the parties did not intend to live together as man and wife, or when the parties to the marriage had not met prior to the marriage. However, when a nonpatrial wife or fiancée sought to join her husband or fiancé in the U.K., she could do so without regard to her husband's nationality or his parents' place of birth. Wives seeking to join their husbands were given indefinite leave to enter, while husbands were admitted initially for twelve months and fiancés or fiancées for three months. All had the possibility of applying later for indefinite leave. These complicated rules simply made the entry of husbands and fiancés much more difficult, or impossible, relative to the entry of wives and fiancées.

The British Nationality Act 1981 replaced the status of CUKC with three categories of citizenship: British citizen, citizen of a British Dependent Territory, and British Overseas citizen. CUKCs with right of abode in Britain became British citizens. The 1982 Immigration Rules provided that for a husband or fiancé to be eligible to enter or remain in the U.K., his wife or fiancée must be a British citizen. The burden of proof was also placed on the husband or fiancé seeking to enter or stay to prove that the marriage was a fully legitimate one. No provision was made in the rules for women settled in the U.K. who were not British citizens to be joined by their husbands or fiancés. The rules respecting entry and abode of wives and fiancées were not materially changed, except for terminology, which is to say that men who were not British citizens but who were permanently settled in the U.K. might be joined by their wives or fiancées, subject, of course, to various other rules.

One stated purpose for these rules was to protect the labor market in the U.K., given a condition of chronic unemployment, from the abode of those who might be expected to become primary wage earners (*Abdulaziz, Cabales and Balkandali,* ser. A, 15). Employing what the U.S. Supreme Court has sometimes called an "archaic and stereotypical generalization," U.K. policy was predicated on the view that males probably would be the primary wage earners. It is worth noting that in *Frontiero v. Richardson* (1973) the U.S. Supreme Court rejected a federal policy based on a similar assumption of who most likely would be the primary wage earner.

An appellate tribunal was established outside the ordinary courts to hear appeals, by leave, from aggrieved applicants whose entry had been denied. No appeal from that tribunal could be had to common law courts, but applicants might be given leave to seek judicial review in the High Court for errors of law, bias, or arbitrary exercise of power.

Respect for Family Life under Art. 8

A brief review of the circumstances of each of the three applicants is essential to the appreciation of their situation (see *Abdulaziz, Cabales and Balkandali,* ser. A, 23–29). Mrs. Abdulaziz was a national of Malawi who entered the U.K. first as a visitor, but eventually was granted permission to settle with her family on the grounds that "she was an unmarried female with little prospect of marriage who formed part of a close family, including her mother and father." She met her husband, a Portuguese national, while he was on a six-month visitor visa in the U.K. They met in mid-October 1979 and were married almost two months later.

Mrs. Cabales was a national of the Philippines with the right of permanent abode in the U.K. She was employed as a state-enrolled nurse. She met her husband while she was on a holiday in the Philippines, where her parents continued to reside.

Mrs. Balkandali was born in Egypt, but like Mrs. Cabales was a permanent resident of the U.K. She became a registered CUKC with right of abode in the U.K. by virtue of her first marriage, which was later dissolved by divorce. Her second husband was a Turkish national who entered the U.K. first as a visitor, but stayed on through a student visa. He married his wife while in the U.K., and they had a son who has the right of abode within the U.K.

In seeking the entry and abode of their husbands the three applicants confronted the identical problem we saw in the *East African Asians* case above. The U.K., having refused to ratify the Fourth Protocol, claimed that the applicants were seeking protection not accorded by the ECHR. The Court noted, however, that the applicants were the wives, not the alien husbands, and the wives all were permanently settled in the U.K. They thus had the status to claim under Art. 8 that U.K. policy failed to respect their family life by denying them the consortium of their husbands. Nonetheless, the Court noted that in the cases of none of the three applicants were there families who had been "left behind" in another country awaiting entry into the U.K. Instead, the applicants had contracted marriages with husbands whose right of entry and abode was limited by U.K. law. Therefore, the Court recognized that the three cases were not "concerned only with family life but also with immigration and that, as a matter of well-established international law . . . a State has the right to control the entry of non-nationals into its territory" (*Abdulaziz, Cabales and Balkandali*, ser. A, 34). The three applicants were in effect on notice of the possible consequences of their actions, and the Court found no violation of Art. 8 *by itself.*

Sex Discrimination under Art. 14 Taken with Art. 8

Art. 14 (which prohibits several forms of categorical discrimination, including sex) taken with Art. 8 is quite another matter. Of course, treating women differently than men does not always violate Art. 14; if the aim is a legitimate one, the means used are proportionate to the aim, and an "objective and reasonable justification" supports the different treatment, a gender-based policy may be sustained. While the words used by the U.S. Supreme Court are somewhat different, the words used by the European Court essentially express the abstract status of law on sex discrimination in the U.S. as well (see, for example, *Michael M. v. Superior Court of Sonoma County* [1981]). That U.K. policy and practice treated men differently than women under the immigration rules was beyond dispute, but was there an objective and reasonable justification for the difference? The aim of protecting the labor market in a time of high unemployment was certainly a legitimate one, but the means chosen, the applicants argued, ignored the "modern role of women" as well as the fact that men or women might be self-employed, rather than seeking employment by others. Moreover, the policy restricting the entry of husbands amounted to a reduction only of about 5,700 entrants per year. To these points the Court added that the objective of the member-states of the Council of Europe of advancing sexual equality meant that "very weighty reasons would have to be advanced" before a sex-based policy could be sustained.

Again, the parallels to decisions of the U.S. Supreme Court are fascinating. In *Frontiero v. Richardson* (1973) the U.S. Supreme Court was only one vote short of holding gender-based discrimination to be a suspect classification, the use of which would have been presumptively invalid and which would have required the government to prove a compelling public interest, were it to survive strict scrutiny. However, in *Craig v. Boren* (1976) a majority of the Court required only that gender-based policies must serve important governmental objectives and be substantially related to the achievement of those objectives. Those words still define the test for gender-based discrimination in the U.S. today.

Not surprisingly, given the European standard that "very weighty reasons would have to be shown if a gender-based policy were to be sustained," the European Court was unconvinced that the different impact of men and women on the labor market was sufficiently important to justify their different treatment as to entry and abode. The three applicants were thus found to be victims of sex discrimination under Art. 14 taken with Art. 8 (*Abdulaziz, Cabales and Balkandali*, ser. A, 39).

Other Issues

The applicants also complained of racial discrimination, but there was a key difference between this case and the *East African Asians* case. The previous case involved CUKCs who had been relegated to second-class status by virtue of U.K. statutes and nationality rules, and the division between first- and second-class status was drawn largely along racial lines. In this case none of the three husbands excluded had any sort of citizenship or special nationality status under U.K. law. While it may have been true that the immigration rules had the intention of lowering the number of "coloured immigrants," on its face the purpose of the exclusion was, as we have seen, to protect the domestic labor market. The Court was quite unwilling to look beneath the surface of the policy, the state's prerogatives over immigration policy being what they are (*Abdulaziz, Cabales and Balkandali*, ser. A, 39–40).

Mrs. Balkandali also claimed that she was the object of discrimination based on birth given the distinction in U.K. policy between female CUKCs born, or having a parent who was born, in the U.K. (whose husbands or fiancés might be admitted) and those with no such ties (whose husbands or fiancés ordinarily would not be admitted)—a policy distinction that was subsequently eliminated by the U.K. The Court found, however, that the U.K.'s cited purpose of favoring those with especially close ties to the country had an objective and reasonable justification (*Abdulaziz, Cabales and Balkandali*, ser. A, 41).

Finally, the Court also found a violation of Art. 13 (absence of an effective remedy in domestic law), which was coupled with the sex discrimination violation under Art. 14 and 8. Their point was that the sex-based violation was a violation only of the ECHR and not of U.K. domestic law. Since the U.K. had not incorporated the ECHR into its domestic law, there could be no effective remedy within the U.K.; consequently, there was a violation of Art. 13 as well.

The British government's response to *Abudulaziz, Cabales and Balkandali* was to amend the immigration rules in 1985 to conform with the decision of the European Court. The amendment, however, did not extend the liberal treatment accorded men to women, but restricted men to the same degree as women. The former rules about the entry of husbands and fiancés now apply equally to wives and fiancées (Bailey et al. 1991, 652). Such outcomes are no doubt a deterrent to applications to the European Commission. While the issue was not litigated, achieving equality for women by reducing the protection already accorded men may constitute a violation of Art. 60 of the ECHR, which provides that nothing in the ECHR shall be construed to limit the rights already ensured by a state member.

POLITICAL ASYLUM AND ADMINISTRATIVE DISCRETION

In addition to possible protection under the ECHR, people who seek political asylum in the United Kingdom potentially are protected under several international conventions. The U.K. has obligations under both the *Convention Relating to the Status of Refugees* (1954) and the *Protocol Relating to the Status of Refugees* (1966). Their key language is that a refugee seeking political asylum must have a "well-founded fear of being persecuted for reasons of race, religion, nationality, membership of a particular social group, or political opinion" in the country of his or her nationality and because of that fear is incapable of being protected by that country (Feldman 1993, 325). In effect the 1954 convention and the 1966 protocol were incorporated into U.K. law in the 1983 immigration rules; however, the potential protection afforded by such words must be transformed into reality, which, as we shall see, is not always easy.

The Plight of Tamil Refugees in Britain

Among the recent cases on claims of political asylum in the United Kingdom are those involving Tamil refugees from Sri Lanka. The first case was brought in a U.K. domestic court and eventually reached the House of Lords as *R. v. Home Secretary, ex parte Sivakumaran et al.* (1988).

Six Tamils had applied to the home secretary for asylum because of their fear of ethnic and religious persecution in Sri Lanka, but their petitions were denied, the home secretary finding that the applicants had no particular reasons to fear persecution. The applicants then applied for judicial review, and the Court of Appeal set aside the home secretary's findings. The home secretary then appealed to the House of Lords.

The issue involved an interpretive choice between subjective and objective tests. In effect the Court of Appeal had adopted a subjective test in which the applicants were required only to show that they did in fact fear persecution and that they had intelligible reasons for their fears, which would have caused persons of reasonable courage to try to avoid returning to their home country. Under such a test they would be entitled to asylum even though it might be shown that they suffered from some misapprehension—that the danger was not in fact as great as they thought. The counsel for the UN High Commissioner for Refugees (who intervened on behalf of the Tamils in the case) argued for the subjective test, in part because his position was that the ECHR and its protocols ought to be liberally construed so as to favor asylum. It would have been difficult for the home secretary, or a court for that matter, to deny the reality of a reasonable, though subjective fear of persecution.

The objective test requires that the objective facts be assessed to determine whether there is, in fact, a real or substantial risk of persecution on grounds recognized by the Convention and Protocol on Refugees. Not surprisingly, given what we have seen before, the House of Lords adopted the more restrictive objective test. Under that test the home secretary has the duty to take into account the facts and circumstances made known to him by applicants (and others) and by the U.K. government (even though the facts are unknown to the applicants) in order to determine whether the applicants' fears of persecution were objectively justified. The crunch, of course, comes once the home secretary has made his decision. Will a U.K. court exercising the power of judicial review be likely to second-guess his judgment? Probably not on factual grounds, if his judgment is surrounded by appropriate words like these: "The Secretary of State has considered the individual circumstances of your case and in addition the situation in Sri Lanka and has concluded that you have not established a well-founded fear of persecution in Sri Lanka." These are the precise words used in the *Vilvarajah* case, so the confirmation of my suggestion that the home secretary's factual finding may be effectively beyond serious judicial review will be found in that case.

Case of Vilvarajah and Others v. United Kingdom (1991)

The report of this judgment of the European Court opens with the case histories of five Tamil men, beginning with Nadarajah Vilvarajah, who will serve here as an example.

Mr. Vilvarajah was born in 1960; he was 27 when he first arrived in London as a refugee. The Sinhalese-dominated Sri Lankan army was active in controlling his home district; later "security" was provided by the Indian Army under a July 1987 accord between Sri Lanka and India. His cousin was killed by the Sri Lankan army in 1986, and his family's shop was raided in 1987. He himself was detained on two occasions in 1986. He claimed that he was beaten, and when escorted back to his home, his captors opened fire and killed three people at random. A firefight ensued between his captors and so-called Tamil terrorists. During a Sri Lankan army offensive in 1987 his family lost their shop and they nearly were killed. In May 1987, his father arranged for his passage to London where he arrived with a forged Malaysian passport. On June 12, 1987, he requested asylum in the United Kingdom.

In August 1987, he received the home secretary's response to his request:

You have applied for asylum in the United Kingdom on the grounds that you hold a well-founded fear of persecution in Sri Lanka for reasons of race, religion, nationality, membership of a social group, or political opinion. You said it was unsafe for you to remain in Sri Lanka due to Government operations around Jaffna. You also said that you had been detained on two occasions in March and April 1986 for 10 hours and 24 hours respectively and that on 28 March 1987 the army raided your family business. But it is noted that the incidents you have related were *random* and part of the army's general activities directed at discovering and dealing with Tamil extremists and that they do not constitute evidence of persecution. (emphasis added, *Vilvarajah v. United Kingdom,* ser. A, 9)

The words of the home secretary denying his application were the ones quoted above. Mr. Vilvarajah next sought judicial review. He was one of the applicants on appeal whose case was included in the opinion of the House of Lords in *R. v. Home Secretary, ex parte Sivakumaran* (1988), reviewed above. When their case was lost in the House of Lords they were sent back to Sri Lanka.

Following his return to Sri Lanka, Vilvarajah was questioned for about three hours by the police, his fingerprints were taken, his address was noted, but eventually he was released. Later he was denounced to the Indian "Peacekeeping Force" (IPKF), questioned, and again released. Still later, he was included in a lineup of suspected terrorists, but he was not identified and again was released.

In March 1989, while Vilvarajah was still in Sri Lanka, an adjudicator of his appeal in the U.K. under section 13 of the Immigration Act 1971 found in his favor. The adjudicator found that as a young Tamil male in Sri Lanka, he was at risk of interrogation, detention, and physical harm. The home secretary then appealed from the decision of the adjudicator to the Immigration Appeal Tribunal, but the home secretary's appeal was rejected for the technical reason of his having failed to meet a deadline for lodging appeals. The home secretary then applied for judicial review of the decisions of the adjudicator and the tribunal on the grounds that Mr. Vilvarajah should not be entitled to claim asylum after having presented a forged Malaysian passport and sought entry as a visitor. The High Court upheld the tribunal in July 1989, but the home secretary appealed again to the Court of Appeal and applied for a stay against Mr. Vilvarajah's return to Britain. The stay was denied, and Mr. Vilvarajah was allowed to return to the United Kingdom in October 1989, where he again made application for asylum. In May 1990, the Court of Appeal rejected the home secretary's appeal from the judgment of the High Court. Mr. Vilvarajah continued to reside in the U.K. while, among other things, his application to the European Commission was under consideration.

The European Commission voted seven to seven on Vilvarajah's (and others') application as to Art. 3 (that to return them to Sri Lanka would threaten to subject them to inhuman or degrading treatment or punishment). The tie vote amounted to a rejection of their claim under Art. 3. However, the Commission did find a violation of Art. 13 (failure to provide an effective domestic remedy) by a vote of thirteen to one.

The Situation in Sri Lanka

Out of a population of about 16 million in Sri Lanka, about 18 percent are Tamil Hindus. The Tamils are concentrated particularly in the northern peninsula of Jaffna. Most of the population of Sri Lanka is Sinhalese. In its decision the European Court presented its review and assessment of the political situation and of the prospects for personal security in Sri Lanka, and the facts recited here are taken from its account.

Conflict between Tamils and Sinhalese dates, for the present case, to the independence of the country in 1948, but in the 1980s the conflict intensified when the Sinhalese-controlled government was contested by various Tamil "liberation groups." The Court's decision focused particularly on the accord between Sri Lanka and India in July 1987, whereby the Indian Army became the guarantor of security in Tamil areas. When Tamil "extremists" rejected that accord, the IPKF became involved in a guerrilla war, which reached its heights in late 1987 (Mr. Vilvarajah fled to Britain in June 1987). At that time the IPKF was engaged in a siege of Jaffna town during which 2,000 to 5,000 civilians were killed. The U.K. represented to the Court that violent conflict "eased off" in December 1987. By that time there was in place a U.N. program of "voluntary repatriation" of Tamils, mostly those having previously taken refuge in India. Some European countries (the Netherlands and France) had begun to send Tamils back; others (Germany and Italy) had not. In December 1987, Amnesty International, the British Refugee Council, and the United Nations High Commissioner for Refugees urged the U.K. government not to send any Tamils back. However, Vilvarajah and the other applicants were returned to Sri Lanka in February 1988.

The adjudicator who found on Mr. Vilvarajah's behalf in March 1989 had jurisdiction through the appellate process set out in section 13 of the 1971 Immigration Act. The difficulty with the process is that ordinarily it may be pursued only from outside the U.K. That was one reason for the European Commission's finding that the review provided under U.K. law was not sufficient to meet the requirements of Art. 13 of the ECHR. However, in Mr. Vilvarajah's instance he prevailed, and it was that process that led to his return to the United Kingdom and through which he ultimately prevailed under the Immigration Act.

The European Court's Decision on Art. 3

While member-states clearly have the right to control immigration, they may not do so in ways that otherwise would violate the ECHR. Political asylum is not directly provided for in either the ECHR or its protocols. Having recognized that, it was nonetheless the case that to expel someone only to return him or her to be tortured or to suffer some form of inhuman or degrading treatment might be a violation of Art. 3. Did the applicants suffer a greater risk of such treatment than did the general Tamil population of Sri Lanka?

Even to ask such a question recalls Yosarian's apprehension in *Catch 22*. When he was ordered to go back outside, where World War II was in hot progress, Yosarian objected, "I'm not going out there; they're trying to kill me!" His friend replied, "Yosarian, they're trying to kill everybody." Yosarian's reply sums up the individualist perspective by saying, "So, what difference does that make?" The U.K. government's point was that whatever danger Vilvarajah and others confronted was *random*, which, of course, was quite immaterial from Vilvarajah's point of view, if the probability was nonetheless high. But the United Kingdom's problem was the consequence of being required to follow a policy under which *anyone* facing random but significant risks of violence in a country torn by civil strife might be entitled to political asylum. Here—as is commonly the case with such governmental decisions—when a collective interest conflicts with an individual right, the result is usually some sort of balancing test. The home secretary concluded that the risk to the applicants was not high enough, nor the threat specific enough to them to justify asylum, a decision which the European Commission on Human Rights upheld by its seven to seven vote.

The European Court of Human Rights upheld the Commission and found no violation, with only one dissenting vote. They found that by February 1988, when the applicants were returned to Sri Lanka, the situation had improved sufficiently to warrant repatriation of many Tamils, and these applicants, the Court concluded, were not at any greater risk than other young Tamil men. Thus there was no violation of Art. 3.

Art. 13 and the Scope of Judicial Review

Art. 13 requires that there be an effective domestic remedy for determining violations of the ECHR. Of course, Britain, as we have seen several times before, is at a disadvantage because it has not incorporated the ECHR into its domestic law and also because it has no rights document of its own with provisions like those of the ECHR. If a state member has incorporated the ECHR, or has essentially the same provision in its own rights document, it is a fairly simple matter for it to show the procedural steps under which a rights complaint may be pursued. But when there is no incorporation of the ECHR—and nothing in domestic law equivalent to it—a state member is required to show that an applicant has some other means for raising the issues that would have been raised had the ECHR been incorporated. In the United Kingdom the only candidate for that is the judicial review process. Not surprisingly, the counsel for applicants and the U.K. government had different views of the potential of judicial review.

Both sides agreed at an abstract level: judicial review is not available either to reassess the facts or to substitute judges' views on the merits of a case for that of the home secretary. But what does that mean? From the applicants' point of view a remedy that allows *only* for a review of the procedural steps whereby a decision is made, or *only* of the factors that lawfully may be taken into account, is not sufficient. The U.K.'s response was that *Wednesbury* principles also are applicable, so that a judge exercising judicial review powers may set aside a home secretary's decision when it is one that no reasonable home secretary could make (*Associated Provincial Picture Houses Ltd. v. Wednesbury Corp.* [1948]). You can imagine how difficult it might be to prove such a condition.

The analysis of excessive and largely unreviewable administrative discretion has been the special contribution of Kenneth Culp Davis (1971, 1976), whose work I mentioned in chapter 1 and whose substantive purpose has been the elimination of unnecessary and excessive discretionary power and the proper confining, structuring, and checking of the discretion that is necessary (and indeed inevitable). In this instance, however, the European Court imposed no real constraints or limitations on the home secretary. Its majority agreed in *Vilvarajah* that U.K. judicial review, as outlined above, provided a sufficiently effective degree of control to satisfy the requirements of Art. 13 (*Vilvarajah and Others v. United Kingdom*, ser. A, 40).

The Convention and the Scope of Judicial Review under British Law

The *Wednesbury* principles are often cited for the view that U.K. courts have the authority through the exercise of judicial review to set aside the clearly unreasonable decisions of executive officers, including the home secretary. While that may be true with respect to judicial review of the authority of a U.K. officer as defined by statute, it is quite a different matter to suggest that such judicial review is sufficient to determine whether or not the actions of executive officers are in violation of the ECHR. Even the possibility of review of statutory authority is problematic when the statute vests broad discretion in the home secretary and does not define the criteria that he is to use in his decisions, as we have previously seen in the home secretary's powers under the Defence of the Realm and Prevention of Terrorism Acts. In the context of this chapter the Alien Restrictions (Amendment) Act 1919 is another example; it gave the home secretary the authority to exclude aliens whose presence in the country is "not conducive to the public good."

David Feldman's recent book suggests the difficulty in seeking judicial review when a British administrative official fails to take into account the provision of the ECHR (1993, 331). As Feldman notes, language in the case of *R. v. Home Secretary, ex parte Brind* (1991) suggested that a U.K. judge is not obliged to take the ECHR into account in his decisions, and also that it is not clearly unreasonable for an executive officer to fail to do so. According to this recent precedent, British judges have no such obligation. This is not to suggest that British courts have no power of judicial review over administrative discretion, but that they only "are entitled to exercise a secondary judgement by asking whether a reasonable Secretary of State, on the material before him, could reasonably [have made such a] primary judgment" (*ex parte Brind*, 749). This point was also made by Lord Denning in *R. v. Home Secretary, ex parte Bhajan Singh* (1975, 1083) in one of the first opinions by a British judge to refer to the ECHR:

> What is the position of the convention in our English law? I would not depart in the least from what I said in the recent case of *Birdi v. Secretary of State for Home Affairs* [an unreported decision]. The court can and should take the convention into account. They should take it into account whenever interpreting a statute which affects the rights and liberties of the individual. It is to be assumed that the Crown, in taking its part in legislation, would do nothing that was in conflict with treaties. So the court should now construe the Immigration Act so as to be in conformity with a convention and not against it. . . .
>
> . . . I would, however, like to correct one sentence in my judgment in *Birdi's* case. I said: "If [an Act of Parliament] did not conform [to the convention] I might be inclined to hold it invalid." That was a very tentative statement but it went too far. There are many cases in which it has been said, as plainly as can be, that a treaty does not become part of our English law except and insofar as it is made so by Parliament. If an Act of Parliament contained any provisions contrary to the convention, the Act of Parliament must prevail. But I hope that no Act ever will be contrary to the convention. So the point should not arise.

I would repeat that when anyone is to consider a problem concerning human rights, we should seek to solve it in the light of the convention and in conformity with it.

Lord Bridge clearly states a different position in *R. v. Home Secretary, ex parte Brind* (1991) when suggesting that British judges need not take the ECHR into account, but his is the prevailing view.

Nonetheless, the European Court of Human Rights was persuaded that the judicial review provided under British practice was sufficient under Art. 13. The *Vilvarajah* decision cited the case of *Bugdaycay v. Home Secretary* (1987) for the views expressed by Lord Bridge and Lord Templeman that when life and liberty are at stake British judges have a "special responsibility" in conducting judicial review to be sure that the home secretary's decisions are in "no way flawed" (*Vilvarajah,* ser. A, 30). The European Court's decision noted that in *Bugdaycay* the home secretary's removal order had indeed been set aside, albeit for only one of four applicants. A careful reading of *Bugdaycay* demonstrates, however, that the exercise of judicial review there does not provide a full-fledged "appeal for formal reconsideration of the decision," as suggested by U.N. procedures—the *Handbook on Procedures and Criteria for Determining Refugees Status* published by the United Nations High Commissioner for Refugees contains these quoted words. However, in *Bugdaycay* (1987, 953) the House of Lords found only that the home secretary had failed to take into account the prospect that the applicant, if returned to Kenya, might immediately be sent home to Uganda, where his life and liberty were in danger. A British court may merely require the home secretary to take a certain factor into account, if the record suggests that he failed to do so. The European Court in *Vilvarajah* also cited *R. v. Home Secretary, ex parte Jeyakumaran* (1985) for a slightly broader point: that the failure of the home secretary to take certain factors into account may cause a judge exercising the power of judicial review to examine the evidence "in some detail." Thus the judge in *Jeyakumaran* quashed the home secretary's denial of the claim for asylum on the grounds that "in reaching his decision he took into account matters which ought not to have been taken into account and failed to take into account matters he should" (*Vilvarajah,* 31). *Gaima v. Home Secretary* (1989), also cited by the European Court, demonstrates that judicial review may also be used to quash a decision of the home secretary in order to require procedural fairness, in this instance to allow the applicant to respond to assertions that challenged her credibility (1989, 209).

Given these precedents, it is understandable that a majority of the European Court might conclude that judicial review satisfies the requirements of

Art. 13 of the ECHR. However, as we have seen, *R. v. Home Secretary, ex parte Brind* (1991) casts doubt on that conclusion.

The implications of *Brind* can readily be seen in the recent case of *R. v. Home Secretary, ex parte Chahal* (1993), another political asylum case. There Judge Potts of the Queen's Bench specifically adopted Lord Bridge's language in *Brind* (*Chahal*, Queen's Bench, 1993, 380). *Chahal* involved a petition for political asylum filed by a member of the International Sikh Youth Federation who, according to the home secretary, had been "actively involved in terrorism in the United Kingdom and India" (Queen's Bench, 1993, 362). Chahal had entered the U.K. in 1971 unlawfully, but was allowed to remain under the terms of a 1974 amnesty for illegal entrants. In 1987 he was convicted of the offense of affray and unlawful wounding and received a sentence of nine months, but his conviction was set aside by the Court of Appeal in July 1992. His alleged offense was related to a disturbance at the East Ham Gurdwara, a Sikh center. In April 1989, his application for registration as a British citizen was denied, and in August 1990 the home secretary decided that he should be deported. Following the service of his notice of deportation he was detained, and while in custody he applied for political asylum. The home secretary's first refusal of Chahal's request for asylum was overturned by the High Court in December 1991. After reconsideration, the home secretary again decided that Chahal should be deported and affirmed a deportation notice in July 1992, whereupon Chahal again sought judicial review. In February 1993, the Queen's Bench through Judge Potts refused the judicial review application and a renewed request for bail.

Apart from U.K. immigration and nationality statutes, Judge Potts specifically mentioned Art. 3 of the ECHR and Art. 3(1) of the U.N. Convention against Torture, both of which prohibit, directly or indirectly, the expulsion and repatriation of someone who may be subjected to torture or inhuman or degrading treatment when returned to his or her home country. While neither of those provisions was incorporated into U.K. law, Art. 32 and 33 of the U.N. Convention on the Status of Refugees had been incorporated into the U.K. Immigration Rules. Art. 32 provided that a refugee may be expelled *only* on grounds of national security or public order and *only* through a decision reached in accordance with due process of law. Art. 33 provided that a refugee shall not be returned to a country where his or her life or freedom would be threatened on grounds of race, religion, nationality, membership of a particular social group, or political opinion, but exempted from that protection is any refugee who constitutes a "serious danger to the security of the country" in which he or she claims asylum, or who has been convicted of a serious crime and thereby represents a danger to the community in the country of his or her asylum.

While these applicable provisions seem clear enough, the real issues once again were who is to make the primary judgment on the factual questions and on what grounds and what standard of secondary review is to be accorded those primary judgments? Under U.K. law the primary judgment is clearly that of the home secretary. But once again (in addition to the other international obligation reviewed above) Art. 13 of the ECHR requires that an applicant be afforded an effective remedy in domestic law whereby such judgments can be contested and reviewed.

Having adopted Lord Bridge's language in *Brind*, the standard for secondary review of the home secretary's primary judgment was simply whether a reasonable home secretary could have made such a judgment on the facts before him. To that standard, however, Judge Potts added the following revealing explanation, "[T]his court cannot judge the quality of, or the weight to be attached to, the evidence going to the risk to the national security posed by this applicant. The only person who can do that is the Secretary of State who has all the available information, and this court must accept his assessment of the extent of the risk" (*Chahal*, Queen's Bench, 1993, 380).

The Court of Appeal's judgment was much the same. Thus, in the words of Lord Justice Staughton, "We can only interfere if this decision was irrational or perverse or otherwise unlawful. In my judgment it is not shown to be any of those things, still less if one weighs against any threat of persecution the risk which Mr. Chahal poses to the national security of this country (*Chahal*, Court of Appeal, 1993, 669).

Thus, it seems clear that judicial review does not offer a full-scale appellate review of the merits of a decision. For this reason, Judges Walsh and Russo dissented from the European Court's decision respecting Art. 13 in the case of *Vilvarajah*, and they dissented almost two years before Judge Potts wrote the words above in *Chahal*. The dissenters in *Vilvarajah* quoted the following language from *Chief Constable of the North Wales Police v. Evans* (1982, 1173–74), "Judicial review is concerned not with the decision, but with the decision making procedure. Unless that restriction on the power of the court is observed, the court will in my view, under the guise of preventing the abuse of power, be itself guilty of usurping power. . . . Judicial review, as the words imply, is not an appeal from a decision, but a review of the manner in which a decision was made." They also cited the *Wednesbury* case for the observation that to prove as grounds for setting aside a discretionary executive judgment that no reasonable authority could have made such a decision "would require something overwhelming" (*Vilvarajah*, ser. A, 42). Considering the language from *Brind* and *Chahal* to *Evans* and *Wednesbury* seems to give the two dissenters in *Vilvarajah* the better conclusion as to Art. 13.

In effect, their conclusion was sustained by the European Commission on

Human Rights when it unanimously concluded in *The Chahal Family v. United Kingdom* (1995) that there had been a violation of Art. 13 because the power of review offered by U.K. domestic courts "when national security was invoked is too restrictive" (1995, CD40). The Commission also unanimously found violations of Art. 3 (because of Chahal's prospect of inhuman or degrading treatment or punishment, should he be deported to India), of Art. 5.1 (because of Chahal's detention for almost five years), and of respect for family life under Art. 8 (because his deportation after having lived more than nineteen years in the United Kingdom would separate him from his wife of nineteen years and their two children, who were born and raised in the United Kingdom). As yet there has been no decision by the European Court.

CONCLUSION

Since the cases reviewed in this chapter were decided, the United Kingdom has adopted the Asylum and Immigration Appeals Act 1993. Since that legislation was enacted, the number of those allowed to stay in the United Kingdom on "exceptional leave to remain" has declined dramatically. Exceptional leave to remain is a category open to those who, while not directly the object of persecution, flee from "war, civil war or anarchy or ecological disaster." The 1993 Act has led to expedited procedures for reviewing asylum claims, reducing the process from one of years to months (*Statewatch* 1995a, 6). In April 1995, the asylum and special cases division of the Home Office announced a "pilot scheme" for an even shorter asylum determination procedure. Applicants from a list of "safe countries" were to be interviewed upon making their asylum claim and given five working days from the interviews to submit supportive documentary evidence. Sri Lanka was among the countries placed on the "safe list," despite a recent Amnesty International report of continuing human rights abuses in that country and despite reports of heavy fighting between Sri Lanka and "Tamil Tiger" forces late in 1995 (*Statewatch* 1995b, 1). Finally, late in 1995, Home Secretary Michael Howard and Social Security Secretary Peter Lilley published another Asylum and Immigration Bill, which proposes a continuation of the "fast track" appeals and the publication of a list of safe countries so that those seeking refugee status from those countries will have to overcome a legal presumption of their safety. The first list, announced in December, included India and Pakistan, but not Sri Lanka (*Statewatch* 1995e, 17–18). While the United Kingdom is not the only European country deciding recently to intensify its efforts to stem the tide of refugees, the United Kingdom's experience before the European Court in the *Vilvarajah* case and the European Commission's report in the *Chahal* case place these recent developments in an interesting if problematic context.

While all of the cases considered in this chapter involve immigration and nationality issues, they are diffuse in their understanding of the relationship between British domestic law and the ECHR. Yet whether the prospect of exclusion, deportation, or refusal of asylum involves the possibility of inhuman or degrading treatment under Art. 3; whether the denial of entry and abode involves interference with the right to respect for family life under Art. 8, or amounts to racial or sexual discrimination under Art. 14 (coupled with Art. 8); or whether U.K. law provides an effective remedy through which all these decisions of the Home Office can be reviewed, they all share the centrality and finality of official discretion. As Ewing and Gearty suggest in their book on civil liberties in Britain (1990, 6–7), "The lack of any real constraints on the executive branch has led to a crisis in overgovernability, in which executive proposals quickly become law via a quiescent Parliament without sufficient consultation, scrutiny, or debate and without any possibility of subsequent judicial challenge."

While effective solutions to this problem are not easy, the prospect for review by the European Court of Human Rights is, at least, one ingredient for a complex recipe.

6

Freedom of Expression and the Convention

This chapter will focus on three key cases, all of them involving the Times Newspaper Group. Two cases involved *The Sunday Times;* in both, the European Court of Human Rights found the United Kingdom to be in violation of Art. 10 of the ECHR. The interactions between developments in the common law as determined by British courts and the decisions of the European Court of Human Rights in Strasbourg probably have been more extensive on the subject of freedom of expression than on any of the other rights protected by the ECHR. This is most prominently illustrated by the third key case, a 1993 decision of the House of Lords in *Derbyshire County Council v. Times Newspapers.*

On February 18, 1993, four "Law Lords" joined Lord Keith in a unanimous House of Lords decision holding that English common law encompasses a right to free expression, which limits the law of libel to protect the freedom of the press. Most interesting was the fact that at the very end of his opinion Lord Keith found it appropriate to comment that he had reached his conclusion "upon the common law of England *without finding any need to rely on the European Convention*" (*Derbyshire County Council v. Times Newspapers,* 1021; emphasis added). In contrast, John Gardner's essay on "Freedom of Expression" (McCrudden and Chambers 1994, 209) argues that there is no such thing as a general *legal* right to freedom of expression in English domestic law. So, were Lord Keith's words a serious, substantive observation on the state of the common law, or were they, more likely, gratuitous, defensive, and self-serving? Either way, his words reflect the recent conceptual development of freedom of the press in the U.K., both under Art. 10 of the ECHR and under the English common law, chiefly as represented in the *Derbyshire County Council* case and the two cases decided by the European Court of Human Rights, beginning with the first *Sunday Times Case* in 1979.

The first *Sunday Times* case was notable for its rarity, for during the first thirty years of its decision making, Art. 10's provisions for freedom of expression were judged by the Court twelve times and only three violations were found. The other two violations of the first thirty years were in *Barthold v.*

Germany (1985) and *Lingens v. Austria* (1986). Since 1989, the frequency of Art. 10 cases has picked up considerably. Violations of Art. 10 have been found in eighteen additional instances, four of them being the second *Sunday Times* case, its companion case involving *The Observer* and *The Guardian, Tolstoy Miloslavsky v. United Kingdom* (1995), and the recent case of *Goodwin v. United Kingdom* (1996). These fifteen violations are counted from the judgments that have been published since 1989 through June 1996, reported either in the Series A reports of the Court or in the *European Human Rights Reports*.[1] Apart from the four additional violations by the United Kingdom, the other violations since 1989 were found in *Weber v. Switzerland* (1990), *Autronic AG v. Switzerland* (1990), *Oberschlick v. Austria* (1991), *Castells v. Spain* (1992), *Thorgeir Thorgeirson v. Iceland* (1992), *Schwabe v. Austria* (1993), *Herczegfalvy v. Austria* (1992), *Open Door and Dublin Well Woman v. Ireland* (1992), *Infor-mationsverein Lentia and Others v. Austria* (1993), *Jersild v. Denmark* (1994), *Vereinigung Demokratischer Soldaten Österreichs and Gubi v. Austria* (1994), *Piermont v. France* (1995), *Vereniging Weekblad Bluf! v. The Netherlands* (1995), and *Vogt v. Germany* (1995). As can be seen in these results, since 1989 Austria has replaced the United Kingdom as the most frequent offender in Art. 10 cases. It has now been held in violation six times.

The United Kingdom, Art. 10, and the European Court

We begin with a brief overview of the two *Sunday Times* cases. The first case involved a conflict between the freedom of the press and the contempt powers of British courts, applied to the press through an injunction to prevent the publication of an article that allegedly would have tended to "obstruct, prejudice or abuse the administration of justice." The article that *The Sunday Times* proposed to publish was about the development, sale, and prescription of the drug thalidomide, which had resulted in the birth of a number of children with serious deformities. One possible purpose of the proposed article was to influence the payment of damages offered by the defendant pharmaceutical company for the deformities suffered from thalidomide treatment. However, the House of Lords Appellate Committee, the court of last resort for the U.K., sustained an injunction against *The Sunday Times* in 1973. It was that injunction which the European Court eventually held (in 1979, by eleven votes to nine) to violate Art. 10 of the ECHR.

The second *Sunday Times Case* (1991), with its companion cases for *The Guardian* and *The Observer,* involved the proposed publication by the three newspapers of articles about or excerpts from *Spycatcher,* Peter Wright's memoirs of his service as a senior member of the British Security Service (MI5) between 1955 and 1976. Peter Wright's book, *Spycatcher,* was first published in Australia and then in the United States in 1987. Among other accusations, the book suggested that MI5 had attempted in 1974–75 to destabilize the Labour government led by Prime Minister Harold Wilson. Interlocutory injunctions were finally sustained in this case by the House of Lords Appellate Committee in 1987. In 1991, however, these were held by the European Court of Human Rights to be (in part) in violation of Art. 10 of the ECHR.

The English case that resulted in 1993 in the enhancement of common law freedom of expression was brought by the Derbyshire County Council against *The Sunday Times* in 1989. The *Derbyshire County Council* case may seem trifling in comparison to the two *Sunday Times* cases that previously had been decided by the European Court of Human Rights. The Derbyshire County Council brought an action of damages for libel against *The Sunday Times* for its questioning of the propriety of certain investments made for the council's superannuation fund. *The Sunday Times* article criticized pension fund deals that involved the then council leader, David Bookbinder, which Derbyshire Council lawyers argued brought the authority into "public scandal, odium and contempt." *The Sunday Times* article on the eventual victory for press freedom in the House of Lords quoted Anthony Lewis, "The judges have emphasised the right of the public to comment freely on politicians, which is bread and butter in the US, but has not exactly been overemphasised in the U.K." (*The Sunday Times*, February 21, 1993).

Again, in stressing the grounding of the House of Lords opinion in the common law, it should be noted that the U.K. Court of Appeal had also upheld the freedom of the press from this sort of libel action, but had done so by relying on Art. 10 of the ECHR. These differing decisional grounds illustrate once again the tension experienced in the U.K. between its domestic institutions and common law, on the one hand, and the ECHR, the European Commission and Court of Human Rights in Strasbourg, and transnational human rights, on the other.

As we have previously noted, a leading review of this tension is contained in Françoise Hampson's article, "The United Kingdom before the European Court of Human Rights" (1990). Hampson comments on the frequently made points that among the reasons cited for the frequency of the U.K.'s appearance as a state defendant before the European Court of Human Rights are the facts that the U.K. has no written constitution and that it has not incorporated the provisions of the ECHR into its domestic law. She notes that there is no way to evaluate the first claim, since the U.K. is alone amongst the members of the Council of Europe in having no written constitution. As we mentioned in passing in chapter 2, the second point is challenged by the finding that other countries that have not incorporated the ECHR into their domestic law have not been frequent offenders, while Belgium and Austria, both relatively frequent offenders, allow the provisions of the ECHR to be pleaded before their domestic courts (Hampson 1990, 122).

Rather than simply counting cases or violations, Hampson examines the ways in which the U.K. has responded to cases before the European Court. Cases may be referred to the European Court of Human Rights by a state member acting as an applicant, but the U.K. has never done that. In most cases either a state defendant or the European Commission on Human Rights, or both, are competent to refer a case from the European Commission on Human Rights to the European Court. While there is no particular pattern in the manner in which cases involving the U.K. as a state defendant before the European Court have been brought, Hampson found it remarkable that the U.K. has consistently defended cases "in which defeat was very predictable" (Hampson 1990, 130). In that connection her most interesting conclusion is as follows:

> The British Government is committed to the *idea* of human rights but it appears complacently to assume that, as a Western European democracy, its practices are in conformity with its legal obligations. Its commitment to human rights in practice is tested when the Government is confronted with a judgment of the European Court of Human Rights in which a violation has been found. If the Government's reaction is anything less than a full implementation of the changes shown to be necessary, it is legitimate to question that commitment. Certain highly predictable findings of a violation of the ECHR and the continuing incidence of cases involving prisoners' rights give rise to concern. (Hampson 1990, 131)

Hampson is, at the least, skeptical about the commitment of the British *government* to the protection of human rights. As to whether the *judges* in the U.K. are committed to human rights, Hampson notes near the conclusion of her article that if they are, they could interpret statutes to ensure conformity with the ECHR, consider not only the text of the ECHR but the decisions of the European Court interpreting the ECHR as they may affect their decisions, give human rights a priority in its own reasoning, and resist the tendency to be complacent about the capacity of the legal system to protect individual rights (Hampson 1990, 168–69). Toward the end of this chapter we will examine the House of Lords Appellate Committee's recent efforts (however stringent) to accomplish the first three goals listed above through the vehicle of the *Derbyshire County Council* case.

Among Hampson's other analytic contributions is her division of breaches of the ECHR into three types. The first, she suggests, consists of landmark cases, whose importance lies in the broad interpretation of an article of the

ECHR and whose connection to any particular state defendant is not of key importance. The second kind of case is one of "system breach," which amounts to a test case that reviews a system, practice, or procedure, and in which the particular facts are not of great importance. The third type is the "application breach," which involves a violation of a particular individual on particular facts (Hampson 1990, 134–35). How do these concepts bear on violations of Art. 10 by the U.K.?

THE FIRST *Sunday Times* CASE (1979)

The Sunday Times v. United Kingdom in 1979 was but one outgrowth of the seventy original lawsuits filed by parents of "thalidomide" children between 1962 and 1966. Sixty-five of those cases had been settled in 1968. The remaining five cases and 261 additional claims were granted leave under English law to be exempted from the usual three-year statute of limitations on such cases. Another 123 claimants had notified the defendant company of the intent to file but had not initiated formal proceedings. Thus, in 1971, 389 claims were still pending, and the defendant proposed to create a charitable trust for the benefit of these remaining children. Over the years a number of newspaper articles had been written about the thalidomide scandal. In December 1971 *The Daily Mail* had published an article that caused certain parents of thalidomide children to complain that additional articles might jeopardize their pending settlement negotiations. *The Daily Mail* was effectively "warned off" by a letter from the attorney general threatening contempt of court (*Sunday Times v. United Kingdom*, Ser. A, 8–9).

On September 24, 1992, *The Sunday Times* published an article entitled "Our Thalidomide Children: A Cause for National Shame." It was noted in the article that a *future* article would "trace how the tragedy occurred," but on November 17, 1972, an injunction was issued on the application of the attorney general that publication of the future article would constitute contempt of court. The key point was that the arguable purpose of the article was to influence the defendant to increase its settlement offer. It was held by a trial judge to be contempt of court for a party in a pending suit to be subjected to such pressure. The test for contempt was whether the words "created a serious risk that the course of justice might be interfered with" (*Attorney-General v. Times Newspapers Ltd.* [Queen's Bench] 1972, 1145). At about the same time, the trial judge decided that a single showing of a television program on the plight of the thalidomide children was not a contempt of court because it had not been established that the producers of the show deliberately intended to influence the pending cases. (*Attorney-General v. London Weekend Television*, 1972).

While the injunction against *The Sunday Times* continued in force, articles were published in other journals and a parliamentary debate focused on the thalidomide controversy. By January 1973, the defendant had increased its trust fund offer from £3,250,000 to £20,000,000. The original injunction against *The Sunday Times* was overturned by the Court of Appeal in February 1973 on the grounds that the public interest in discussion of the thalidomide issue outweighed the prejudice that might be suffered by the defendant pharmaceutical firm (*Attorney-General v. Times Newspapers Ltd.* [Court of Appeal] 1973), but the injunction was restored on appeal by the House of Lords in July 1973 on the grounds that it was a contempt of court to hold the pharmaceutical firm up to "public obloquy" for exercising its right to have legal rights and duties ascertained in a court of law (*Attorney-General v. Times Newspapers Ltd.* [House of Lords] 1973). Most of the damage suits were settled in July 1973 without admission of negligence by the defendant. The injunction against *The Sunday Times* was eventually discharged in June 1976, and four days later the intended article was published (*Sunday Times v. United Kingdom*, 1979, 11–12). Meanwhile *The Sunday Times* had filed a complaint with the European Commission on Human Rights in January 1974, following the House of Lords' opinion upholding the finding of contempt. In May 1977, the Commission agreed (eight to five) that Art. 10 of the ECHR had been breached. The Commission referred the case to the Court, which sustained the Commission in finding a violation (eleven to nine) of Art. 10 in March 1979. How did the House of Lords and the European Court of Human Rights differ in their conclusions?

We should be mindful that Lord Denning's judgment for the Court of Appeal discharged the injunction because he found that the public interest in discussion of the issues outweighed potential prejudice and that it was discriminatory to enjoin *The Sunday Times* when other newspapers had published and Parliament had debated the settlement.

The five law lords led by Lord Reid had concluded, however, that prejudgment of issues through trial by newspaper should be prevented:

> Responsible "mass media" will do their best to be fair, but there will also be ill-informed, slapdash or prejudicial attempts to influence the public. If people are led to think that it is easy to find the truth, disrespect for the processes of the law could follow, and if mass media are allowed to judge, unpopular people and unpopular causes will fare very badly. Most cases of prejudging of issues fall within the existing authorities on contempt. I do not think that the freedom of the press would suffer, and I think that the law would be clearer and easier to apply in practice if it is made a *general rule* that it is not permissible to prejudge issues in pending cases. (*Attorney-General v. Times Newspapers*, House of Lords, 1973, 65, emphasis added)

Lord Cross added that an absolute rule against prejudging an issue in pending litigation was "necessary in order to prevent a gradual slide towards trial by newspaper or by television" (*Attorney-General v. Times Newspapers,* House of Lords, 1973, 84). None of their lordships mentioned Art. 10 of the ECHR.

A *general rule* against press coverage of pending litigation that might have the effect of prejudging the issues in the litigation might be reviewable before the European Court as a "system breach," but when the injunction was actually reviewed by the Court, Hampson concluded (1990, 142) that it was only an "application breach"—a much narrower and more fact-bound determination. In other words, while it was clear to all the judges of the European Court that the injunction was a violation of section 1 of Art. 10, the question remained whether it nonetheless had a legitimate aim and was "necessary in a democratic society" under section 2. The asserted aim of "maintaining the authority and impartiality of the judiciary" was included in section 2, so the key question remained the injunction's necessity in a democratic society. Lowe (1983, 320) notes that the proviso of Art. 10.2 relative to "maintaining the authority and impartiality of the judiciary" was proposed by the British delegation that participated in drafting the ECHR.

After lengthy consideration, the European Court of Human Rights came to the question of whether the interference with freedom of the press through the injunction corresponded to a "pressing social need sufficient to outweigh public interest in freedom of expression" and was proportionate to the legitimate aim pursued under section 2—much the same evaluation as the balancing of public interest against potential prejudice weighed by the Court of Appeal. Eleven members of the European Court found that the injunction did not represent a pressing social need sufficient to outweigh the right to freedom of expression. Nine members disagreed. Unlike American appellate opinions, the judges of the European Court of Human Rights do not write extended justifications for their conclusions, but the members of the Court differed principally on how they viewed the "margin of appreciation" accorded state members under the ECHR.

The margin of appreciation amounts to a zone of discretion accorded national authorities by a transnational institution. While the House of Lords eventually concluded that it had to strike a balance between two conflicting principles—the public interest in freedom of expression on one hand and the public interest in the fair administration of justice on the other—a majority of the European Court wrote that they "were not faced with a choice between two conflicting principles, but with a principle of freedom of expression that is subject to a number of exceptions which must be narrowly interpreted" (*Sunday Times v. United Kingdom,* Ser. A, 41). It is Art. 10 of the ECHR that imposes this "European supervision" on the Court (Ser. A, 36). This presumption in favor of freedom of expression is not unlike that expressed by the U.S. Supreme Court when assessing intrusions upon "preferred or fundamental freedoms." The "preferred freedoms" doctrine comes from Justice Stone's famous footnote 4 in *United States v. Carolene Products Co.* (1938). Much like the "preferred freedoms" position, the European Court majority's approach also seems to amount to something more than a finding of a narrow "application breach," which might be limited to the particular facts. The dissents support this conclusion.

According to the joint dissent of nine members of the Court, even though any judge of the European Court of Human Rights might differ with a conclusion reached by the House of Lords, if their lordships acted in good faith, with due care and in a reasonable manner, the margin of appreciation granted by the ECHR requires that deference be accorded their judgment. Thus, for the majority of the European Court to reject the conclusions reached by the five law lords, they in effect must have found them to be unreasonable and not made in good faith—strong words indeed, according to the dissenters.

Following the European Court's decision in 1979, Parliament passed the Contempt of Court Act 1981. The "real impetus" for this legislation was the European Court's decision (Bailey, Harris, and Jones 1991, 346), but the statute was also responsive to the report of the Phillimore Committee on Contempt of Court (1974). The Phillimore Report had recommended that conduct amounting to intimidation or threats ought to count as contempt (1974, 25–30). Section 1 of the Contempt of Court Act 1981 provides for the rule of strict liability, which means that conduct which, in fact, interferes with the course of justice may be contemptuous without proof of any intent to do so. However, section 2(2) of the act provides that strict liability for contempt is allowable only when the publication "creates a substantial risk that the course of justice in the proceedings in question will be seriously impeded or prejudiced." Section 5 of the 1981 act provides that a publication, made in good faith as part of a discussion of public affairs or matters of general public interest, shall not be subject to the strict liability rule of section 1 if the risk of impediment or prejudice to legal proceedings is merely incidental to the discussion. These provisions might have made it more difficult for an injunction to be issued against *The Sunday Times* in the thalidomide controversy. But whether the Contempt of Court Act has accomplished that purpose is a matter of some controversy (Arlidge and Eady 1982; Lowe, 1983). In 1983, Times Newspapers and Others applied again to the European Commission, arguing that the Contempt of Court Act 1981 had been interpreted by the House of Lords in the case of the *Attorney-General v. English* (1982) in a manner that did not fully implement the judgment of the European Court of Human Rights in the *Sunday Times* case. They suggested that the state of the English domestic law was at the least ambiguous and placed the applicants in the position of reasonably fearing that their publications might again be held in contempt of court. The Commission concluded that the applicants' complaint was as yet hypothetical since they had not themselves been the victims of an adverse ruling (*Times Newspapers Ltd. and Others v. United Kingdom,* 1984). So the law at that point remained uncertain. We shall see whether, in a quite different context, a strong presumption in favor of freedom of the press is sustained by the second *Sunday Times* case.

THE CASE OF *The Observer* AND *The Guardian* AND THE SECOND *Sunday Times v. United Kingdom* CASE (1991)

The events leading to these cases began when Granada television presented an extended interview in July 1984 with Peter Wright, a former British Security Service (MI5) agent. As noted in the introduction above, the second *Sunday Times* case and the companion cases of *The Observer* and *The Guardian* first involved an interlocutory injunction brought against *The Observer* and *The Guardian* in response to articles published by them in June 1986. The articles contained disclosures concerning the British Security Service from Peter Wright's book, *Spycatcher.* While the articles contained many of the same allegations as did the 1984 Granada television interview, the initial *ex parte* injunctions were nonetheless granted on June 27, 1986. On July 11 these injunctions were modified but continued, and they were upheld on July 25, 1986, by the Court of Appeal.

In the meantime, the U.K. government had brought an action in Australia in September 1985 to prevent the publication there of *Spycatcher,* but the Australian trial court ruled against the U.K. in mid-March 1987.

Articles were published in British newspapers, *The Independent, The Evening Standard,* and *The London Daily News,* in late April 1987. Also in late April 1987, counsel for *The Observer* and *The Guardian* moved for discharge of the interlocutory injunction in the U.K. because of the events in Australia and widespread newspaper accounts of those proceedings and of *Spycatcher's* disclosures. A hearing was held on the discharge motion but judgment was reserved. In May 1987, a major publisher announced its intention to publish *Spycatcher* in the United States. In June 1987, Vice Chancellor Browne-Wilkinson of the Chancery Division rejected contempt proceedings against *The Independent,* the *Evening Standard,* and the *London Daily News* on the grounds that they had not been parties to the July 1986 injunction against *The Observer* and *The Guardian* (*Attorney-General v. Newspaper Publishing plc and Others* (1987). On July 12, 1987, *The Sunday Times* published its first installment of a series of excerpts from *Spycatcher,* its publication being designed to coincide with publication of the book in the U.S. On July 13, the U.K.

attorney general applied to have *The Sunday Times* held in contempt of court on the grounds that its publication frustrated the purpose of the July 11, 1986, interlocutory injunction against *The Observer* and *The Guardian*. On the following day, *Spycatcher* was published in the U.S. and a number of copies of the book were thereafter brought into the U.K. The U.K. government made no effort to prevent the private importation of the book. Nevertheless, on July 16 the Attorney General applied for an injunction against *The Sunday Times* to restrain the publication of any additional excerpts. This application was granted and a temporary injunction was issued to last until July 21, when the application of *The Observer* and *The Guardian* to discharge the original interlocutory injunction would be taken up.

On July 22, 1987, the trial judge discharged the original interlocutory injunction against *The Observer* and *The Guardian* and dismissed the application for an injunction against *The Sunday Times* to prevent publication of additional excerpts (*Attorney General v. Guardian Newspapers and Others*, Chancery Division, 1987). Probably the key factors in this result were that the proceedings in Australia, the publication of the book in the U.S., and overall publicity surrounding these events had so destroyed the purpose of the injunctions that the courts "were manifestly incapable of achieving their purpose." Even so, the attorney general appealed and on July 24 the Court of Appeal held that, while it was inappropriate to continue the interlocutory injunction in its original form, it *was* appropriate to vary the injunction to restrain the publication of all or part of the book (*Attorney General v. Guardian Newspapers and Others*, Court of Appeal, 1987). Leave was given to appeal to the House of Lords, which by a vote of three to two gave judgment on July 30, 1987, that the modified interlocutory judgment should continue in force (which it did until a trial on the merits of the confidentiality issues in November and December 1987) (*Attorney General v. Guardian Newspapers and Others*, House of Lords, 1987).

On July 31, 1987, the day following the judgment of the House of Lords, *The Sunday Times* filed a complaint with the European Commission on Human Rights on the grounds that the interlocutory injunction violated Art. 10 of the ECHR.

In September 1987 the U.K.'s appeal from the Australian trial court's denial of an injunction was denied by the New South Wales Court of Appeal and its further appeal was dismissed in June 1988. Proceedings brought by the U.K. attorney general were successful in Hong Kong, but not in New Zealand.

On October 27, 1987, the attorney general began proceedings against *The Sunday Times* for breach of confidence for publishing the excerpts from *Spycatcher*. The U.K. trial in late 1987 involved both permanent injunctive relief and an action for accounting of profits derived by *The Sunday Times* for the breach of confidence. On December 21, 1987, judgment was given that *The Observer* and *The Guardian* had not breached a duty of confidentiality in their original articles but, rather, had engaged in fair reporting, which was also justified on the ground of disclosure of "iniquity"; *The Sunday Times* had breached a duty of confidentiality in publishing the first extract from the book, and it was liable to account for the profits resulting from that publication; no permanent injunction would be issued because worldwide dissemination of *Spycatcher* had destroyed any element of confidentiality (*Attorney General v. Guardian Newspapers and Others* (No. 2, Chancery Division, 1987). Temporary injunctions were restored pending appeal until October 13, 1988, when the appellate committee of the House of Lords by and large sustained the trial judgment and held that *The Sunday Times* had indeed breached a duty of confidentiality and should be required to account for its profits (*Attorney General v. Guardian Newspapers and Others* (No. 2, House of Lords, 1988). In May 1989, *The Sunday Times* was fined £50,000 and costs for its contempt of the July 11, 1986, injunction. According to the House of Lords, one finding that strongly supported the contempt judgment against *The Sunday Times* was the newspaper's decision to withhold the extract from the first edition of its July 12 issue so as to avoid the risk of an *ex parte* temporary injunction (*Attorney General v. Times Newspapers Ltd.*, House of Lords, 1991, 408). Lustgarten and Leigh (1994, 265) note that Sunday newspapers are "particularly vulnerable" to *ex parte* temporary injunctions, for such an injunction granted on a Friday afternoon, even if set aside the following Monday, will defer publication for a Sunday only paper.

The judgment against *The Sunday Times* for £50,000 and costs was upheld as to the payment of costs only (the fines being overturned) by the Court of Appeal in February 1990 and by the House of Lords on April 11, 1991 (*Attorney General v. Times Newspapers Ltd. and Another*, House of Lords, 1991). Note that the European Court of Human Rights' decision on the original interlocutory judgments was not rendered until late November 1991.

This abbreviated though still complicated recital of events is necessary to understand the decisional context of the European Court. The Court had the advantage of being able to oversee from a distance the continuing global efforts of the U.K. government to prevent publication of *Spycatcher* and to punish those who effected or threatened disclosures. These efforts led eventually to a context in which *only* the residents of the U.K. (and probably few even of those) could have remained ignorant of *Spycatcher*'s disclosures. Keep in mind that *only* the propriety of the interlocutory injunctions was before the European Court in its reported decisions of November 26, 1991.

It is important also to note that the House of Lords' affirmation of the interlocutory injunctions on July 30, 1987, did include a reference by Lord

Brandon to Art. 10 of the ECHR. Even though Lord Brandon's reference was to section 2, which contains the exception for the protection of national security, the potential application of the ECHR was at least recognized—as it had not been by the majority of the House of Lords in the first *Sunday Times* case.

Even more notable was the dissenting opinion of Lord Bridge, who wrote that:

> Having no written constitution, we have no equivalent in our law to the First Amendment to the Constitution of the United States of America. Some think that puts freedom of speech on too lofty a pedestal. Perhaps they are right. We have not adopted as part of our law the European Convention for the Protection of Human Rights and Fundamental Freedoms . . . to which this country is signatory. Many think that we should. I have hitherto not been of that persuasion, in the large part because I have had confidence in the capacity of the common law to safeguard the fundamental freedoms essential to a free society. . . . *My confidence is seriously undermined by your Lordships' decision. . . .*

> Freedom of speech is always the first casualty under a totalitarian regime. Such a regime cannot afford to allow the free circulation of information and ideas among its citizens. Censorship is the indispensable tool to regulate what the public may and what they may not know. The present attempt to insulate the public in this country from information which is freely available elsewhere is a significant step down that very dangerous road. The maintenance of the ban, as more and more copies of the book *Spycatcher* enter this country and circulate here, will seem more and more ridiculous. If the Government are determined to fight to maintain the ban to the end, *they will face inevitable condemnation and humiliation by the European Court of Human Rights in Strasbourg.* Long before that they will have been condemned at the bar of public opinion in the free world. (*Attorney-General v. Guardian Newspapers and Others*, House of Lords, 1987, 346–47; emphasis added)

It was not disputed before the European Court that the interlocutory injunctions violated section 1 of Art. 10, so the only questions were whether the injunctions were covered by the national security exception of section 2 and were "necessary in a democratic society." "Necessary" was again taken to refer to a "pressing social need," and the "margin of appreciation" accorded the U.K. again became the central concern. For the majority the exception had to be "proportionate to the legitimate aim pursued," and the reasons asserted to support it had to be "relevant and sufficient" (*The Observer and Guardian v.*

United Kingdom, Ser. A, 30; *The Sunday Times v. United Kingdom, No. 2*, Ser. A, 29). The most interesting point made by the European Court's judgments was about *prior restraints*.

While Art. 10 does not expressly prohibit prior restraints (and the first *Sunday Times* case certainly had not entirely excluded them), the European Court noted that "the dangers inherent in prior restraints are such that they call for the most careful scrutiny on the part of the Court." This is reminiscent of the presumption against prior restraints first expressed in *Near v. Minnesota* (1931) and restated in *New York Times v. U.S.* (1971). The U.S. Supreme Court so far has been consistent in rejecting prior restraints. According to the European Court, careful scrutiny is especially required when newspapers are concerned, "for news is a perishable commodity and to delay its publication, even for a short period, may well deprive it of all value and interest" (*The Observer and Guardian v. United Kingdom*, Ser. A, 30; *The Sunday Times v. United Kingdom, No. 2*, Ser. A, 29–30).

With respect to *The Observer* and *The Guardian*, the European Court found that during the period from July 11, 1986, through July 30, 1987, the interlocutory injunctions against *The Observer* and *The Guardian* had indirectly served the purpose of protecting national security. The Court also found that the injunctions had the valid aim of maintaining the authority of the judiciary. Thus, the European Court concluded (fourteen to ten) that U.K. authorities were entitled to conclude that the interference with freedom of expression complained of by both newspapers was necessary in a democratic society, but *only* with regard to the period from July 11, 1986, to July 30, 1987 (*The Observer and Guardian v. United Kingdom*, Ser. A: 33). The Court held unanimously that *after* July 30 (the date of the House of Lords judgment continuing the injunctions) the injunctions were no longer necessary.

Conceding that the House of Lords had taken some notice of the requirements of Art. 10 in their judgment of July 30, the judges of the European Court nonetheless found unanimously that the confidentiality sought through the interlocutory injunctions had been effectively destroyed by publication of *Spycatcher* in the United States. The European Court found that the U.K.'s interest in confidentiality had expired by July 30, 1987 (*The Sunday Times* having filed its complaint with the Commission on July 31 and *The Observer* and *The Guardian* having filed subsequently in January 1988). However, the House of Lords' judgment upholding the modified interlocutory injunction had been continued through its subsequent decision of December 21, 1987, which also required *The Sunday Times* to account for its profits for having published the first excerpt. Once confidentiality had been lost, the only purpose in continuing the injunctions was, in the view of the European Court, "to deter others who might be tempted to follow in Mr. Wright's footsteps" and to demonstrate that the Security Service would not "countenance unauthorised publication." The Court did not regard "these objectives as sufficient to justify the interference complained of" (*The Sunday Times v. United Kingdom,* No. 2, Ser. A, 31).

The dissents of European Court judges were in favor of even stronger protection for freedom of the press and would have found a violation of Art. 10 during the period from July 11, 1986, to July 30, 1987. The partially dissenting opinion of Judge DeMeyer of Belgium (joined by Pettiti, Russo, Foighel, and Bigi) is most interesting for its strong position against prior restraints: "Under no circumstances, however, can prior restraint, even in the form of judicial injunctions, either temporary or permanent, be accepted, except in what the Convention describes as a 'time of war or other public emergency threatening the life of the nation' and, even then only 'to the extent strictly required by the exigencies of the situation'" (*The Observer and Guardian v. United Kingdom,* Ser. A, 46).

Overall the ten dissenters were more concerned about the propriety of prior restraints and more reluctant to accept the necessity of the interlocutory injunctions than were the fourteen members of the majority. But some of the dissenters, at least, were clearly inclined to declare a "systems breach" (in terms of the concepts suggested by Hampson) by enforcing presumptions against prior restraints. Lord Bridge's dissent from the House of Lords was largely in agreement, and his strong words were perhaps the stimulus for the defensive decision of Lord Keith in the *Derbyshire County Council* case.

Derbyshire County Council v. Times Newspapers et al. (1993)

In three articles published in September 1989, *The Sunday Times* questioned the propriety of certain investments made by the Derbyshire County Council in its superannuation fund. The articles were headlined, "Revealed: Socialist Tycoon's Deals with a Labour Chief," "Bizarre Deal of a Council Leader and the Media Tycoon" and "Council Share Deals under Scrutiny." The council leader was David Bookbinder and the tycoon was Owen Oyston. An action for libel was brought by the Derbyshire County Council and by Bookbinder and Oyston against the publishers of *The Sunday Times,* its editor, and the journalists who wrote the articles. According to their suit, the alleged libel brought the county council into "public scandal, odium and contempt" (*Derbyshire C.C. v. Times Newspapers,* 1013).

The preliminary point of law in the case was whether a local authority was entitled to maintain an action for libel. This was decided in the council's favor by a judge of the Queen's Bench, but was reversed by the Court of Appeal. There were two key but conflicting common law precedents. The first, *Manchester Corporation v. Williams,* had held in 1891 that a municipal corporation could not recover in a libel action for damages resulting from charges of bribery and corruption since these were crimes that could not be committed by a corporation. The second, *Bognor Regis Urban District Council v. Campion* (1972), had held, to the contrary, that a municipal corporation could recover for damages to its reputation, as distinct from the reputations of its members. Thus the most recent common law precedent seemed to support such an action, though neither the Court of Appeal nor the House of Lords had written on the subject.

The Court of Appeal rejected such an action by relying almost entirely on Art. 10 of the ECHR—in the absence of controlling higher court precedent—and found "no pressing social need that a public authority should have the right to sue in damages for protection of its reputation."

Lord Keith reached the same result for the House of Lords, but, as we saw in the introduction to this chapter, he proudly proclaimed that he had *"no need to rely upon the European Convention"* (*Derbyshire C.C. v. Times Newspapers*, 1021; emphasis added). The common law of England would suffice, thank you very much! At least it would if common law (constitutional) authorities from the United States could be borrowed for the purpose. First, Lord Keith took note of the "special position" of a local governmental council. It was, to be sure, a "governmental body," but, more important, it was a "democratically elected" body, elected moreover through a partisan process. Thus, "[it] is of the highest public importance that a democratically elected body, or indeed any governmental body, should be open to uninhibited public criticism. Second, the threat of civil action for defamation must inevitably have an inhibiting effect on freedom of speech" (*Derbyshire C. C. v. Times Newspapers*, 1017, *et seq.*) The precedents?—a 1923 decision of the Supreme Court of Illinois, *City of Chicago v. Tribune Co.* and *New York Times v. Sullivan* (1964). Lord Keith noted that while these decisions rested on U.S. constitutional grounds, "the public interest considerations which underlaid them are no less valid in this country. What has been described as the 'chilling effect' induced by the threat of civil actions for libel is very important" (*Derbyshire C.C. v. Times Newspapers*, 1018).

Lord Keith's words have been characterized (McCrudden and Chambers 1994, 222) as a "disingenuous line that the arguments used in the American constitutional cases are already a recognised part of English law." It certainly is remarkable that Lord Keith did not mention Lord Denning's words in *Associated Newspapers Group v. Wade* (1979, 708) that it was a "fundamental principle of our law that the press shall be free." "In this respect," Denning had written, "our law corresponds with Art. 10(1) of the European Convention." Nor did Lord Keith note that in 1980, Lord Scarman, writing for the House of Lords in *Attorney General v. British Broadcasting Corporation* (1980, 177–

78), had recognized the ruling of the European Court of Human Rights in *The Sunday Times v. United Kingdom* (1979, 177–78):

> This House's decision, even though the European Court has held the rule it declares to be an infringement of the convention, is the law. Our courts must continue to look not to the European court's decision . . . but to the House of Lords decision reported in *Attorney General v. Times Newspapers* . . . for the rule of English law. Yet there is a presumption, albeit rebuttable, that our municipal law will be consistent with our international obligations. . . . If the issue should ultimately be, as I think in this case it is, a question of legal policy, we must have regard to the country's international obligation to observe the European convention as interpreted by the European Court of Human Rights.

In part recognizing the international obligation, the House of Lords in *Attorney General v. BBC* (1980) thus determined not to extend the reach of contempt of court to a local ratings court, and refused to enjoin a broadcast about a religious sect that had a case pending before that court. No doubt it was the traditional discretionary powers of British courts over contempt proceedings that contributed to this outcome, but such discretion also allowed for the influence of Art. 10 of the ECHR.

Another contempt proceeding, *Schering Chemicals Ltd. v. Falkman Ltd.* (1981), had involved a pharmaceutical company's efforts to enjoin the production of a television documentary because of its impact on pending litigation. There Lord Denning found a presumption against prior restraint in the common law—in the cornerstone U.S. precedent of *Near v. Minnesota* (1931) *and* in Art. 10 of the ECHR. While the Court's majority refused to enjoin the film as a contempt of court, they did sustain an injunction as a remedy for a breach of confidence. Denning, however, found that the information in the film was not confidential at all. His conclusion was resounding: "Freedom of the press is of fundamental importance in our society. It covers not only the right of the press to impart information of general interest or concern, but also the right of the public to receive it. It is not to be restricted on the ground of breach of confidence unless there is a 'pressing social need' for such restraint" (*Schering Chemicals Ltd. v. Falkman Ltd.*, 334).

Despite words such as these, keep in mind that the 1987 decision of the House of Lords sustained the interlocutory injunction in the *Spycatcher* case. And it was in the case of *R. v. Secretary of State for the Home Department, ex parte Brind* (1991) that the House of Lords refused to engage in a plenary review of the decision of the home secretary to prohibit the broadcasting of direct statements on the BBC and the Independent Broadcasting Authority (IBA) (now the Independent Television Commission) by representatives of proscribed organizations in Northern Ireland. The House of Lords allowed only for review under *Wednesbury* principles (as we have seen: could a reasonable home secretary have made such a decision?), rather than determining whether the prohibition was strictly necessary because it rested on a pressing social need. Unlike the contempt process (which was within the tradition province of the courts), a statute had given to the home secretary discretion to require either the BBC or the IBA to refrain from broadcasting any matter that the home secretary specified in a notice to them. Counsel for the broadcasters argued that such discretion, if entirely unlimited, would violate Art. 10 of the ECHR. But the House of Lords responded that neither the statute nor the licensing agreement was ambiguous, and that left British courts no power to intervene. Whenever unambiguous administrative discretion is vested by statute in an officer of the Crown, the appropriate British standard, they said, is *Wednesbury* reasonableness. The National Union of Journalists applied to the European Commission for a determination of whether the broadcasting ban violates Art. 10 (Curtis and Jempson 1993), but the ban was lifted by the British government late in 1994 in conjunction with the Northern Ireland cease-fire and ensuing settlement negotiations. The *Brind* case itself was held to be inadmissible by the European Commission in May 1994, chiefly on the grounds that the restrictions on broadcasting were based on a pressing social need, determined to be within the margin of appreciation accorded a state member under Art. 10.2 (*Brind and Others v. United Kingdom* [1994]).

CONCLUSION

As of this writing the last words on freedom of expression under English law or under Art. 10 of the ECHR are those in *Rantzen v. Mirror Group of Newspapers* (1993), *Attorney-General v. Associated Newspapers* (1994), and in *Tolstoy Miloslavsky v. United Kingdom* (1995), and *Goodwin v. United Kingdom* (1996).

In *Rantzen*, after considering the same precedents we have already reviewed in this chapter, Lord Justice Neill concluded that "we have come to the conclusion that we must interpret our power so as to give proper weight to the guidance given by the House of Lords *and* by the European Court of Human Rights" (*Rantzen*, 972, emphasis added). The result was that the Court of Appeal was willing to exercise its powers under the Courts and Legal Services Act 1990 to examine the amount of damages awarded in a libel case against a newspaper to determine whether the amount awarded was necessary to compensate the plaintiff and to reestablish his reputation and was justified by a pressing social need, or whether it was an excessive burden on the freedom of the press. In the end the Court of Appeal reduced the award of damages from £250,000 to £110,000. However, in the 1994 *Associated Newspapers* case the House of Lords upheld a contempt of court judgment against *The Mail on Sunday* for its having published the deliberations of jurors in a jury room (which had been obtained from a source other than the jurors themselves), despite the newspaper's claim of protection under Art. 10 of the ECHR. Their lordships found that both the proscription against disclosures by the jurors themselves and the publication of such disclosures were in response to a pressing social need to protect the integrity of the judicial process, consistent with the provisos of Art. 10.2. Section 8 of the Contempt of Court Act 1981 provides that "it is a contempt of court to obtain, disclose or solicit any particulars of statements made, opinions expressed, arguments advanced or votes cast by members of a jury in the court of their deliberations in any legal proceedings." And so a fine for contempt of £60,000 was upheld.

The recent (July 1995) decision of the European Court of Human Rights in *Tolstoy Miloslavsky v. United Kingdom* fits into an interesting niche in these recent English cases. There the European Court ruled that a jury award of £1,500,000 in a libel was "not necessary in a democratic society." The English domestic law applicable at the time, they held, "did not offer adequate and effective safeguards against a disproportionately large award," and thus the judgment violated the freedom of expression protection by Art. 10. The key was that the alleged libel by Tolstoy Miloslavsky preceded the effective date (February 1, 1991) of the Courts and Legal Service Act 1990; the domestic law then applicable did not include the power for the Court of Appeal to substitute its own assessment of damages for that of a jury. Of course, that was precisely the power exercised in the 1993 *Rantzen* case reviewed above. Since the power to review such jury awards was severely limited under the domestic law applicable to Tolstoy Miloslavsky, the European Court found that a disproportionately large jury award violated the freedom of expression protected by Art. 10. So the European Court's 1995 judgment in the *Tolstoy Miloslavsky* case applies only to the niche in time of the particular libel, and thus we see that the recent interactions between the ECHR, and the European Court, on the one hand, and English courts and English domestic law, on the other, have become both frequent and complex.

The most recent decision (March 1996) of the European Court of Human Rights in *Goodwin v. United Kindom* held that there had been a violation of Art. 10 by virtue of a court order requiring a journalist to reveal the identity of a source. That order had been upheld both by the Court of Appeal and the House of Lords. They applied a balancing test and found that the interest of confidentiality, which had been upheld by holding the journalist in contempt for refusing to identify the source of a leak of confidential information outweighed the public interest of disclosure. The U.K. government did not dispute that the disclosure order interfered with the journalist's freedom of expression under Art. 10 but urged that the interference was justifiable under Art. 10.2 as being "necessary in a democratic society" to protect confidential information. This conclusion was rejected by the European Court, which held that the interest asserted was not sufficient "to outweigh the vital public interest in the protection of the applicant's journalist's source" (*Goodwin v. U.K.*, 145).[2]

Occasionally some longstanding, presumptively permanent, and fundamental feature of our reality changes quickly—to our amazement—before our very eyes. The demise of the Soviet Union and Soviet-supported governments in Eastern Europe was like that. It certainly is not the purpose of this chapter to suggest that the recent evolution of freedom of the press in the United Kingdom—under either the common law or Art. 10—has been of a magnitude or importance equal to that of the demise of Soviet-led Marxism-Leninism. And legal transitions rarely are as quick or as profound as that. Still, the cases featured in this chapter do present a vivid example of a judicial system's struggle to adapt to a changing environment. Hampson has suggested that U.K. judges ought to give human rights a higher priority in their reasoning. She concluded her article by suggesting that "What is needed is a change of attitude on the part not only of the institutions of government but also of the public at large. They need to learn to think in terms of rights" (Hampson 1990, 173). That, perhaps, is what we are beginning to witness. But, the law being as it is, smug complacency and dogged resistance to change remain real possibilities. For example, in reaching his "common law" judgment in the *Derbyshire County Council* case, Lord Keith cited with approval Lord Goff's words in the *Spycatcher* case. You can judge whether they are smug or insightful:

> Finally I wish to observe that I can see no inconsistency between English law on this subject and art 10 of the Convention. . . . This is scarcely surprising, since we may pride ourselves on the fact that freedom of speech has existed in this country perhaps as long as, if not longer than, it has existed in any other country in the world. The only difference is that whereas art 10 of the convention, in accordance with its avowed purpose, proceeds to state a fundamental right and then to qualify it, we in this country (where everybody is free to do anything, subject only to the provisions of the law) proceed rather on an assumption of freedom of speech, and turn to our law to discover the established exceptions to it. (*Attorney-General v. Guardian Newspapers [No. 2]*, 660)

In closing we should note that in February 1994 the attorney general obtained an injunction in the Chancery Division against the impending opening of "Maxwell, The Musical" at London's Criterion Theatre. The attorney general sought the injunction "because he said that the musical, based on the life of deceased financier Robert Maxwell would create a serious risk of prejudice in the forthcoming trial of his sons, Kevin and Ian Maxwell, on fraud charges—which they strenuously deny" (*The Sunday Times*, February 13, 1994). According to *The Times*, the injunction would put almost 100 people out of work and would cost the producer £600,000. We should also note that concern over the highly intrusive conduct of some journalists and their sometimes inaccurate stories led to the appointment and charge in 1992 of Sir David Calcutt, Q.C., to conduct a review of the voluntary nongovernmental Press Complaints Commission, which had been at work since January 1991. Calcutt's 1993 report recommended the creation of a Press Complaints Tribunal that, among other powers, would have had the power to restrain the publication of materials that breached a code of journalistic practices. The code would be drawn up by the Tribunal (*Calcutt Report* 1993, 46).

Clearly, prior restraint is not dead in English law or practice, and the balance between freedom of the press and a proper defense of other values still hangs in the balance.

7

The Convention in United Kingdom Courts

The four previous chapters on the prevention of terrorism and due process, on prisoners' rights, on nationality and immigration, and on freedom of expression have focused on specific interactions between English cases, statutes, or administrative law and practice on those subjects, on the consequential rulings of the European Court of Human Rights, and on the impact of European Court rulings on English domestic law and practice. This chapter will review the references in English cases to the ECHR chronologically, article by article. My purpose is to show how English courts have characterized and treated the ECHR in general, or its specific articles, especially to determine whether there has been any discernible evolution in the characterization or treatment of the ECHR by English courts since the beginning.

To recall briefly a few facts from chapter 1: The ECHR was drafted in 1950, first went into effect in 1959, the first judges were elected in 1959, and the first decision of the European court was in 1960. Through 1973, the Court had decided only seventeen cases. The first decision of the European Court of Human Rights that involved the United Kingdom as a state defendant was the *Golder* case, decided in 1975. The first reference to a European Court decision found through a computer search of English cases was in the case of *Hubbard and Others v. Pitt and Others* (Queen's Bench Division, 1974).

Table 7.1 displays the results of a LEXIS search of English case references to the ECHR, from the first citation in 1974 through the end of 1993. This produced 169 case references.[1] Of these, 150 cases contained some sort of substantive reference to the ECHR, however minimal, while there were nineteen citations with no significant substantive content, apart from the citation itself. From these 150 cases, sixty-two cases were selected for review in this chapter as relatively important ones. However, only Art. 5, 6, 7, 8, 9, 10, and 11—and the general considerations of the domestic applicability of the ECHR to the United Kingdom—were the subject of more than a single reference in these cases. A review of cases referencing only these articles—and of the general considerations of domestic applicability—involves fifty-eight English cases.

REFERENCES TO ART. 5

Only three cases make more than passing references to Art. 5, and all three are contingent on the 1981 decision of the European Court of Human Rights

Table 7.1. Summary of references to the European Convention in English cases

Provision	Number of cases	Number of important cases
Article 8	32	12
Article 10	31	16
Article 6	24	11
On applicability	14	7
Article 5	8	3
Article 3	8	1
Article 9	7	3
Article 11	7	3
Article 7	6	3
First Protocol, Art. 1	4	—
Article 2	3	—
Article 12	2	1
Article 14	2	1
Article 13	1	1
First Protocol, Art. 2	1	—
References in passing	19	—
Total[a]	169	62

a. Includes multiple references.

in *X v. United Kingdom*. In that case the European Court held that the review provided by the Mental Health Review Tribunal established under the Mental Health Act 1959 was not sufficient to satisfy the requirements of Art. 5.4 because the tribunal had only the power to recommend release, not to order it. This violation was cured by the provision in section 75(1) of the Mental Health Act 1983, for dispositive power by the tribunal. In *R. v. Home Secretary, ex parte K* (1990), however, the Court of Appeal refused to take the ECHR into account beyond the necessary statutory response to *X v. United Kingdom*. The reason for that reticence was the precedent of *R. v. Home Secretary, ex parte Brind* (1990), which, as we have seen before, is the most important recent case on the *applicability* of the ECHR in English domestic law, as we shall see later in this chapter.

In *Pickering v. Liverpool Daily Post and Echo Newspapers plc and Others* (1991) the House of Lords simply referred to the reforms that had followed *X v. United Kingdom* in acknowledging that the Mental Health Review Tribunal was a court for the purposes of the Contempt of Court Act 1981. Finally, in *R. v. Canons Park Mental Health Review Tribunal, ex parte A* (1993) a Queen's Bench Divisional Court refused to accept an interpretation of a statute that it viewed as jeopardizing the effectiveness of the U.K.'s statutory response to the European Court's judgment in *X v. United Kingdom*.

While certainly limited in their scope, these references to Art. 5 at a minimum show the effectiveness of the European Court of Human Rights decision in *X v. United Kingdom.*

REFERENCES TO ART. 6

Guilfoyle v. Home Office (1980), the first significant case reference to Art. 6, questioned whether a prisoner had a right to communicate with his solicitor in connection with an application pending before the European Commission involving an assault by a prison officer. Guilfoyle was one of six suspects, known as the "Birmingham Six," who were convicted of the November 1974 terrorist bombing that killed twenty-one people in Birmingham. The convictions of the six eventually were overturned because the evidence on which they were convicted was deemed unreliable. Lord Denning was apparently outraged by the application of Guilfoyle to the European Commission, for he noted the previous U.K. proceedings regarding the alleged assault and went on to comment, "Yet, despite all these investigations here, Patrick Guilfoyle has the *audacity* to seek to complain to the European Commission of Human Rights" (*Guilfoyle*, 945; emphasis added). As we saw in chapter 4, the prison rules had been amended after the European Court's decision in *Golder v. United Kingdom* (1975) to allow a prisoner to communicate with his solicitor without having his mail read or stopped, but this rule applied only to pending "legal proceedings." As we also saw, Lord Denning eventually concluded that while proceedings before the European Court were "legal proceedings," an application to the Commission was not:

> Translated into the affairs of the European Convention, the proceedings in the European *Court* of Human Rights are "legal proceedings" because that court exercises judicial functions: but the proceedings in the European *Commission* are not, because the commission exercises no judicial function. They only make a report on the facts and state their opinion. They make no order at all, nothing which can be enforced by anyone.
>
> Even if proceedings in the European Commission could be considered to be "legal proceedings," when does an applicant become a "party" to the legal proceedings? I think an applicant only becomes a "party" when his application is accepted as admissible by the commission such that the other party is called to answer it. (*Guilfoyle*, 946)

So Guilfoyle's correspondence with his solicitor could be read and examined by the prison governor, although it could not be stopped. Clearly this was a calculated narrow construction of the prison rules.

It is interesting that two years later in *Raymond v. Honey* (1982) the House of Lords held that the statutory authorization for prison authorities to make rules for the "discipline and control of prisoners" was not sufficient to sustain "hindrance or interference" with the right of a citizen to unimpeded access to the courts. The opinions of Lord Wilberforce and Lord Bridge both discuss the *Golder* case and its aftermath and note the protection afforded by Art. 6 of the ECHR. Eventually, however, their decision rested, they said, on two common law principles. The first was that interference with a citizen's access to the courts was a common law contempt of court, and the second was that a prisoner retains all civil rights that are not expressly or "by necessary implication" taken away. Lord Bridge's effort to found rights on the common law certainly is consistent with his efforts to found freedom of expression on the common law, rather than on Art. 10 of the ECHR, as we saw in the *Derbyshire County Council* case in chapter 6.

And despite the protestations of Lord Denning, in the case of *Campbell v. United Kingdom* (1992), the European Court of Human Rights held that the screening of letters between a prisoner and his solicitor was a violation of the attorney-client privilege and an invasion of privacy under Art. 8 (also as we saw in chapter 6). Finally, in May 1993 the Court of Appeal in *R. v. Home Secretary, ex parte Leech* entirely overturned the prison rule that allowed officers to read prisoners' correspondence with their solicitors about pending or prospective legal proceedings.

Another case that considered Art. 6 was the 1981 decision of the Privy Council in *Haw Tua Tau v. Public Prosecutor*. The case involved three appeals in capital cases from Singapore involving the privilege against self-incrimination. Singapore's criminal procedure had been amended in 1976 to allow judges to call upon defendants to give evidence and, upon their refusal, to draw inferences from their silence. Lord Diplock's opinion found this procedure neither to violate "fundamental rules of natural justice" nor to be protected by the ECHR by virtue of the presumption of innocence required by Art. 6.2. He noted that

in many countries of the non-communist world, whose legal systems are not derived from the common law, the court itself has an investigatory role to play in the judicial process for the trial of criminal offences. In such systems interrogation of the accused by a judge, though not direct interrogation by the prosecution, forms an essential part of the proceedings. (*Haw Tua Tau*, 21)

The right to silence was limited in Northern Ireland by the Criminal Evidence (Northern Ireland) Order of November 1988. Under that order, a defendant is required to account for his conduct to the police. Failure to do so may be offered as evidence of guilt. Early in 1994, the European Commission on Human Rights held admissible the application of Anthony Murray, who was convicted of a terrorist-related crime in 1991. Murray's application alleged that the 1988 Criminal Evidence Order violates Art. 6 of the ECHR (*John Murray v. United Kingdom*, 1994). We should also note that the Criminal Justice Act 1994 reduces the right to silence in England and Wales, much as did the 1988 order for Northern Ireland.

Home Office v. Harman, decided by the House of Lords in 1982, primarily was an Art. 10 case, but Art. 6, through its requirement of a fair and public trial, was peripherally involved. The question was whether an undertaking to keep confidential certain government documents (obtained through discovery) was still binding on a litigant once the documents were read in open court. The majority upheld the contempt finding, but Lord Scarman's dissent, upholding the disclosure of the documents, noted the Art. 6 requirement of a public hearing (which meant that the documents, when read, must have been in the public domain), and it contains an extended discussion of freedom of expression under Art. 10 (see below).

R. v. Home Secretary, ex parte Tarrant and another (1983) and *Hone v. Maze Prison Board of Visitors* (1988) both refer to the right to counsel under Art. 6.3(c) of the ECHR. *Tarrant* was decided by a Queen's Bench Divisional Court. The applicants were prisoners who were charged with offenses against prison discipline. Their request for legal representation before the Prison Board of Visitors was denied. While their application for judicial review of this denial was before the Queen's Bench, the European Commission had reported its finding that prisoners charged with "especially grave offenses" were entitled to the assistance of counsel under Art. 6.3(c). This the Court noted in its opinion in *Tarrant*, while holding that a Prison Board of Visitors had the discretion to grant requests for legal representation "under our law, including the principles of natural justice" (*Tarrant*, 824). In 1984 the European Commission's report sustaining the right to counsel in especially grave prison offenses was upheld by the European Court of Human Rights in its judgment in *Campbell and Fell v. United Kingdom*. However, in *Hone v. Maze Prison Board of Visitors* (1988) the House of Lords considered the European Court's judgments on the right to counsel and concluded that the European Court applying Art. 6.3(c) and British courts applying natural justice both ended at the same place. The right to counsel in prison disciplinary proceedings was not absolute but discretionary, depending, for the most part, on the seriousness of the disciplinary violation and the severity of the consequences for the prisoner.

Three cases have referred to Art. 6 in the context of a parent's right to a hearing on the termination of parental rights by the state. All three cases sought to take into account the decision of the European Court of Human Rights in *R. v. United Kingdom* (1987). When the issues in that case arose, U.K. law did not provide for a hearing for either a parent or a guardian of a minor child to review the decision of a local authority in refusing or terminating access to a child, when the authority already had custody of the child. The European Court held both that there was a right to such a hearing under Art. 6.1 and that the U.K. had also violated the right to respect for family life of Art. 8. Anticipating that decision, in 1983 Parliament amended the statute to provide for a hearing in that specific context. However, the three cases reviewed here refused to extend the protection required by the European Court in its decision.

The first case, *Re K D (a minor)* (1988), while mentioning Art. 6, primarily focused on parental rights under Art. 8, but the second, *M v. H and Others* (1988) conceded that even if the applicant (the father of an illegitimate child) was correct that the denial of his right of access violated both Art. 6 and 8, British courts had no duty to enforce the provisions of the ECHR. It was Parliament's responsibility to amend the law to provide for a hearing in this context, as it had done in 1983 in anticipating an adverse ruling in Strasbourg. Finally, in *F v. Wirral Metropolitan Borough Council* (1990), the Court of Appeal expressly relied on its own 1990 decision on applicability of the ECHR in *R. v. Home Secretary, ex parte Brind* (the House of Lords decision came later) and also disclaimed any responsibility for resolving conflicts between the ECHR and the actions of local authorities or others who might interfere with parental rights.

Two opinions on the same case, *R v. Home Secretary, ex parte Wynne* (1991) and *Wynne v. Home Secretary* (1993), the first from the Court of Appeal and the second from the House of Lords, involved the issue of whether a prisoner who had been granted leave to apply for judicial review of his conviction of a disciplinary violation could be required to pay £419 toward the cost of escorting and transporting him to the High Court in London for his hearing.

The applicant claimed that interference with his attendance at the hearing was a violation both of chapter 40 of Magna Carta (which provides that "To no one will we deny, or delay or sell right and justice") and of Art. 6.1 of the ECHR. Lord Justice Staughton accepted that the ECHR was not part of U.K. law, but volunteered that "it is important to pay attention to it" (*ex parte Wynne*, 315). The United Kingdom's response was that attendance was denied (or the costs assessed) only when the home secretary was satisfied that the prisoner's presence in court was not necessary in the interests of justice. The Court's reluctance to accept that response was that it, in effect, placed the Home Office in the position of determining the merits of an action brought against itself (*ex parte Wynne*, 316), but a majority reluctantly concluded that the home secretary had not acted unreasonably.

The House of Lords dismissed the prisoner's appeal on technical grounds, but Lord Goff volunteered at some length a "practical solution," under which the home secretary might seek a judicial determination of the question of the prisoner's attendance at a hearing. In discussing his "practical solution" he noted that the right of access to courts was not absolute even under *Golder v. United Kingdom* (1979, 581), but he clearly placed some value on the right of access protected by Art. 6.

The last Art. 6 case, *R. v. Redbourne* (1992), was an appeal from a confiscation order under the Drug Trafficking Offences Act 1986. The case is not particularly important or interesting, and it is mentioned here only for the novelty that it was the counsel for the prosecution who invoked Art. 6 and 7 of the ECHR in support of a particular statutory interpretation. To decide otherwise, he argued, would make statute inconsistent with those articles of the ECHR.

References to Art. 7

Not surprisingly, the provision of Art. 7 against ex post facto laws has been infrequently referenced. Five of the six cases in which reference has been made have been decided within the past five years, but only three of these are of particular interest.

In the first important reference, *Jones and Lee v. Miah and Miah* (1992), the Court of Appeal introduced the nuance of the adoption of ECHR by the Court of Justice of the European Community (as it was then) as part of the "common law" of the community. While that meant that the ECHR might be applied in cases before community courts or when community obligations were at stake, was it also the means by which the ECHR would be introduced into British courts? The opinion of the Court of Appeal does give due regard for Art. 7's prohibition of ex post facto criminal laws, but in the end avoided the issue of applicability by deciding that the provisions in question were civil rather than criminal. The provisions of the Housing Act 1988 had imposed tort liability with punitive damages on landlords who unlawfully deprived tenants of their premises.

We have already briefly reviewed *R. v. Redbourne* (1992) under our discussion of Art. 6. The issue there was whether a provision for confiscation of property under the Drug Trafficking Offences Act (1986) could be applied retroactively, in this instance to property acquired by Redbourne six years before his conviction. However, once again the confiscation was held to be civil rather than criminal. And *R. v. Brown* (1993) made only a slight reference to Art. 7, and then moved on to a serious discussion of privacy rights under Art. 8 and under the common law, as we shall see below.

Finally, in *L'Office Cherifien des Phosphates v. Yamashita-Shinnihon Steamship Co.* (The Boucraa) (1993) the Court of Appeal held that acts of Parliament were presumed not to operate retrospectively, unless the intention for retrospective application was clearly expressed or necessarily implied, and this was not limited to criminal statutes. To sustain that conclusion the Court cited legal maxims (*nullum crimen nulla poena sine lege* [no crime may be punished without a law] and *lex prospicit no respicit* [the law looks forward not backwards]), the French Civil Code (*la loi ne dispose que pour l'avenir, elle n'a point d'effet retroactif* [the law is directed only toward the future; it has no retroactive application]), common law maxims of statutory construction, and Art. 7 of the ECHR (1993, 691). The Court of Appeal was, however, reversed by the House of Lords and allowed retrospective application, without citing either broad principles or Art. 7.

REFERENCES TO ART. 8

The first three cases we review here involve immigration and the right to respect for family life under Art. 8. In *R. v. Home Secretary, ex parte Phansopkar* (1975)(also discussed in chapter 5) and its companion case, *ex parte Begum*, both applicants were Indian nationals who were the wives of *patrials* and who sought entry into the U.K. Their difficulty was that they were required to obtain their entry papers in India, where they confronted a queue of fourteen months or longer, and where by making application for such papers they stood to lose their Indian citizenship, so they came to the United Kingdom without their papers. The airport immigration officer refused to believe that they were the lawful wives of *patrial* husbands without their papers, and denied them entry. While still in England they applied to the home secretary for the necessary certificates acknowledging that they were the wives of *patrials*, but his response was that it was "more convenient" and "more satisfactory" for the requests to be dealt with in India, despite the queue. They won their case in the Court of Appeal, Lord Denning and Lord Scarman both agreeing that a writ of mandamus ought to be issued to the home secretary, but it was in Scarman's opinion that both Magna Carta and Art. 8 were cited in support of their right to have a decision made on their applications by the home secretary while they were in England: "This hallowed principle of our law [Magna Carta] is now reinforced by the European Convention for the Protection of Human Rights 1950 to which it is now the duty of our public authorities in administering the law, including the Immigration Act 1971 and of our courts in interpreting and applying the law, including the Act to have regard" (1975, 511). He concluded that the immigration rules did not specify that certificates had to be issued outside the U.K., but, to the contrary, said that they could be issued overseas or by the Home Office.

Mistry v. The Entry Clearance Officer, Bombay (1975) (also reviewed in chapter 5) was a case decided by the Immigration Appeal Tribunal before Lord Denning's several meandering decisions as to the application of the ECHR were delivered (see section on applicability later in this chapter). While the outcome in the case rejected the application of a twenty-five-year-old son to join his parents in the United Kingdom, finding no violation of Art. 8 in the refusal of entry, the tribunal at that time expressed its willingness to take the ECHR into account.

But only a year later, in *R. v. Chief Immigration Officer, Heathrow Airport, ex parte Salamat Bibi* (1976), Lord Denning and Lord Justice Roskill made it clear that the ECHR was to be considered by judges only as an aid in construing the meaning of an ambiguous statute. The immigration officer in this case had denied entry to a woman (and her two children) who arrived from Pakistan and sought entry, saying that she was there only for a two-week visit. She had not obtained an entry visa from the British embassy in Pakistan, as required by law should she wish to reside with her husband in the United Kingdom, Pakistan no longer being a commonwealth country. She was met at the airport by a man who claimed to be her husband and who told the immigration officer that he wanted her to live with him permanently. That was the basis for the immigration officer's denying her a visitor's visa. The Court of Appeal found no ambiguity either in the statute or in the immigration rules and therefore no basis for the application of Art. 8.

Wiretapping as an alleged violation of privacy rights under Art. 8 was the subject of *Malone v. Commissioner of Police of the Metropolis* (no. 2) (1979). The difficulty was that there was no specific authorization for the police to engage in wiretapping under either the common law or by statute, but neither was there any statute or common law rule against it. Vice Chancellor Megarry of the Chancery Division covered the familiar ground that the ECHR by itself had no direct application in the United Kingdom, but could it influence an outcome in the silence of common and statutory law? Megarry declined the possibility. Under English legal tradition when something is not expressly prohibited by statute, or by necessary implication of law, it is permitted. This was not, he said, an instance of statutory ambiguity in which the ECHR might be used as an aid in construction, and the ECHR conferred no direct rights on Malone. He went on to admit, however, that it was "becoming abundantly clear that a system which has no legal safeguards whatever has small chance of satisfying the requirements of [the European] court" (1979, 648). It was plain, he said, "that telephone tapping is a subject which cries out for legislation" (1979, 649). But it was not for the courts to address this complex subject through common law rules.

So the European Court resolved the issue instead, for in *Malone v. United Kingdom* (1984) the Court unanimously found that the U.K.'s wiretapping was a violation of Art. 8. And the ruling in *Malone v. United Kingdom* made an important contribution to the passage of the Interception of Communications Act 1985, as noted by Lord Mustill in *R. v. Preston and Others* (House of Lords, 1993, 650).

The next two cases, *Fernandes v. Home Secretary* (1980) and *Guilfoyle v. Home Office* (1980), contain words directed toward the ECHR and the European Commission and Court that verge on hostility. As we saw at the beginning of the chapter, *Guilfoyle* was the case in which Lord Denning remarked on the audacity of Guilfoyle (as we have seen, one of the Birmingham Six) in complaining to the European Commission about his alleged assault by a prison officer. Even so, Denning admitted, "It looks as if they did get a little bit of rough handling by someone or other. They were bruised and received black eyes, but nothing more. It may have been done when they were trying to escape, or when they refused to do what they were told. At all events their complaints have been fully investigated in this country (*Guilfoyle*, 1980, 945). Guilfoyle's complaint relative to Art. 8 was for interference with his correspondence; it was rejected on the grounds that Guilfoyle was not a party to legal proceedings within the meaning of the prison rules, as we saw above in this chapter under our review of Art. 6 cases.

Fernandes involved an Indian woman who was the mother of adult children who resided in the U.K. She was the subject of a deportation order for overstaying her visitor's visa. She sought to stop the deportation on the grounds that it would result in the breakup of her family in violation of Art. 8. While the deportation order was pending, she notified the home secretary that she would be filing an application with the European Commission. She did so, and in October 1980, while she was still in the U.K., the Commission asked the government of the U.K. to comment on the admissibility and merits of her application. Her case was presented to the Commission in November 1980, and four days later her application for judicial review was denied by a Queen's Bench Divisional Court. During her appeal from this denial, her application was under consideration by the Commission, but the Commission did not request a stay of her deportation by the U.K., as it had done in another case. Her principal point was that her deportation should be stayed, pending the outcome of her application to the Commission. It would have been easy for the home secretary to do so, but he refused.

Her appeal was dismissed by the Court of Appeal on the ground that she had not shown that the home secretary's refusal to stay her deportation was a decision that no reasonable home secretary could have made (per *Wednesbury* reasonableness). That outcome is not surprising, given other decisions we have seen, but Lord Justice Waller volunteered the following: "In my judgment, there was no legal obligation on the Secretary of State to consider whether or not this [the deportation] was a contravention of the Articles of the Convention" (*Fernandes*, 1980, 6).

And Lord Justice Watkins added, "The Secretary of State so it seems to me has, having regard to the facts of the case, shown a degree of tolerance which by itself is a manifestation of the fair way in which he treated the repeated applications of this applicant to stay in the country" (*Fernandes*, 1980, 7).

Watkins was persuaded that Mrs. Fernandes's application to the Commission was simply another dilatory effort to delay her deportation. In a footnote to his opinion he also quoted with approval *dicta* from Lord Denning's opinion in *R. v. Chief Immigration Officer, Heathrow Airport, ex parte Salamat Bibi*:

> The Convention is drafted in a style very different from the way we are used to in legislation. It contains wide general statements of principle. They are apt to lead to much difficulty in application; because they give rise to much uncertainty. *They are not the sort of thing which we can easily digest. Article 8 is an example. It is so wide as to be incapable of practical application. So it is much better for us to stick to our own statutes and principles, and only look to the Convention for guidance in case of doubt* (1980, 7; emphasis added).

In 1987 in *R. v. Immigration Appeal Tribunal, ex parte Chundawadra*, a Queen's Bench Divisional Court rejected a claim under Art. 8 brought by a male of 26 years who had resided with his parents in the United Kingdom since he was eighteen. Having been convicted of a serious drug offense, he had been ordered deported on the home secretary's determination that his deportation would be "conducive to the public good." The opinion recites the words that British courts commonly use when holding that the ECHR has no direct domestic application. The only reason the case is particularly interesting is that one year later in *Berrehab v. Netherlands* (1988) the European Court sustained a claim under Art. 8 of a Moroccan national who had been expelled by the Netherlands after his divorce from his Dutch spouse. And that case was followed by two cases in 1991, one in 1992, and another in 1993, all of which involved persons who were ordered deported because of the commission of crimes within their host country. In *Moustaquim v. Belgium* (1991) the European Court ruled in favor of a man who had come to Belgium when one year old and who had a long history of juvenile and adult crime, while in *Djeroud v. France* (1991) a friendly settlement was reached through which a deportation order was revoked and compensation of Fr 150,000 was paid by France. *Beldjoudi v. France* (1992) involved a repeat offender who had been born in France of Algerian parents in 1950 and who was ordered to be deported in 1979. The European Court also ruled in his favor. The Court had written in *Moustaquim* that for a deportation order to be sustainable against an Art. 8

claim for respect of family life, it must be justified by "a pressing social need" and must be "proportionate to the legitimate aim [the maintenance of public order] pursued."

The direct contradiction to the outcome in *Chundawadra* in 1987 came in 1993 when a friendly settlement was reached in the case of *Lamguindaz v. United Kingdom*, then pending before the European Court. Lamguindaz was a twenty-three-year-old Moroccan immigrant whose conviction for a number of offenses, including crimes of violence, had led the home secretary to determine in 1990 that his exclusion would be "conducive to the public good." However, given the European Court's precedents, the United Kingdom agreed to revoke the deportation, to grant him the right to remain indefinitely, and to pay him more than £8,000 costs and expenses.

We reviewed *Re K D (a minor)* (1988), *M v. H and Others* (1988), and *F v. Wirral Metropolitan Borough Council* (1990) under the right to a hearing accorded by Art. 6. Despite the outcome of *R v. United Kingdom* in 1987 (which required the United Kingdom to amend its statutes to provide a hearing through which the rights of parents to have access to their children might be determined), in none of these three cases were parental rights under Art. 8 further extended.

R. v. Governor of Pentonville Prison, ex parte Chinoy (1990) involved a novel point, in that evidence secured through wiretapping conducted by U.S. undercover agents in France in violation both of French law and Art. 8 (which applied domestically in France) was offered in an extradition proceeding in the United Kingdom. The evidence was, however, legitimate under English law, and English law did not provide for a comprehensive exclusionary rule even for evidence secured in violation of English law. The evidence was admitted and the admission was upheld on appeal.

Over the dissents of Lord Mustill and Lord Slynn, the House of Lords in *R. v. Brown and other appeals* (1993) upheld the assault convictions of appellants. The accused were a group of sadomasochistic homosexual adults who voluntarily participated in acts of violence against one another, including genital torture. The question was whether the violent acts of consenting adults in private were protected by privacy rights. The majority had no difficulty in rejecting that argument, and the opinion of Lord Templeman apparently forgot for the occasion that the ECHR had no direct application in British courts, for he explicitly determined that a prosecution in such circumstances did not violate Art. 8: "I do not consider that art 8 invalidates a law which forbids violence which is intentionally harmful to body and mind. . . . Society is entitled and bound to protect itself against a cult of violence. Pleasure derived from the infliction of pain is an evil thing. Cruelty is uncivilised" (1993, 84).

Lord Mustill was no enthusiast for the ECHR. His view of Art. 8 follows:

The jurisprudence with which this article, in common with other terms of the convention, is rapidly becoming encrusted shows that in order to condemn acts which appear worthy of censure they have had to be forced into the mould of art 8, and referred to the concept of privacy, for want of any other provision which will serve. I do not deny that the privacy of the conduct was an important element in the present case, but I cannot accept that this fact on its own can yield an answer (*R. v. Brown*, 115).

Nonetheless, Lord Mustill conceded that the "general tenor of the decisions of the European Court of Human Rights does furnish valuable guidance on the approach which the English courts should adopt, if free to do so." Like the European Court, he believed in "balancing the personal considerations invoked by art 8(1) against the public interest considerations called up by art 8(2)" and favored "the right of appellants to conduct their private lives undisturbed by the criminal law," although his conclusion was based on statutory interpretation and public policy, rather than on the ECHR alone (1993, 115).

Lord Slynn agreed that the question was one of statutory interpretation, although he found Art. 8 entirely irrelevant to his conclusion that the acts of consenting adults in private were not made criminal by the extant statute. If these acts were to be made criminal, that was up to Parliament, and he expressed no opinion on whether such a decision would be acceptable under Art. 8.2 of the ECHR.

The most recent Art. 8 case, like those at the beginning of this section, involved immigration. *Iye v. Home Secretary* (1993) involved a man of Nigerian nationality who had illegally entered the United Kingdom on a false passport in 1986. When he was convicted of social security fraud in 1993, he was sentenced to two years in prison, and the judge recommended that he be deported. The home secretary decided to expel him. The difficulty was that by 1993 Iye was the father of a two-year-old child, and, as we have seen, under the European Court's decisions in *Berrehab* (1988), *Moustaquim* (1991), and *Beldjoudi* (1992), as well as the friendly settlement in *Lamguindaz* (1993), the expulsion order seems highly questionable.

The Court of Appeal took note of an internal document, "The Home Office Enforcement Policy Group Instruction" (DP/2/93) of January 1993, through which the Home Office attempted to guide its officers in cases like Iye's. The document advised officers of the outcomes of the cases cited above and suggested that these be taken into account in weighing the compassionate circumstances in a case. Despite that, the officer in Iye's case still ordered his exclusion. Could such a decision be *Wednesbury* reasonable in the face of the

Home Office document? Two members of the Court of Appeal took the position that the European Court's precedents were instructive but not dispositive, so that an officer could, on the facts of a particular case, reasonably decide in favor of exclusion. The majority of the Court of Appeal took the position that both Iye's initial entry by fraud and the seriousness of his crime (a two-year sentence and a recommendation of deportation) could be taken into account in deciding whether to expel him.

Lord Justice Evans reluctantly joined the decision, but wanted clarification by the Home Office as to the intent and purpose of its internal document: "I find it unsatisfactory that in a case of this sort, involving the removal of an applicant from this country after many years here, the respondents are unable to make clear . . . the position of the Secretary of State" (*Iye*, 1993, 67).

REFERENCES TO ART. 9

Only three cases have made serious references to Art. 9. All three cases were followed by applications to the European Commission after they had been lost in British courts. Unlike the First Amendment to the U.S. Constitution, which has both a free exercise and an establishment of religion clause, Art. 9 has only what amounts to a free exercise provision in Art. 9.1, and 9.2 sets out explicit limitations even on that. It appears from the Commission's reports on these three cases that a state adhering to the ECHR may have a relatively easier burden in showing necessity under Art. 9.2 than would be the case under the U.S. First Amendment.

In *Ahmad v. Inner London Education Authority* (1977) a devout Muslim employed as a teacher in London sought to have recognized his right to be absent from school for about forty-five minutes each Friday afternoon to attend prayers at a nearby mosque. He had not claimed this right when initially employed, but did so only after he was transferred to a school sufficiently near a mosque that he might attend. Only Lord Scarman was much impressed by the possible application of Art. 9. Lord Denning found that Ahmad's contractual employment obligation ought to prevail over any implication contained in the pertinent statute. Section 30 of the Education Act 1944 provides that "no teacher in any school shall be required to give religious instruction or receive any less emolument or be deprived of or disqualified for, any promotion or other advantage by reason of the fact that he does or does not give religious instruction or by reason of his religious opinion or of his attending or omitting to attend religious worship." Nonetheless, Lord Denning wrote:

> I venture to suggest that it would do the Moslem community no good,
> if they were to be given preferential treatment over the great majority
> of people. If it should happen that, in the name of religious freedom,

they were given special privileges or advantages, it would provoke discontent, and even resentment among those with whom they work. As indeed, it has done so in this very case. And so the cause of racial integration would suffer. So, whilst upholding religious freedom to the full, I would suggest that it should be applied with caution, especially having regard for the setting in which it is sought. . . . I see nothing in the European Convention to give Mr Ahmad any right to manifest his religion on Friday afternoons in derogation of his contract of employment, and certainly not on full pay. (*Ahmad*, 577–78)

As noted above, only Lord Scarman was more sympathetic, and his dissent made one of the strongest comments on the ECHR that we have seen. Here are two quotes:

Today, therefore, we have to construe and apply s 30 not against the background of the law and society of 1944 but in a multi-racial society which has accepted international obligations and enacted statutes designed to eliminate discrimination. (*Ahmad*, 583)

In modern British society, with its elaborate statutory protection of the individual from discrimination arising from race, colour, religion or sex, and against the background of the European Convention this [a narrow construction of section 30] is unacceptable, inconsistent with the policy of modern statute law and almost certainly a breach of our international obligations. (*Ahmad*, 585)

Lord Scarman is often alone in his comments and conclusions about the ECHR. In *Ahmad v. United Kingdom* (1981), even the European Commission of Human Rights unanimously concluded that the right to exercise freedom of religion was not absolute but was subject to contractual obligations of employment.

In *R. v. Lemon* and its companion case *R. v. Gay News Ltd.*, the editor and publishers of a newspaper for homosexuals were prosecuted for blasphemous libel through a private prosecution. The offending publication was of a poem, with illustrations, that purported to display certain sexual acts with the crucified body of Jesus. The trial judge instructed the jury that the defendants need not have a specific intent to blaspheme if they intentionally published material that was itself blasphemous. The defendants were convicted and their appeal eventually came to the House of Lords, which sustained the conviction. Lord Scarman agreed, and again in considering the implications of Art. 9, he concluded "that a due respect for freedom of religion" includes the duty "to refrain from insulting or outraging the religious feelings of others" (*Lemon*, 927). The defendants took their case to the European Commission in *Gay News*

Ltd. and Lemon v. United Kingdom (1982), which also had little difficulty in concluding that the prosecution was sustainable under the provisos of Art. 9.2.

The last case under Art. 9 was another private prosecution, this one being brought against Salman Rushdie and Viking Penguin Publishing Company for blasphemous libel in the publication of *Satanic Verses*. When the prosecution was dismissed, the applicant sought judicial review in the High Court of the dismissal in the case of *R. v. Chief Metropolitan Stipendiary Magistrate, ex parte Choudhury* (1990). The Queen's Bench Divisional Court concluded that the common law offense of blasphemous libel was confined to protecting the Christian religion, an outcome that certainly would be problematic under the First Amendment in the United States. Art. 9, however, has no establishment clause, and the idea of an established religion is, of course, the generally accepted tradition in the United Kingdom. It is not surprising that British courts sustained the dismissal and that they held Art. 9 not to be applicable since the Christian objective of blasphemous libel under the common law was, "without doubt, certain" (*Choudhury*, 320). It perhaps is a bit surprising that the European Commission unanimously found a subsequent application to it inadmissible in *Choudhury v. United Kingdom* (1991). The Commission found no right to prosecute for malicious libel under Art. 9. What was surprising was that Choudhury also alleged religious discrimination under Art. 14 and the Commission concluded only that since there was no right to prosecute for blasphemous libel protected by Art. 9, there could be no discrimination under Art. 14. Unlike establishment clause cases in the United States, where singling out a single religion for the protection of a blasphemy statute would clearly have violated the First Amendment, Art. 9 has no comparable prohibition.

REFERENCES TO ART. 10

As we have already witnessed in chapter 6, Art. 10 has produced more serious references by English courts than any other provision of the ECHR. The opinions of English courts also treat the provisions of Art. 10 far more seriously than we have seen with other articles of the ECHR. Two reasons for this come to mind. The first is the pride the English judiciary takes in the tradition of freedom of expression. The second is that the law on freedom of expression is mostly judge-made. But even if these observations are true in general, none of the opinions of English courts in the thalidomide contempt of court case, which led to the first *Sunday Times* case—decided by the European Court in 1979—even mentioned the ECHR.

The first serious reference to Art. 10 was contained in Lord Scarman's dissent in *R. v. Lemon* and *R. v. Gay News Ltd.* (1979) (which we just reviewed as religious freedom cases under Art. 9 above). As we have seen several times,

Lord Scarman has been more favorably disposed toward the ECHR than any other member of the House of Lords. Even so, just as was the case with the application of Art. 9 in *R. v. Lemon*, Scarman had no difficulty in finding that the freedom of expression guaranteed by Art. 10.1 was not violated by this prosecution for blasphemy of the editor and publishers of a magazine. To be sure, most readers would have found the publication offensive in its portrayal of Jesus. Scarman found the prosecution of the publication to be acceptable within the limitations prescribed in Art. 10.2: "It would be intolerable if by allowing an author or publisher to plead the excellence of his motives and the right of free speech he could evade the penalties of the law even though his words were blasphemous in the sense of constituting an outrage on the religious feelings of his fellow citizens" (*Lemon*, 927).

It must be said, however, that much the same point was made by *Choudhury* in seeking to prosecute Salman Rushdie for blasphemy in his *Satanic Verses*, but Rushdie's book, of course, did not blaspheme Jesus.

The next case found Lord Denning making another of his many uneven references to the ECHR. This one was in the context of an application for an injunction against a trade union for "blacking" (refusing to print) the advertisements of certain advertisers who did business with the papers printed by publishers who had not recognized the union. In *Associated Newspapers Group v. Wade* (1979), Denning commented that it was a "fundamental principle of our law that the press shall be free." "In this respect," he wrote (1979, 708), "our law corresponds with article 10(1) of the European Convention."

Gleaves v. Deakin (1979) was brought as a private criminal prosecution for defamatory libel. In the House of Lords, Lord Diplock considered the common law of criminal defamatory libel at some length, and reflected on its possible conflict with the requirements of Art. 10. He noted that the original purpose of criminal defamatory libel was to allow a wronged person to seek the punishment of his defamer by law, rather than by personal vengeance, but this purpose of preventing breaches of the peace was now anachronistic. The common remedy these days was through a civil action for damages, sometimes coupled with a prayer for injunctive relief. Noting that the restrictions permissible under Art. 10.2 were to be narrowly construed, Lord Diplock found the common law of defamatory libel to be quite the opposite:

> In contrast to this the truth of the defamatory statement is not in itself a defence to a charge of defamatory libel under our criminal law; so here is a restriction on the freedom to impart information which states that are parties to the Convention have expressly undertaken to secure to everyone within their jurisdiction. No onus lies on the prosecution to show that the defamatory matter was of a kind that it is necessary in a demo-

cratic society to suppress or penalise in order to protect the public interest. On the contrary, even though no public interest can be shown to be injuriously affected by imparting to others accurate information about seriously discreditable conduct of an individual, the publisher of the information must be convicted unless he himself can prove to the satisfaction of a jury that the publication of it was for the public benefit.

This is to turn art 10 of the Convention on its head. (*Gleaves*, 498–99)

His solution was to propose that the consent of the attorney general be obtained before initiating any prosecution for criminal libel; the attorney general, he said, ought to have the responsibility for determining whether prosecution was necessary on any of the grounds stated in Art. 10.2.

Viscount Dilhorne (*Gleaves*, 502) and Lord Scarman (*Gleaves*, 509) agreed that the attorney general or the director of public prosecutions ought to screen cases to see whether they were in the public interest, but neither of them mentioned Art. 10.

A year later in *Attorney General v. British Broadcasting Corp.* (1980) the House of Lords refused to recognize a local tax valuation court as a court exercising a judicial function and therefore avoided the question of whether to protect the valuation court under the contempt powers of the Queen's Bench. More important was the fact that Lord Scarman's opinion in the BBC case was the first opportunity for the House of Lords to note the ruling of the European Court of Human Rights in the first *Sunday Times* case (1979), as we considered in chapter 6.

Schering Chemicals Ltd. v. Falkman Ltd. (1981) and *Home Office v. Harman* (1982) were reviewed in chapter 6 as examples of contempt proceedings involved with the evolution of common law freedom of expression. We need not cover the same ground here.

In *Wheeler v. Leicester City Council* (1985) we find an example of political correctness before that subject became a popular journalistic topic. The Leicester City Council passed a resolution banning for twelve months a local rugby football club from using a city-owned recreation ground. This was done to penalize three members of the club for joining an English team selected to tour South Africa during the time of apartheid and the sports boycott of South Africa. Was the players' right to join the tour protected by freedom of expression, so that the Council's decision violated their freedom? A majority of the Court of Appeal found the Leicester Council's decision to be *Wednesbury* reasonable; only Lord Justice Browne-Wilkinson disagreed. He noted that the Universal Declaration of Human Rights and the ECHR both included freedom of conscience and speech among basic human rights, and he found that English law contained the same principles. If the Council were to be given the power by Parliament to discriminate in the use of public facilities according to the views of those who use them, Parliament should have "expressed such intention in the clearest terms" (1985, 158).

Next came the second *Sunday Times* case and the companion cases of *The Guardian* and *The Observer*. Given the extensive discussion of the *Spycatcher* cases in chapter 6, we need not repeat that review here.

The next case certainly is mundane in comparison to the *Spycatcher* cases. In *R. v. General Medical Council, ex parte Colman* (1989) the question was whether the General Medical Council's restrictions on advertising created an unnecessary and unreasonable restraint of trade and whether the powers conferred on the council by the Medical Act 1983 ought to be narrowly construed so as to avoid a conflict with Art. 10. Through the opinion of Lord Justice Gibson, the Court of Appeals declined to be bound always to assess the nature of the "pressing social need" under Art. 10. Once again, the key precedent was *R. v. Secretary of State for the Home Department, ex parte Brind* (1990, 1991) on the applicability of the ECHR in Britain, as we shall see below.

We come now to the last few cases that have referenced Art. 10. In *Dobson v. Hastings* (1991) we find another contempt case, this one involving a journalist who sought permission to see a closed file in a case of a public company that was in liquidation (in effect, a corporate bankruptcy proceeding). She was handed the file, along with a form, and was told that she must complete the form and get the permission of the registrar to see the file. When she spoke with the registrar, he told her she would have to make a formal request to see the file. She told him she already had it and had looked through it. The registrar then phoned the editor of the newspaper for which she worked. The editor understood that there was an ethical problem but did not get the impression that publication was forbidden by law, so an article was published. Eventually, a contempt proceeding was brought against the editor, and an injunction was sought against further publication. The judge in the Chancery Division again reviewed Art. 10 and the precedents of the European Court that require that restrictions on the freedom of the press must represent a pressing social need. This was rejected by the court, at least as an abstraction, while making the point that not all files in a proceeding like this one are in the public domain. The safeguard to the public was the procedure for applying to the registrar, who would consider the need for confidentiality, for permission to see the file. However, the court found neither the reporter nor the editor in contempt. The reporter having been given the file by mistake, and the editor not having been fully informed of the confidentiality of the file, neither of them was found to be in willful contempt of court.

We have previously seen the next case under our review of religious freedom under Art. 9. *R. v. Chief Metropolitan Stipendiary Magistrate, ex parte Choudhury* (1990) was the private prosecution brought by Choudhury against Salman Rushdie and Penguin Publishing Company for blasphemy. While the Queen's Bench Divisional Court had no difficulty in rejecting Choudhury's claim under Art. 9, it did acknowledge that one consequence of accepting this prosecution for blasphemy (had the court allowed it) might be the violation of both Art. 7 (by making an act criminal that was not at the time of commission) and Art. 10 (invasion of Rushdie's and Penguin's freedom of expression through publication of a book).

Derbyshire County Council v. Times Newspapers Ltd. (1993), which, you will recall, held that a public agency's right to sue for libel ought to be limited by common law freedom of expression, was featured as a key case in chapter 6 and need not be reviewed again here.

The most recent use of Art. 10 in *Rantzen v. Mirror Group Newspapers* (1993) was also reviewed in chapter 6. You may recall that there the Court of Appeal determined whether the punitive damages awarded by a jury in a defamatory libel case against a newspaper represented an excessive intrusion on freedom of the press. In the end the court accepted a statutory duty to review the verdict in that regard and it reduced the jury's award of punitive damages from £250,000 to £110,000 (*Rantzen*, 976).

The *Rantzen* case is most interesting for its extensive review of the precedents we have covered in this section, and in its efforts to trace both the common law and the precedents of the European court on freedom of expression— all the while repeating (with pride) that there are *no* important differences between the two traditions on this subject.

References to Art. 11

Only three cases have made significant references to Art. 11. The first, *United Kingdom Association of Professional Engineers (UKAPE) v. Advisory Conciliation and Arbitration Service (ACAS)* (1979, 1980), was brought against ACAS for a report that recommended against recognition of UKAPE as a collective bargaining agent. The Court of Appeal set aside the report on the ground that it had not made proper findings of fact as required by statute, but Lord Denning went on to suggest that ACAS had also failed to give proper weight to the rights of association of individual members of UKAPE. Once again, it was declared that the ECHR and the common law were alike in protecting individual rights:

> That article [Art. 11] only states a basic principle of English law. The common law has always recognised that everyone has the right to freedom of association; provided always that the association does not pursue

any unlawful end or use any unlawful means and is motivated, not by a desire to injure others, but by a desire to protect the interests of its members. . . .

. . . The European Convention has not yet been formally introduced into our statute law. . . . But the proposition in art 11 accurately states the common law; and for myself, I think that when Parliament enacts legislation on trade unions, it must be taken not to intend to contravene that basic right. (*UKAPE v. ACAS*, Court of Appeal, 486)

However, the House of Lords was of a different mind:

Finally, the point on the European Convention. I agree with Lord Denning MR that art 11 of the convention and common law recognise and protect the right of association, which in the present context includes the right to join a trade union. But it does not follow from the existence of the right that every trade union which can show it has members employed by a particular company or in a particular industry has a right to recognition for the purposes of collective bargaining. I would be surprised if either the convention or the common law could be interpreted as compelling so chaotic a conclusion. . . . Until such time as the Act is amended or the convention both becomes part of our law and is authoritatively interpreted in a way proposed by Lord Denning MR, the point is a bad one. (*UKAPE v. ACAS*, House of Lords, 622)

The next case referencing Art. 11 also went all the way to the House of Lords. *Cheall v. Association of Professional, Executive, Clerical and Computer Staff* (1981, 1983) involved a dispute between two trade unions over their acceptance for membership of one of the other's former members. When it was found that the acceptance had not been in compliance with rules that required the second union to seek the approval of the first, the second terminated Cheall's membership. "The Bridlington principles" applied to such interunion disputes through a Trades Union Congress (TUC) committee. Writing for the Queen's Bench, Justice Bingham noted the potential application of Art. 11 in the context of the European Court's decision in *Young, James and Webster v. United Kingdom* (1981). That case involved a closed shop and the dismissal of the three applicants when they refused to join a recognized trade union. The European Court upheld their freedom not to join under Art. 11, but *dicta* in the case also suggested an Art. 11 right to choose the union one joins. The other side of that point was that the right of choice had to exist in the real world in which a single union ordinarily was recognized as the collective bargaining agent for a particular trade in a particular company.

Lord Denning wrote another of his idiosyncratic opinions in the Court of Appeal:

I reach the conclusion that *art 11(1) of the convention is part of the law of England or at any rate the same as the law of England.* The courts of England should themselves give effect to it rather than put a citizen to all the trouble and expense of going to the Court of Human Rights. Our courts should themselves uphold the right of every man to join a trade union of his choice for the protection of his interests. (*Cheall*, 879; emphasis added)

This opinion was rejected outright in the words of Lord Diplock in the House of Lords:

Finally it was argued that . . . the Bridlington principles, which have been in operation since as long ago as 1939, are contrary to public policy, since they restrict the right of the individual to join and remain a member of a trade union of his choice; and that any attempt to give effect to any such restriction would, on application by the individuals affected by it, be prevented by the courts.

This supposed rule of public policy has, it is claimed, always formed part of the common law of England but it has now been reinforced by the accession of the United Kingdom to the European Convention. (*Cheall*, 1135)

This "reinforcement" by the ECHR was firmly rejected by Lord Diplock.

Finally, in *Taylor v. Co-operative Retail Services Ltd.* (1982) we found Lord Denning once again on his own, this time conforming to the inevitable by rejecting the application of the ECHR but making his point nonetheless. Taylor was a milkman who, with others, withdrew from one union and joined another. Thus the dispute was almost exactly like that in *Cheall* above, and a TUC disputes committee advised the second union to terminate the membership of Taylor and his associates. When Taylor refused to rejoin the first union, he was dismissed. To this Lord Denning responded, while agreeing to the dismissal of Taylor's appeal, that:

Mr. Taylor was subjected to a degree of compulsion which was contrary to the freedom guaranteed by the European Convention on Human Rights. He was dismissed by his employers because he refused to join a trade union which operated a "closed shop." He cannot recover any compensation from his employers under English law because, under the [Trade Union] Acts of 1974 and 1976, his dismissal is to be regarded as fair. But those Acts themselves are inconsistent with the freedom guaranteed by the European Convention. The United Kingdom Government is responsible for passing those Acts and should pay him compensation. He can recover it by applying to the European Court of Human Rights. But I see no reason why his employers should pay him compensation. They only did what the trade unions compelled them to do. He cannot sue the trade unions. They are immune from suit. This means that the appeal must be dismissed. He cannot recover any compensation in these courts. *But, if he applies to the European Court of Human Rights, he may in the long run—and I am afraid it may be a long run—obtain compensation there. So in the end justice may be done. But not here.* (*Taylor,* 610; emphasis added)

References on Applicability of the Convention

Probably the discussions found in the opinions of English courts regarding the domestic applicability of the ECHR are the most important and serve best to illustrate the views of various judges regarding the ECHR. So this indeed is a case of being last but not least, as we shall see.

One of the most important early opinions on the applicability of the ECHR in the United Kingdom was that of the Master of the Rolls Lord Denning in *R. v. Home Secretary, ex parte Bhajan Singh* (1975). Bhajan Singh was an Indian national, illegally in Britain, who sought to marry before being deported. He claimed the right to marry under Art. 12 of the ECHR.

In considering the application of Art. 12 to Bhajan Singh's claim, Lord Denning referred to his own words in a previously unreported decision. There he had conceded that British courts ought to take the ECHR into account "whenever interpreting a statute which affects the rights and liberties of an individual." He also was willing to assume that the Crown would do nothing that would conflict with its treaty obligations, so that British courts ought to construe statutes "so as to be in conformity with a convention and not against it" (*Bhajan Singh,* 1083).

But Lord Denning then retracted one sentence of his previous unreported decision. While previously he had said that he might be inclined to hold an act of Parliament invalid if it conflicted with a convention, now he said that there were many cases in which it had been held that a treaty does not become part of "English law except and insofar as it is made to do so by Parliament." Therefore, "[if] an Act of Parliament contained any provisions contrary to the convention, the Act of Parliament must prevail" (*Bhajan Singh,* 1083).

Still, Lord Denning also commented that

immigration officers and the Secretary of State in exercising their duties ought to bear in mind the principles stated in the convention. They ought, consciously or subconsciously, to have regard to the principles in it—because, after all, the principles stated in the convention are only a statement of the principles of fair dealing; and it is their duty to act fairly. (*Bhajan Singh*, 1083)

In the meantime Lord Denning's opinion in *Bhajan Singh* was cited with approval by the Immigration Appeal Tribunal in *Mistry v. The Entry Clearance Officer, Bombay* (1975), although the tribunal followed the rule that nothing in the ECHR guaranteed the right to enter and reside in a particular country.

But in *R. v. Chief Immigration Officer, Heathrow Airport and another, ex parte Salamat Bibi* (1976), Lord Denning expressly rejected his previous words and said instead that immigration officers "cannot be expected to know or to apply the ECHR. They must go simply by the immigration rule laid down by the Secretary of State and not by the Convention" (*Salamat Bibi*, 847).

Lord Justice Roskill's opinion in the *Salamat Bibi* case concurred with Denning's several retractions and also expressly disavowed Lord Scarman's even more generous appreciation of the application of the ECHR. In *R. v. Secretary of State for Home Affairs, ex parte Phansopkar* (1975), Lord Scarman had said that it was "now the duty of our public authorities in administering the law . . . and of our courts in interpreting and applying the law . . . to have regard" for the ECHR (*Phansopkar*, 511). Scarman went on to note that British courts could not "defy or disregard clear unequivocal provisions" in statutes, so his notion of having "regard" for the ECHR was that it was possible only when two competing interpretations are "reasonably open to the Court," a point he made clearly in his opinion in *Pan-American World Airways v. Department of Trade* (1975). But even that was too much for Lord Justice Roskill, who was careful to brand any broad implication in Scarman's language as mere dicta.

The narrower interpretation eventually preferred by Denning and Roskill has ever since been the established law on applicability of the ECHR, although Denning himself has been quite inconsistent.

In 1987 in *R. v. Immigration Appeal Tribunal, ex parte Chundawadra*, an opinion of Justice Taylor clearly put the ECHR at arm's length in affirming that the home secretary was not bound to take into account the provisions of Art. 8 requiring respect for family life in the case of a man who was to be deported to Tanzania, after eight years' residence in Britain (from the age of 18), because of his conviction of a serious drug offense—despite his admittedly strong family ties in Britain to his parents, his wife, and his daughter. Thus the current majority view is that the only possible application of the ECHR is when there is some ambiguity in a British statute, or some uncertainty in the common law, in which event the ECHR may be used by a British court as an aid to resolve the ambiguity or uncertainty and avoid a conflict. Otherwise, British litigants must seek their remedy under the ECHR in Strasbourg. Even so, the opinions and outcomes have not always been consistent, especially in Art. 10 cases.

Among many other decisions, the recent opinion of Lord Bridge in *R. v. Home Secretary, ex parte Brind* (1991) broadly affirms the narrow view and goes on to embellish and fortify the point:

> Hence it is submitted, when a statute confers upon an administrative authority a discretion capable of being exercised in a way which infringes any basic human right protected by the convention, it may similarly be presumed that the legislative intention was that the discretion should be exercised within the limitation which the convention imposes. I confess that I found considerable persuasive force in this submission. But in the end I have been convinced that the logic of it is flawed. When confronted with a simple choice between two possible interpretations of some specific statutory provision, the presumption whereby the courts prefer that which avoids conflict between our domestic legislation and our international treaty obligations is a mere canon of construction which involves no importation of international law into the domestic field. But where Parliament has conferred on the executive an administrative discretion without indicating the precise limits within which it must be exercised, to presume that it must be exercised within convention limits would be to go far beyond the resolution of ambiguity. It would be to impute to Parliament an intention not only that the executive should exercise the discretion in conformity with the Convention, but also that the domestic courts should enforce that conformity by the importation into domestic administrative law of the text of the convention and the jurisprudence of the European Court of Human Rights in the interpretation and application of it. . . . When Parliament has been content for so long to leave those who complain that their convention rights have been infringed to seek their remedy in Strasbourg, it would be surprising suddenly to find that the judiciary had, without Parliament's aid, the means to incorporate the convention into such an important area of domestic law and I cannot escape the conclusion that this would be a judicial usurpation of the legislative function. (*Brind*, House of Lords, 723)

Brind clearly is the most important recent precedent on applicability, and it represents the most restrictive view, so far, on the domestic application of the ECHR.

CONCLUSION

A few clear patterns emerge from this section-by-section review of references to the ECHR. The most important pattern is that English courts have struggled—from almost their earliest references to the ECHR (in 1974) to their most recent—to find some basis for upholding an asserted right under English law, rather than under the ECHR. Note the following examples and their sequence:

1975 Respect for family rights under Magna Carta, rather than under Art. 8 (*R. v. Home Secretary, ex parte Phansopkar*).

1979 Common law protection of freedom of association, rather than under Art. 11 (*United Kingdom Association of Professional Engineers and another v. Advisory Conciliation and Arbitration Service*).

1979 Common law protection of freedom of expression, rather than under Art. 10 (*Associated Newspapers Group Ltd. and Others v. Wade*).

1982 Common law right of access to courts, rather than under Art. 5 (*Raymond v. Honey*).

1985 Common law protection of freedom of expression, rather than under Art. 10 (*Wheeler and Others v. Leicester City Council*).

1988 Common law right to counsel, rather than under Art. 6 (*Hone v. Maze Prison Board of Visitors*).

1991 Common law restrictions on prior restraints, rather than under Art. 10 (*Derbyshire County Council v. Times Newspapers Ltd. and Others*).

1993 Presumption against retrospective application of legislation, rather than under Art. 7—overruled, however, by the House of Lords (*L'Office Cherifien des Phosphates and another v. Yamashita-Shinnihon Steamship Co. Ltd.*, Court of Appeal).

1993 Respect for privacy under public policy considerations, rather than under Art. 8 (*R. v. Brown and Other Appeals*).

1993 Common law freedom of expression, rather than under Art. 10 (*Rantzen v. Mirror Group Newspapers Ltd. and Others*).

And when English courts have not found it possible to reconcile the common law and the protections accorded by the ECHR, they sometimes note that the solution is for Parliament, rather than the courts (see *Malone v. Commissioner of Police of the Metropolis* [No. 2] [1979] and *M v. H and Others* [1988]).

Occasionally judicial opinions contain expressions approaching hostility to the breadth, inclusiveness, and intrusiveness of a rights document like the ECHR (see *R. v. Chief Immigration Officer, Heathrow Airport and another, ex parte Salamat Bibi* [1976]). The most important recent statement of the House of Lords on the domestic applicability of the ECHR in *Brind* certainly is not particularly friendly or open to the ECHR.

The exceptions to these findings are most often found in the opinions of Lord Scarman, while the various opinions of Lord Denning are notable for their inconsistency.

The implications of these findings, as well as the lessons to be gleaned from the previous six chapters, are the subject of the next chapter.

8

<hr>

A Charter of Rights for the United Kingdom?

At the beginning of this book, I proposed to review in depth four subjects of human rights violations by the United Kingdom drawn from its forty-one violations of the ECHR—from the first violation in the *Golder* case in 1975 through the case of *Benham v. United Kingdom* in June 1996. The four topics were selected for the frequency of their violations and for their intrinsic importance and interest as human rights issues. The issues involved in the prevention of terrorism in Northern Ireland, in the operation of British prisons, in British immigration and citizenship policy, and in freedom of expression (freedom of the press) have been considered at some length. However, table 8.1 presents the entire array of U.K. violations. Nearly half of the forty-one violations represented in table 8.1 are subsumed under the four topics already presented in chapters 3–6. The only other specific topics in table 8.1 represented by more than a single case are various parents' rights cases (involving several different ECHR articles), represented by eight cases, and corporal punishment, which was involved in two cases, *Tyrer* and *Campbell and Cosans.* Art. 8 (respect for private and family life, home, and correspondence) was also involved in several cases other than those involving prisoners' correspondence, and several cases involved due process rights under Art. 5 or 6, albeit in different settings.

Despite our common expectations about the strength of the liberal tradition of the British political system, table 8.1 reveals the various circumstances under which the United Kingdom became the most frequent violator of the ECHR from 1959 through 1989, the first thirty years of the European Court of Human Rights, and its eighteen additional violations since 1989.

Lest this book seem too critical of the human rights shortcomings of the United Kingdom at the European Court and seriously myopic with respect to those of the United States, we should note that in the list of cases in table 8.1 involving issues other than those covered in our previous chapters, there are at least three instances of decisions by the European Court of Human Rights that are more supportive of the human rights issues raised there than are comparable decisions of the Supreme Court of the United States. The European Court's decision in the *Dudgeon* case (1981) encompassed homosexual conduct of consenting adults in Northern Ireland within the right of privacy pro

Table 8.1. United Kingdom's violations of the European Convention of Human Rights through June 1996

Case name	Citation Series A	Subject	Decision date	Breach
1. *Golder*	18	prisoners' rights	2/75	Art. 6,8
2. *Ireland v. U.K.* [a]	25	terrorism	1/78	Art. 3[a]
3. *Tyrer* [b]	26	corporal punishment	4/78	Art. 3
4. *Sunday Times*	30	press freedom	4/79	Art. 10
5. *Young, James & Webster*	44	freedom of association	8/81	Art. 11
6. *Dudgeon*	45	homosexuality, privacy rights	10/81	Art. 8
7. *X vs. U.K.*	46	mental illness	11/81	Art. 5.4
8. *Campbell and Cosans*	48	parents' rights of conscience	2/82	Protocol 1, Art. 2
9. *Silver and others*	61	prisoners' rights	3/83	Art. 6.1, 8, 13
10. *Campbell and Fell*	80	prisoners' rights	6/84	Art. 6, 8, 13
11. *Malone*	82	wiretapping	8/84	Art. 8
12. *Abdulaziz, Cabales and Balkandali*	94	immigration, gender discrimination	5/85	Art. 13, 8w/14
13. *Gillow* [c]	109	residential qualifications	11/86	Art. 8
14. *Weeks*	114	prisoners' rights due process	7/87	Art. 5.4
15–19. *O, H, W, B, and R* [d]	120	parents' rights due process	7/87	Art. 6.1, 8
20. *Boyle and Rice*	131	prisoners' rights	4/88	Art. 8
21. *Brogan and others*	145B	terrorism	11/88	Art. 5.3, 5.5
22. *Gaskin*	160	access to personal records	7/89	Art. 8
23. *Soering*	161	extradition/ murder charge	7/89	Art. 3
24. *Granger*	174	prisoners' rights	3/90	Art. 6.1, 6.3c
25. *Fox, Campbell and Hartley*	182	terrorism	8/90	Art. 5.1, 5.5
26. *McCallum*	183	prisoners' rights	8/90	Art. 8

27. *Thynne, Wilson and Gunnell*	190A	prisoners' rights	10/90	Art. 5.4, 5.5
28. *The Observer and The Guardian*	216	press freedom	11/91	Art. 10
29. *Sunday Times (No. 2)*	217	press freedom	11/91	Art. 10
30. *Campbell*	233	prisoners' rights	3/92	Art. 8
31. *Darnell*	272	delay, civil proceedings	10/93	Art. 6.1
32. *Boner*	300B	right to counsel	10/94	Art. 6.3c
33. *Maxwell*	300C	right to counsel	10/94	Art. 6.3c
34. *Welch*	307A	parents' rights	2/95	Art. 7.1
35. *McMichael*	308	parents' rights	2/95	Art. 6.1, 8
36. *Tolstoy Miloslavsky*	323	freedom of expression	7/95	Art. 10
37. *McCann and Others*	324	right to life	9/95	Art. 2
38. *John Murray*	e	terrorism	2/96	Art. 6.1, 6.3c
39. *Hussain*	e	due process	2/96	Art. 5.4
40. *Goodwin*	e	press freedom	3/96	Art. 10
41. *Benham*	e	right to counsel	6/96	Art. 6.1, 6.3c

a. Violations of Articles 5 and 6 subject to derogation under Article 15.

b. Case from the Isle of Man.

c. Case from Guernsey.

d. These are counted as separate cases because they are reported separately.

e. Official Series A version not yet published.

tected by Art. 8, while the U.S. Supreme Court in *Bowers v. Hardwick* (1986) sustained the criminalization of such conduct against a privacy claim. The conclusion of the European Court in *Campbell and Cosans* that parents had the right to object to the corporal punishment of their children by school officials was not matched with equal concern by the U.S. Supreme Court's ruling in *Ingraham v. Wright* (1977), which supported the continuation of corporal punishment in American public schools. And recent developments in American public education have brought "zero tolerance" of student misconduct, in which due process often has been relegated to the back burner. The European Court's judgment in the *Soering* case (1989) expressed grave reservations about the process (especially the lengthy appeals) through which capital punishment is administered in the State of Virginia, while the majority of the U.S. Supreme Court in *Gregg v. Georgia* (1976) and subsequent "guided discretion" decisions usually has not exhibited such sensitivity to the "death row phenomenon." To be sure, the U.S. Supreme Court has been concerned to shorten the time between the death sentence and the imposition of that punishment, but the concerns of the court's majority have had more to do with striving to make the death penalty a more effective deterrent than with the conditions of inmates on death row or the psychological toll involved in the death row phenomenon.

What inferences should be drawn from the list of violations contained in table 8.1? Some judges and scholars have concluded from the record of such violations that Britain needs a bill of rights, whether accomplished through the adoption of the ECHR by statute for domestic application or through a rights document developed specifically for the purpose. But that is by no means a unanimous conclusion.

Some observers have concluded that the ECHR has already had a great impact on the United Kingdom. Note, for example, these words from an editorial that recently launched a new law review:

> The influence of the Convention on the law of the United Kingdom is nowadays undeniable. A growing list of remedial statutes owe their origins directly to decisions of the European Court of Human Rights. The Law Commission has begun to use conformity with the Convention as one of its key criteria for assessing current and proposed legislation. And the European Court of Justice has held that the Convention is an implicit part of Community law. Within the sphere of Community competence at least, the Convention now has a form of direct applicability in the domestic courts of this country. ("Editorial," *European Human Rights Law Review* 1995, 1)

The editorial goes on to claim that in the past two or three years the most important development has been in the impact that the ECHR has had on the common law. To some extent that is the same development that we noted in chapter 6 in our review of the *Derbyshire County Council* case (1992), and the editorial cites that case as one example. At the end of chapter 7, however, we showed how English courts have attempted to find human rights under the common law, rather than under the ECHR. Overall, the editorial probably claims too much for the impact of the ECHR, given the persistent application of *Wednesbury* principles and the precedent of *R. v. Home Secretary, ex parte Brind* (1990), but no doubt change is in the wind. It is a good question whether change will come case by case, by the statutory adoption of the ECHR as part of U.K. domestic law, or by the adoption of a rights document.

Perhaps the most telling criticism by those who oppose the adoption of a rights document for the United Kingdom is that the presence of a rights document, and the power of courts to enforce it, has not proven to be a consistent and effective remedy in the United States. That trenchant criticism deserves a serious response, but necessarily a brief one within the context of this book.

We should begin by admitting that there have been some long-standing and conspicuous failures in American constitutional history, and by remembering that the vigilant protection of civil rights and liberties by the Supreme Court of the United States has mostly been accomplished within the past sixty years.

THE EFFICACY OF JUDICIAL REVIEW IN THE UNITED STATES

No doubt the most egregious failure of American constitutional law was the legally constituted racial segregation in the United States that thrived (beginning in the last quarter of the nineteenth century) despite the ratification of the Fourteenth Amendment in 1868. *De jure* segregation endured until the decision in *Brown v. Board of Education* (1954), and segregationists fought a determined retreat after 1954. Racism has been such a central and enduring feature of American society that it deserves a more complete treatment than can be given here (see Jackson 1992). Still, there certainly is sufficient merit in the argument that constitutional judicial review in the U.S. has provided inadequate protection for human rights in other instances for it to deserve serious analysis. One way to do that is through a brief comparative analysis; that is, to examine the issues presented in chapters 3 through 6 of this book to see what sort of constitutional protection has been afforded in the U.S. in comparable situations. Of course, this also could be the subject of a separate book (or, indeed, of several books). This review will offer only a few key examples.

Violence, "Terrorism," and Threats to National Security

What is the best U.S. example to compare with Britain's efforts to control political terrorism in Northern Ireland? We should set aside the depredations suffered both by American settlers and by various Indian tribes and the related Indian wars in the West as suitable examples, for they had no constitutional significance, which is only to say that the Supreme Court of the United States did not attempt to bring the subject under the protection of the Bill of Rights. We should also set aside the experience of the American Civil War, for the federal courts were not a key forum for judging policies during that conflict and the Supreme Court of the United States enforced no important constitutional constraints over executive war powers. Indeed, the Supreme Court's decision in *Dred Scott v. Sanford* (1856) had the effect of seriously eroding its legitimacy—and that of lower federal courts—as constitutional arbiters during that conflict. The Supreme Court did make a modest effort in *ex parte Milligan* (1866), but only after the war was concluded. Of course it can and perhaps should be argued that the absence of any important constitutional constraints imposed by the Supreme Court on these two occasions is itself excellent evidence that the Supreme Court has not been very effective as a protector of human rights. One answer to that is that such criticism is anachronistic, but a better conclusion is simply to acknowledge the point and meld it with later evidence that tends to point in the same direction, as we shall see.

Probably the best example of federal courts being confronted with demands for enforcement of policies designed for a perceived threat to national security is offered by the policies of the federal government toward persons of Japanese ancestry during World War II. The leading cases are *Hirabayashi v. U.S.* (1943), *Korematsu v. U.S* (1944), and *ex parte Endo* (1944), which, together, represent a signal failure of due process.

Hirabayashi involved the first and, relatively speaking, least intrusive regulation, a curfew order applied to persons of Japanese ancestry on the West Coast shortly after the attack on Pearl Harbor. Of course, the order was categorical—as were all the other orders directed toward persons of Japanese ancestry—no assessment of any individual's prospect of actually engaging in espionage or sabotage was attempted. Instead, the orders were based on a racial category, allied with a judgment of military necessity and intended to prevent espionage and sabotage in the event of an invasion. Despite the racial category, the Supreme Court upheld Hirabayashi's conviction for violating the curfew, the majority admitting that "We cannot say that the war-making branches of the Government did not have grounds for believing that in a critical hour such persons could not readily be isolated and separately dealt with, and constituted a menace to the national defense and safety, which demanded that prompt and adequate measures be taken to guard against it" (*Hirabayashi,* 99).

Korematsu was the next step. It involved an order of "temporary exclusion" from the West Coast of persons of Japanese ancestry, but those so excluded were usually interned in "relocation centers," and Korematsu had appealed his conviction for refusing to leave his home. This time Justice Black, a justice usually of impeccable rectitude on matters of civil rights and liberties, wrote for the court's majority in upholding the discretion of military authorities over civilians in a time of perceived emergency:

> We uphold the exclusion order as of the time it was made and when the petitioner violated it. [H]ardships are part of war, and war is an aggregation of hardships. . . . Citizenship has its responsibilities as well as its privileges, and in time of war the burden is always heavier. Compulsory exclusion of large groups of citizens from their homes, except under the direst emergency and peril is inconsistent with our basic governmental institutions. But when under conditions of modern warfare our shores are threatened by hostile forces, the power to protect must be commensurate with the threatened danger. (*Korematsu,* 219–20)

Thus, the court's majority upheld the exclusion of 112,000 persons of Japanese ancestry, including more than 70,000 native-born American citizens (Dembitz 1945, 175). The dissents of three justices, but especially that of Mr. Justice Jackson (later chief U.S. prosecutor at the Nuremberg trial of leading Nazis), were strong: "I should hold," Jackson wrote, "that a *civil court* cannot be made to enforce an order which violates constitutional limitations *even if it is a reasonable exercise of military authority*" (*Korematsu,* 247; emphasis added).

It was not until *ex parte Endo,* decided the same day as *Korematsu,* that the Supreme Court unanimously denied that military authorities had any power to continue to detain American citizens of Japanese ancestry, such as Mitsue Endo, whose loyalty to the United States had been conceded by those same authorities. So the United States has indeed had its equivalent of the *Liversidge* and *Greene* cases, even if it has not had anything like the conflict over Northern Ireland—at least not since the American Civil War. Indeed, the American practice in World War II may have been worse than Britain's, since the American exclusion and internment was conceded by civilian authorities to military authorities, while Britain was careful to use civilian authority over civilians (Dembitz 1945, 179). The key point, however, is that the Bill of Rights offered no effective protection for citizens against initial exclusion and internment, even though Mitsue Endo eventually secured her freedom. Nonetheless, to acknowledge a signal failure of constitutional due process during a perceived World War II emergency is not to accept the inevitability of failure in all emergencies. It can of course be argued that rules of law and the institutions that enforce them are ill equipped to deal with the conduct of conflicts that are resolved through military force. But to concede the inevitability of failure or defeat is to give up too much. When and under what circumstances judges ought to be prepared to intervene to ensure due process of law—and what the consequences may be—are not easy questions, as we have seen in chapter 3.

Due Process and Prisons

In the 1960s American federal judges began to intervene in the administration of state prisons and jails, deriving their authority from the due process clause of the Fourteenth Amendment. The "criminal due process revolution" that had begun symbolically with the extension of exclusionary rule protection to the states in *Mapp v. Ohio* (1961) soon entered other contexts, for example, legislative apportionment in *Baker v. Carr* (1962), welfare policy in *Shapiro v. Thompson* (1969), and public schools in *Tinker v. Des Moines* (1969). Prisons became another context for federal enforcement of due process. Probably the best example of American prison litigation is *Ruiz v. Estelle*, filed in 1972 and practically concluded in 1986.

The *Ruiz* case went to trial in 1978, and in 1980 federal district judge William Justice issued a 248-page memorandum opinion detailing the changes he would require in the way Texas ran its state prison system. Judge Justice's central finding that the system's treatment of inmates was cruel and unusual punishment under the Eighth and Fourteenth Amendments was upheld by the 5th Circuit Court in 1982. The crucial point for this review was the willingness of a federal court to intervene in the day-to-day prison regime. Who indeed ought to have final authority over public prisons?

> The structure of authority frequently is determined by who has the last say in any given dispute. In the years before active court intervention, prison administrators were for all intents and purposes the court of last resort. When the federal courts began to intervene and rule on the legitimacy of prison conditions, the balance of authority shifted. Court intrusion means there was another ear to listen and other voices to be heard. By definition, this disrupted the existing equilibrium of legitimate authority. (Eklund-Olson and Martin 1990, 83)

Again, recognizing a pattern is not necessarily to approve it, and scholars have been bitterly divided over the propriety and efficacy of this instance of judicial intervention. For example, one observation has been that "Critics . . . maintain that court orders have made prisons and jails more unruly and difficult to manage and fostered violence among inmates" (Feeley and Hanson 1990, 16). Still even the most skeptical critics of judicial intervention agree that "the impact of judicial intervention into prisons and jails over the last two decades has been positive—a qualified success, but a success just the same" (Dilulio 1990, 291). However, the purpose of this review is neither to approve nor disapprove of such intervention but, rather, to admit that we are, at the least, uncertain as to when and to what extent judges ought to intervene in prison administration, and we usually are in the dark as to the probable consequences of intervention.

Nationality and Alienage

The treatment of aliens in American constitutional law has had a long history. One of the early decisions was that in *Yick Wo v. Hopkins* (1886), when it was written that the equal protection of law protected by the Fourteenth Amendment was not confined to the protection of citizens and that its provisions were "universal in their application." A more recent view was expressed in *Graham v. Richardson* (1971), which struck down state laws that denied welfare benefits to resident aliens. The key language in that case seemed to describe alienage as a *suspect classification,* which, like a racial category, is "inherently suspect and subject to close judicial scrutiny." However, since the *Graham* decision the court has vacillated, sometimes moving away from viewing alienage as a suspect classification. In *Foley v. Connelie* (1978) the court, led by then Chief Justice Warren Burger, suggested that the state need only show some rational justification for a policy that treated aliens differently than citizens when a state acted on matters "firmly within [its] constitutional prerogative." Yet that language was belied by Mr. Justice Brennan's majority opinion in *Toll v. Moreno* (1982), holding that the supremacy clause prevented states from imposing burdens on aliens beyond those contemplated by Congress.

Probably the most famous alienage decision was that of *Plyler v. Doe* in 1982. Both Texas state law and the policies of certain local school districts denied access to free public education to children of undocumented illegal aliens. The Supreme Court held five to four that even illegal aliens were protected by the Fourteenth Amendment. Justice Brennan wrote for the majority that, while neither undocumented aliens nor their children could be treated under the suspect classification rule, and while public education is not a constitutionally guaranteed right, Texas policy nonetheless had "impose[d] a lifetime hardship on a discrete class of children not accountable for their disabling status" (*Plyler,* 223). In the majority's opinion the hardship of the children was real and enduring, but Texas had achieved no substantial state interest to offset this hardship.

While the Fourteenth Amendment clearly has afforded some protection even to illegal aliens, this is not to suggest that the position of aliens has forever been secured in the U.S. The enactment of Proposition 187 (which denies a number of public benefits and programs to illegal aliens who reside in the state) in California in November 1994 is testimony that such conflicts may be fought generation after generation, and late in 1994, the new Republican majority in Congress was offering to cut welfare costs by denying benefits to aliens *lawfully* in the country, possibly in direct violation of the precedent in *Graham v. Richardson* (1971). Eventually these issues will be determined by a Supreme Court which, at present, retains only one member from the key alienage decisions made in the 1970s and early 1980s. So once again we must concede the point that constitutional rights adjudication in the U.S. has not always—and certainly not easily—provided secure protection to aliens. And there are few, if any, constant guarantees for the future.

Freedom of the Press

Unlike the other topics in this brief review, the First Amendment's protection for freedom of the press has been cited in the judgments of the House of Lords regarding the protection of freedom of the press in the United Kingdom. For example, as we saw at length in chapter 6, the U.S. Supreme Court's decision in *New York Times v. Sullivan* (1964) was explicitly relied on by the House of Lords in *Derbyshire County Council v. Times Newspapers* (1993). It is clear that First Amendment protection for freedom of the press offers the best example for this review of an instance in which U.S. constitutional law affords greater protection than does the common law of England. To a large extent that is due to the primacy given the First Amendment by the Supreme Court in the last sixty years or so. And any comparison of the Pentagon Papers case (*New York Times v. U.S.*, 1971) with the *Spycatcher* cases will indicate that both the First Amendment and the presumption against prior restraints that has obtained in the U.S., at least since the decision in *Near v. Minnesota* in 1931, afford a level of protection for freedom of the press that is not often matched in the United Kingdom. Whether the U.S. position is the better one is, of course, a matter of some dispute. It probably is the case that the First Amendment affords greater protection for freedom of expression than does any other rights document, as interpreted through judicial review by any other national or international court. But there are those who say that the U.S. sometimes has gone beyond freedom to license. See, for example, the words of Lord Ackner in the *Spycatcher* case: "There the [U.S.] courts, by virtue of the First Amendment, are, I understand, powerless to control the press. Fortunately, the press in this country is, as yet, not above the law, although like some other powerful organisations they would like that to be so, that is until they require the law's protection" (*Attorney General v. Guardian Newspapers Ltd. and Others*, House of Lords, 1987, 363). Yet there are also those who admire and envy the accomplishments of the First Amendment and the Supreme Court of the United States in protecting freedom of expression (Gardner 1994, 222). Such assessments, pro or con, are easy to make, but more difficult to justify.

Adding to the difficulty of comparing the human rights records of the United States and the United Kingdom, even in a few examples like those above, are the difficulties in comparing the record of the United Kingdom before the European Court with those of other Western European countries. For example, it *may be* the case that the United Kingdom is a country sufficiently open to outside scrutiny to make it possible for human rights cases to be brought before the European Commission and Court of Human Rights in Strasbourg, while another country may exercise greater control over access to information, making an appeal to Strasbourg more difficult. A good illustration of that point can be found in the reports of the several official U.K. commissions that were charged with examining the conduct of the prevention of terrorism program in Northern Ireland. Judging from the references made by the European Court, the factual findings contained in those reports must have contributed significantly to the European Court's ruling in *Ireland v. United Kingdom*. In the end, we must admit that the data do not exist through which we can make a valid evaluation of the relative protection of human rights afforded by the countries that are members of the Council of Europe. We can, however, seek to explain why the United Kingdom has been in violation of the ECHR forty-one times through June 1996.

SOME GENERALIZATIONS ABOUT POWER AND DISCRETION

The key failings revealed by the various violations by the United Kingdom of the ECHR are likely to be found in the largely unreviewable discretion of its executive officials. When untrammeled discretion is coupled with an administrative culture that encourages insiders and prefers the exclusion of outsiders, while vigilantly draping their work in a shroud of secrecy, there is created a climate in which human rights abuses are predictable. It was suggested in chapter 1 of this book that Kenneth Culp Davis's book *Discretionary Justice* (1971) offered a useful perspective for evaluating the question of why the United Kingdom has been so frequently in violation of the ECHR. Davis was chiefly concerned with the problem of unreviewable and unaccountable discretion. He began his book by proposing a revision to the aphorism inscribed on the pediment of the Department of Justice building in Washington: "Where law ends tyranny begins." Davis's revision was: "Where law ends, discretion begins," and to that he added the amplification that "the exercise of discretion may mean either beneficence or tyranny, either justice or injustice, either reasonableness or arbitrariness" (Davis 1971, 3). He defined discretion as the freedom to make a choice among alternative courses of action, presumably without serious constraints. Thus elaborated, his revised aphorism is apt and pertinent to Britain's recurrent problems with the ECHR, for the purpose of his book was to explore what might be done to minimize injustice from the exercise of discretionary power. Let the point be made very clearly: executive officials in the United Kingdom exercise a great deal of unreviewable and unaccountable discretion.

Davis's solution for this circumstance (when he observed it in the United States) was to propose that "we should eliminate much unnecessary discretionary power and that we should do much more than we have been doing to confine, to structure and to check necessary discretionary power" (Davis 1971, 4). The elimination of discretionary power, he acknowledged, is both impossible and undesirable, but confining, structuring, and checking discretion are feasible and desirable goals.

Confining discretion, according to Davis, means fixing boundaries and keeping discretion within them, and this is accomplished chiefly through administrative rule-making power: "administrators must strive to do as much as they reasonably can to develop and make known the needed confinements of discretionary power through standards, principles and rules" (Davis 1971, 59).

The structuring of discretionary power involves the use of "open plans, open policy statements, open rules, open findings, open reasons, open precedents and fair informal procedure," and here Davis makes another important point:

> The reason for repeating the word "open" is a powerful one: Openness is the natural enemy of arbitrariness and a natural ally in the fight against injustice. We should enlist it much more than we do. When plans and policies and rules are kept secret, as through confidential instructions to staffs, private parties are prevented from checking arbitrary or unintended departures from them. Findings are a better protection against arbitrariness if affected parties can point to needed corrections. Reasoned opinions pull toward evenhanded justice but the pull is stronger if the opinions are out in the open. (Davis 1971, 98)

The U.K.'s formulation and enforcement of prison rules come to mind.

Checking discretion "includes both administrative and judicial supervision and review" (Davis 1971, 55). The argument was made in chapter 1 that accountability of executive power to the popular sovereignty represented by the British Parliament has long been a myth—presumably a reassuring one to some and an illusion to others. It has become a myth chiefly because of the evolution of the electoral system, the rise of disciplined political parties and the consequent concentration of power in the leaders of the governing party in the United Kingdom. So the "result of this historical trend is a Parliament that for most of the time now exists to do the executive's bidding" (Ewing and Gearty 1990, 4–5). This is what Lord Halisham described as an "elective dictatorship," and the election of this dictatorship may be contingent on less than a majority of the popular votes cast in a general election. The Conservative victory in 1979 that made Margaret Thatcher prime minister rested on 43.9 percent of the popular vote, given Britain's "first past the post electoral system."

We probably should note—as Davis does—that legislative casework may sometimes be important in helping to ensure a more responsible government. He, of course, was referring to congressional casework in the U.S., but the point should be noted for Britain as well. Still, the efforts of some representatives on behalf of individual constituents (sometimes through referrals to the office of the parliamentary ombudsman) are likely to benefit only the few who somehow have commanded the attention of a representative or his or her aide. It also is the case that parliamentary scrutiny through committee hearings is both recent and ineffectual in the United Kingdom relative to the United States. The parliamentary select committee system dates only from 1979, and select committees do not have power over pending legislative proposals.

Even given the relatively greater oversight and power of Congress over broad policy decisions, Davis proposed that there be established a system of "administrative appeals tribunals" that would review federal administrative actions "for which judicial review is now provided either by statute or by common law remedy but which as a practical matter [are] unreviewable because litigation expense equals or exceeds the interests at stake" (Davis 1971, 156–57). Of course, his proposal borrows from the several European countries that have a separate administrative review system—he mentioned West Germany—in which citizens can challenge the abuse of discretionary administrative actions. And West Germany's constitutional court also has the authority to check executive authority through its power of constitutional judicial review. But there are two points that we should note concerning the relevancy and efficacy of such a solution for the United Kingdom. The first is to remember once again that there is no rights document in the U.K., and, of course, no courts with power of constitutional judicial review as it is known in the United States. The second is while there is a judicial review procedure in the United Kingdom, and while it has the same name as in the United States and elsewhere, its content is quite different.

Current U.K. judicial review practice dates largely from reforms made in 1977. As the term is used in the United Kingdom, "judicial review refers to the process by which those aggrieved by actions of public authorities may challenge those authorities in the High Court on the grounds that they have (or will do so) abused (or exceeded) their legal powers" (Sunkin 1992, 145). This form of judicial review sounds very much like the administrative appeals tribunals suggested by Davis, but the British judicial review procedure is intended for legal rather than factual disputes. Applications for judicial review ordinarily involve questions of whether an administrative officer has acted within the scope of the authority delegated by statute and has followed prescribed procedures. Judicial review may also be used when an official acts in a grossly unreasonable way or abuses the "rules of natural justice" governing fair procedures (Griffith 1977, 125). Usually in judicial review cases officials either have authority, or they do not; they have followed prescribed procedures, or they have not. British judicial review procedure ordinarily is not available either for considering the adequacy of the evidence on which a decision has been predicated or for evaluating the factual grounds on which discretionary authority has been exercised. Despite that limitation, the judicial review procedure is relatively prompt, at least through the decision on application for leave to seek judicial review, and the costs of a judicial review application may be covered by legal aid.

Maurice Sunkin is a leading scholar on contemporary judicial review in the United Kingdom. Sunkin and his colleagues compiled and analyzed data on judicial review applications filed within calendar years 1987–89 and for the first quarter of 1991, and traced each filing through to decision. They found that the three largest categories for judicial review applications were in criminal cases and, on the civil side, in immigration and housing cases (which account for over half of all applications). Sunkin's major conclusions about judicial review were that:

> judicial review is used regularly in only a very few subject areas against a correspondingly narrow range of public agencies, by litigants advised by a small band of lawyers. Despite general impressions, judicial review litigation impinges only upon a tiny fraction of governmental decision making, vast tracts of which remain free from legal challenge and resulting judicial scrutiny. (Sunkin 1992, 143)

So it seems that while the British version of judicial review may be an approximation of Davis's administrative appeal tribunal, it has had limited scope and impact. And it is isolated as a checking procedure, given the absence of constitutional judicial review in the U.K.

In chapter 5's review of cases on immigration and nationality, we suggested that judicial accountability under *Wednesbury* principles usually would not be sufficient to determine whether actions of executive officials are in violation of the ECHR. Art. 13 of the ECHR requires that there be an effective domestic remedy for protecting the human rights set out in the ECHR, and when, for example, official actions are taken under the authority of the home secretary, *Wednesbury* principles provide that a U.K. judge exercising judicial review may set aside a home secretary's decision, but only when the decision is shown to be one that no reasonable home secretary could have made. In the case of *Associated Provincial Picture Houses, Ltd. v. Wednesbury Corp.* (1947, Court of Appeal, 682–83) the Court of Appeal defined the word unreasonable for the purpose of judicial review:

> Lawyers familiar with the phraseology commonly used in relation to exercise of statutory discretion often use the word "unreasonable" in a rather comprehensive sense. It has frequently been used as a general description of things that must not be done. For instance, a person entrusted with a discretion must, so to speak, direct himself properly in law. He must call his own attention to the matters which he is bound to consider. He must exclude from his consideration matters which are irrelevant to what he has to consider. If he does not obey those rules, he may truly be said, and often is said, to be acting "unreasonably." Similarly there may be something so absurd that no sensible person could ever dream that it lay within the powers of the authority.

This quote gives the same meaning of unreasonable as that enunciated by Lord Bridge in *R. v. Home Secretary, ex parte Brind* (1991), reviewed at length in chapter 7. In *Brind* the House of Lords held that it was not unreasonable for the home secretary to fail entirely to take the freedom of expression provision of Art. 10 of the ECHR into account in his decision to ban from public broadcasting in Britain the words of anyone "who supported or invited support of a terrorist organization" such as the IRA.

The problem with the limited scope of judicial review does not stop with Art. 13's right to an effective domestic remedy. The European Commission and Court often will reach a different conclusion from that of English judges because the Commission and Court, in applying the second paragraphs of Art. 8, 9, 10, 11, and 14, use the concept of "proportionality." Proportionality has a lower threshold than *Wednesbury* reasonableness. Proportionality is a recognized principle of European Union law and, in that context, is applied by English judges. In *Brind*, however, the House of Lords refused to apply proportionality to the exercise of administrative discretion.

We also saw in chapter 3 that, following the precedents of *Green v. Secretary of State for Home Affairs* (1941) and *Liversidge v. Anderson* (1941), the decisions in *Ex parte Lynch* (1980) and in *McKee v. Chief Constable for Northern Ireland* (1984) allowed a constable to effect an arrest based on subjective suspicion, with no requirement that the objective reasonableness of the suspicion be proven to a court. And in chapter 4 we saw that in the recent case of *R. v. Home Secretary, ex parte Chahal* (1993), Judge Potts said:

> [T]his court cannot judge the quality of, or the weight to be attached to, the evidence going to the risk to that national security posed by this applicant. The only person who can do that is the Secretary of State who has all the available information, and this court must accept his assessment of the extent of the risk. (*Chahal*, 380).

The key point is that British "[j]udicial review is concerned not with the decision, but with the decision making procedure" (*Chief Constable of the North Wales Police v. Evans*, 1980, 173–74).

Such examples should suffice to illustrate the limitations of judicial review in the United Kingdom. In their recent book, *In from the Cold: National Security and Parliamentary Democracy*, Lustgarten and Leigh (1994, 330–31) argue that contemporary British judges don't like to admit openly to the abdication of their potential power to the executive, so the judges play word games to disguise that reality. Officialdom's assertions of national security interests, supported by an affidavit avowing such reasons for executive action, usually will carry the day. This is especially true, when, as in almost all national security matters, the executive has exclusive control of relevant information. To compound that circumstance, British judges also may be fearful that official secrets may become public knowledge through judicial intervention. Lustgarten and Leigh also point out the long history of British courts having "a record of faithful trust in government motives," and in support of that observation they cite a comment by Lord Reading: "It is of course always to be assumed that the executive will act honestly and that its powers will be reasonably exercised" (1993, 332). This tradition indeed suggests that we should expect little executive accountability to the traditionally deferential British judiciary. Griffiths (1991, 153–54) quotes Lord Denning on this point:

> There is a conflict between the interests of national security on the one hand and the freedom of the individual on the other. The balance between these two is not for a court of law. It is for the home secretary. He is the person entrusted by Parliament with the task. In some parts of the world national security has on occasion been used as an excuse for all sorts of infringements of individual liberty. But not in England. Both during the wars and after them successive ministers have discharged their duties to the complete satisfaction of the people at large. . . . They have

never interfered with the liberty or the freedom of movement of any
individual except where it is absolutely necessary for the safety of the
state.

Surely nothing more needs to be said about the views of British judges. We
should note, however, that there are those who question the efficacy of Kenneth Davis's proposals to constrain administrative discretion through legal
processes. One of the most trenchant criticisms is contained in a chapter by
Nicola Lacey, "The Jurisprudence of Discretion: Escaping the Legal Paradigm,"
in Keith Hawkins's recent book, *The Uses of Discretion* (1992). Her overarching
concern is that the world view of lawyers and legal theorists may represent an
inappropriate or incomplete way of viewing administrative discretion. No doubt
that is a legitimate concern, but the point of this chapter is that discretion
ought to be reviewable by and accountable to *some independent authority*
who is charged with the application of human rights principles (such as those
in the ECHR) and who is separate from the structure that produced an original decision. Whether to accomplish that through administrative tribunals or
through common law courts, through domestic application of the ECHR or
through a new rights document, is a secondary question.

   In another important book, *Discretionary Powers: A Legal Study of Official Discretion*, D. J. Galligan suggests (1986, 227) that judicial review under
the *Wednesbury* standard can result either in judicial restraint or judicial
assertiveness, and he argues that British judges have become more assertive in
recent years. While that may appear to be so in some highly visible cases,
Sunkin's research reviewed earlier in this chapter does not support the conclusion that British judges have become highly assertive in their everyday
decisions across most policy arenas through their power of judicial review.
Nonetheless, Galligan does cite a number of examples (1986, 253 *et seq.*) to
describe a trend toward increasing assertiveness. He also notes the concerns of
those who view the extension of judicial review with alarm. One concern is
that, absent a rights document, British judges have no sure guide to the principles they ought to apply. That, of course, overlooks the potential of the ECHR.
There is little in Galligan's book about the conflicts between British courts
and the European Commission and Court of Human Rights that have been
the subject of this book, but he does acknowledge (1986, 299) that the ECHR
is a potential source of constitutional constraints, yet to be incorporated fully
in English domestic law.

   Another concern that Galligan notes (1986, 239–40) is the question of
whether judicial review is democratic. The basis for that question is the asser-
tion that courts *are not* politically accountable. While that no doubt is true,
the next step of that argument, if it is to be taken seriously, must be the claim

that ministers of state and the state bureaucracy *are* politically accountable.

In reality, there is no likely prospect for real accountability of executive power to Parliament. As Anthony Lester has written (1984, 47), "The main safeguards against abuse of power" in Britain mostly depend "upon the sense of fair play of Ministers and civil servants; the vigilance of the Opposition and individual Members of Parliament; the influence of a free press and of an informed public opinion; and the periodic opportunity of changing the Government through free and secret elections." But Lustgarten and Leigh describe the more likely reality of traditional British political culture in this regard (1994, 413):

> Within this culture the conduct of government is seen as something for the knowledgeable and well-intentioned (and often well-connected) parties. The masses are let in on the act only so far as is good for them or is politically unavoidable. This ethos, though now attenuated, still pervades the entire administration, and is responsible among other things for the extreme secrecy of the British government, which virtually alone among Western democracies refuses to enact access or freedom of information legislation. And unrestricted executive discretion mixed with secrecy is witches' brew, at its most potent in those areas where the "mysteries of state" are most jealously guarded by all governments: foreign relations, military matters, and "national security."

Anthony Lester (1984, 63) describes a "political machine," including the civil service, that jealously guards its power:

> It is entirely understandable that the mandarins of Whitehall should be opposed to the creation of speedy and effective legal remedies for breaches of the Convention by public authorities, including themselves. The argument which they use to great effect with Ministers is that incorporation would transfer power from Parliament to the judiciary.

Whether such conclusions seem excessively harsh, it is important to remember a point made repeatedly in this book: the actual system of Westminster parliamentary democracy has not sustained real accountability of the executive to Parliament for a long time. Lustgarten and Leigh note this as well, and they cite the irony of this reality in an observation of Colin Turpin (1994, 413): "It is indeed a paradoxical feature of the modern constitution that for the control and accountability of the government we rely mainly upon an elected House in which the majority see it as their principal function to maintain the Government in power." Another dimension should always be added to this observation: many of the members of Parliament who vote to sustain the government of the day do so in the hope that one day they will have ministerial responsibility themselves. Ewing and Gearty (1990, 6) refer to these circumstances as having created "a crisis of over governability." While there may be some independence and safety for parliamentary rebels in numbers sufficient to create a coalition of dissidents, John Major's decision in 1994 to withdraw the whip (that is, party recognition) from dissident Tory "Euroskeptics" illustrates the usual fate of those who are unwilling "to go along in order to get along."

Is a Bill of Rights a Viable Solution?

None of the solutions for excessive and unaccountable executive discretion are easy or unequivocal. It is easy to suggest that unnecessary discretion ought to be reduced, but quite another thing to determine in advance when discretion is unnecessary. Confining discretion by filling in detailed policy through published administrative rules and regulations is a partial solution, but only to the extent that the rules and regulations themselves are reasonable and accessible. Remember from chapter 4 the prison rules that first required prior ventilation of prisoners' complaints, only to replace that requirement with simultaneous ventilation. Such rules usually are the product of a closed administrative structure, one that has the protection and convenience of those inside the system as a prime motivation. Officialdom thus rules supreme! That is why structuring discretion by publishing plans, policy statements, and rules— as Davis emphasizes, through open procedures, open findings, open rules, and open precedents—is so important. Secrecy, as many have commented, is a serious "neurosis" of British officialdom.

Davis's third remedy, checking discretion through some sort of accountability review, as we have discussed, is not effectively established in the current British judicial review process. The most commonly suggested remedy is that Britain ought to have a bill of rights and that its courts ought to have full power of judicial review in human rights cases, whether that be accomplished by incorporating the ECHR into British domestic law or by the creation of a new document.

We noted in chapter 1 that the Charter 88 movement in Britain had as its goal the adoption of a constitutional document, and that Lord Scarman, the law lord whose opinions have been most consistently supportive of human rights in general and of the ECHR in particular, has been a leading advocate for the safeguards provided by a written constitution. Lord Scarman has insisted on four essential safeguards: the protection of human rights, the setting of constitutional limits for legislative and executive power, the protection of regional and local government, and the establishment of an independent judiciary with the power of judicial review (1994, 15).

We also noted in chapter 1 that legal philosopher Ronald Dworkin concluded in his pamphlet *A Bill of Rights for Britain: Why British Liberty Needs Protecting* (1990) that "Liberty Is Ill in Britain," but he found that the illness is not the work of despots, but of those who "have a more mundane and corrupting insensitivity to liberty" (1990, 9–10). Given the decline in what he calls the "culture of liberty," he favors incorporation of the ECHR: "With very little procedural fuss Parliament could enact a statute providing that the principles of that convention are henceforth part of the law of Britain, enforceable by British judges in British courts" (1990, 15–16). However, Ewing and Gearty (1990, 275) believe that the problems of civil liberties in Britain are "much too serious to be met by glib proposals for the introduction of a bill of rights as a panacea to all our problems." They argue that a more fundamental redistribution of power is necessary. They also note three particular problems with the bill of rights remedy. The first problem is one of finding a way to make either the ECHR or a specially written bill of rights superior to the subsequent will of parliament. Under the tradition of parliamentary sovereignty one session of parliament has no power to bind a subsequent one. This is called the problem of entrenchment. There is no tradition in Britain for a constitutional document that is superior to ordinary legislation. Robert Kerridge's article on incorporation of the ECHR (1993, 276) considers this problem and argues that while some solutions might require some sort of new constitutional settlement in the United Kingdom, others might be accomplished by rules of interpretation so that the ECHR would prevail except when in direct and express conflict with subsequent legislation.

The second problem is that of vesting the ultimate power of civil liberties adjudication in "unaccountable" judges who are appointed for life and whose appointment is not subject to parliamentary review or approval. The third problem is related to the second: no one knows how British judges might exercise such power. Dworkin's pamphlet proposes answers to each of these concerns, but there is no objective way to determine who is right.

The strongest critic of giving more power to British judges is J. A. G. Griffith, whose two books, *The Politics of the Judiciary* (1991) and *Judicial Politics since 1920* (1993), are pioneering efforts to consider judges in Britain as political actors. Among his chief concerns about British judges is the fact that they are the most elite members of an elite profession, drawn from a narrow range of socioeconomic and educational backgrounds that often include public schools (elite private schools) and an "Oxbridge" education. Such judges usually are the willing defenders of established authority in what he believes to be an "increasingly authoritarian society" (1991, 332). Thus he concludes (1991, 282) that "One of the greatest myths is that the courts of this country are alert to protect the individual against the power of the state." For these reasons he doubts that the power of judicial review is the solution:

> Far more than on the judiciary, our freedoms depend on the willing- ness of the press, politicians and others to publicize the breach of these freedoms and on the continuing vulnerability of ministers, civil servants, the police, other public officials and powerful private interests to accusa- tions that these freedoms are being infringed. In other words we depend far more on the political climate and on the vigilance of those members of society who for a variety of reasons, some political and some humani- tarian, make it their business to seek to hold public authorities to their proper limits. That those limits are also prescribed by law and that judges may be asked to maintain them is not without significance. But the judges are not, as in a different dispensation and under a different social order they might be, the strong natural defenders of liberty. (1991, 327–28)

I think it clear that the agents and means that Griffith proposes for safe- guarding human rights, while also important in the United States, have not done much to protect human rights, especially the rights claimed by minority groups and interests, certainly not as much as have the constitutional deci- sions of federal judges during the past forty years or so. Admittedly that has not been the case for all of U.S. history, and there certainly are no guarantees for the future. But Griffith may be right with respect to Britain. Only the incorporation of the ECHR and the actual experience of judicial review exer- cised by British judges will provide a more certain answer.

Appendix

Selected Provisions from the Convention for the Protection of Human Rights and Fundamental Freedoms

The Governments signatory hereto, being Members of the Council of Europe,

Considering the Universal Declaration of Human Rights proclaimed by the General Assembly of the United Nations on 10th December 1948;

Considering that this Declaration aims at securing the universal and effective recognition and observance of the Rights therein declared;

Considering that the aim of the Council of Europe is the achievement of greater unity between its Members and that one of the methods by which that aim is to be pursued is the maintenance and further realisation of Human Rights and Fundamental Freedoms;

Reaffirming their profound belief in those Fundamental Freedoms which are the foundation of justice and peace in the world and are best maintained on the one hand by an effective political democracy and on the other by a common understanding and observance of the Human Rights upon which they depend;

Being resolved, as the Governments of European countries which are like-minded and have a common heritage of political traditions, ideals, freedom and the rule of law to take the first steps for the collective enforcement of certain of the Rights stated in the Universal Declaration,

Have agreed as follows:

Article 1

The High Contracting Parties shall secure to everyone within their jurisdiction the rights and freedoms defined in Section 1 of this Convention.

SECTION I

Article 2

1. Everyone's right to life shall be protected by law. No one shall be deprived of his life intentionally save in the execution of a sentence of a court following his conviction of a crime for which this penalty is provided by law.
2. Deprivation of life shall not be regarded as inflicted in contravention of this Article when it results from the use of force which is no more than absolutely necessary:
(a) in defence of any person from unlawful violence;

(b) in order to effect a lawful arrest or to prevent the escape of a person lawfully detained;

(c) in action lawfully taken for the purpose of quelling a riot or insurrection.

Article 3

No one shall be subjected to torture or to inhuman or degrading treatment or punishment.

Article 4

1. No one shall be held in slavery or servitude.

2. No one shall be required to perform forced or compulsory labour.

3. For the purpose of this Article the term "forced or compulsory labour" shall not include:

a) any work required to be done in the ordinary course of detention imposed according to the provisions of Article 5 of this Convention or during conditional release from such detention;

(b) any service of a military character or, in case of conscientious objectors in countries where they are recognised, service exacted instead of compulsory military service;

(c) any service exacted in case of an emergency or calamity threatening the life or well-being of the community;

(d) any work or service which forms part of normal civic obligations.

Article 5

1. Everyone has the right to liberty and security of person. No one shall be deprived of his liberty save in the following cases and in accordance with a procedure prescribed by law;

(a) the lawful detention of a person after conviction by a competent court;

(b) the lawful arrest or detention of a person for non-compliance with the lawful order of a court or in order to secure the fulfilment of any obligation prescribed by law;

(c) the lawful arrest or detention of a person effected for the purpose of bringing him before the competent legal authority on reasonable suspicion of having committed an offence or when it is reasonably considered necessary to prevent his committing an offence or fleeing after having done so;

(d) the detention of a minor by lawful order for the purpose of educational supervision or his lawful detention for the purpose of bringing him before the competent legal authority;

(e) the lawful detention of persons for the prevention of the spreading of infectious diseases, of persons of unsound mind, alcoholics or drug addicts or vagrants;

(f) the lawful arrest or detention of a person to prevent his effecting an unauthorised entry into the country or of a person against whom action is being taken with a view to deportation or extradition.

2. Everyone who is arrested shall be informed promptly, in a language which he understands, of the reasons for his arrest and of any charge against him.

3. Everyone arrested or detained in accordance with the provisions of paragraph 1(c) of

this Article shall be brought promptly before a judge or other officer authorised by law to exercise judicial power and shall be entitled to trial within a reasonable time or to release pending trial. Release may be conditioned by guarantees to appear for trial.

4. Everyone who is deprived of his liberty by arrest or detention shall be entitled to take proceedings by which the lawfulness of his detention shall be decided speedily by a court and his release ordered if the detention is not lawful.

5. Everyone who has been the victim of arrest or detention in contravention of the provisions of this Article shall have an enforceable right to compensation.

Article 6

1. In the determination of his civil rights and obligations or of any criminal charge against him, everyone is entitled to a fair and public hearing within a reasonable time by an independent and impartial tribunal established by law. Judgment shall be pronounced publicly but the press and public may be excluded from all or part of the trial in the interest of morals, public order or national security in a democratic society, where the interests of juveniles or the protection of the private life of the parties so require, or to the extent strictly necessary in the opinion of the court in special circumstances where publicity would prejudice the interests of justice.

2. Everyone charged with a criminal offence shall be presumed innocent until proved guilty according to law.

3. Everyone charged with a criminal offence has the following minimum rights:

(a) to be informed promptly, in a language which he understands and in detail, of the nature and cause of the accusation against him;

(b) to have adequate time and facilities for the preparation of his defence;

(c) to defend himself in person or through legal assistance of his own choosing or, if he has not sufficient means to pay for legal assistance, to be given it free when the interests of justice so require;

(d) to examine or have examined witnesses against him and to obtain the attendance and examination of witnesses on his behalf under the same conditions as witnesses against him;

(e) to have the free assistance of an interpreter if he cannot understand or speak the language used in court.

Article 7

1. No one shall be held guilty of any criminal offence on account of any act or omission which did not constitute a criminal offence under national or international law at the time when it was committed. Nor shall a heavier penalty be imposed than the one that was applicable at the time the criminal offence was committed.

2. This Article shall not prejudice the trial and punishment of any person for any act or omission which at the time when it was committed, was criminal according to the general principles of law recognised by civilised nations.

Article 8

1. Everyone has the right to respect for his private and family life, his home and his correspondence.

2. There shall be no interference by a public authority with the exercise of this right except such as is in accordance with the law and is necessary in a democratic society in the interests of national security, public safety or the economic well-being of the country, for the prevention of disorder or crime, for the protection of health or morals, or for the protection of the rights and freedoms of others.

Article 9

1. Everyone has the right to freedom of thought, conscience and religion; this right includes freedom to change his religion or belief and freedom, either alone or in community with others and in public or private, to manifest his religion or belief, in worship, teaching, practice and observance.

2. Freedom to manifest one's religion or beliefs shall be subject only to such limitations as are prescribed by law and are necessary in a democratic society in the interests of public safety, for the protection of public order, health or morals, or for the protection of the rights and freedoms of others.

Article 10

1. Everyone has the right to freedom of expression. This right shall include freedom to hold opinions and to receive and impart information and ideas without interference by public authority and regardless of frontiers. This Article shall not prevent States from requiring the licensing of broadcasting, television or cinema enterprises.

2. The exercise of these freedoms, since it carries with it duties and responsibilities, may be subject to such formalities, conditions, restrictions or penalties as are prescribed by law and are necessary in a democratic society, in the interests of national security, territorial integrity or public safety, for the prevention of disorder or crime, for the protection of health or morals, for the protection of the reputation or rights of others, for preventing the disclosure of information received in confidence, or for maintaining the authority and impartiality of the judiciary.

Article 11

1. Everyone has the right to freedom of peaceful assembly and to freedom of association with others, including the right to form and to join trade unions for the protection of his interests.

2. No restrictions shall be placed on the exercise of these rights other than such as are prescribed by law and are necessary in a democratic society in the interests of national security or public safety, for the prevention of disorder or crime, for the protection of health or morals or for the protection of the rights and freedoms of others. This Article

shall not prevent the imposition of lawful restrictions on the exercise of these rights by members of the armed forces, of the police or of the administration of the State.

Article 12

Men and women of marriageable age have the right to marry and to found a family, according to the national laws governing the exercise of this right.

Article 13

Everyone whose rights and freedoms as set forth in this Convention are violated shall have an effective remedy before a national authority notwithstanding that the violation has been committed by persons acting in an official capacity.

Article 14

The enjoyment of the rights and freedoms set forth in this Convention shall be secured without discrimination on any ground such as sex, race, colour, language, religion, political or other opinion, national or social origin, association with a national minority, property, birth or other status.

Article 15

1. In time of war or other public emergency threatening the life of the nation any High Contracting Party may take measures derogating from its obligations under this Convention to the extent strictly required by the exigencies of the situation, provided that such measures are not inconsistent with its other obligation under international law.
2. No derogation from Article 2, except in respect of deaths resulting from lawful acts of war, or from Articles 3, 4 (paragraph 1) and 7 shall be made under this provision.
3. Any High Contracting Party availing itself of this right of derogation shall keep the Secretary General of the Council of Europe fully informed of the measures which it has taken and the reasons therefor. It shall also inform the Secretary General of the Council of Europe when such measures have ceased to operate and the provisions of the Convention are again being fully executed.

Article 16

Nothing in Articles 10, 11 and 14 shall be regarded as preventing the High Contracting Parties from imposing restrictions on the political activity of aliens.

Article 17

Nothing in this Convention may be interpreted as implying for any State, group or person any right to engage in any activity or perform any act aimed at the destruction of any of the rights and freedoms set forth herein or at their limitation to a greater extent than is provided for in the Convention.

Article 18

The restrictions permitted under this Convention to the said rights and freedoms shall not be applied for any purpose other than those for which they have been prescribed.

Selected provisions from the Protocols:

FIRST PROTOCOL

Article 1

Every natural or legal person is entitled to the peaceful enjoyment of his possessions. No one shall be deprived of his possessions except in the public interest and subject to the conditions provided for by law and by the general principles of international law.

The preceding provisions shall not, however, in any way impair the right of a State to enforce such laws as it deems necessary to control the use of property in accordance with the general interest or to secure the payment of taxes or other contributions or penalties.

Article 2

No person shall be denied the right to education. In the exercise of any functions which it assumes in relation to education and to teaching, the State shall respect the right of parents to ensure such education and teaching in conformity with their own religious and philosophical convictions.

FOURTH PROTOCOL

Article 1

No one shall be deprived of his liberty on the ground of inability to fulfill a contractual obligation.

Article 2

1. Everyone lawfully within the territory of a State shall, within that territory, have the right to liberty of movement and freedom to choose his residence.

2. Everyone shall be free to leave any country, including his own.

3. No restrictions shall be placed on the exercise of these rights other than such as are in accordance with law and are necessary in a democratic society in the interests of national security or public safety, for the maintenance of *ordre public,* for the prevention of crime, for the protection of health or morals, or for the protection of the rights and freedoms of others.

Article 3

1. No one shall be expelled, by means either of an individual or of a collective measure, from the territory of the State of which he is a national.

2. No one shall be deprived of the right to enter the territory of the State of which he is a national.

Article 4

Collective expulsion of aliens is prohibited.

SIXTH PROTOCOL

Article 1

The death penalty shall be abolished. No one shall be condemned to such penalty or executed.

Article 2

A State may make provision in its law for the death penalty in respect of acts committed in time of war or of imminent threat of war; such penalty shall be applied only in the instances laid down in the law and in accordance with its provisions. The State shall communicate to the Secretary of the Council of Europe the relevant provisions of that law.

Article 3

No derogation from the provisions of this Protocol shall be made under Article 15 of the Convention.

Notes

Chapter 1

1. A complete text of Section I of the European Convention for the Protection of Human Rights and Fundamental Freedoms can be found in the appendix. Section I contains Articles 1 through 18, which provide for specific rights and freedoms.

2. These citations were found through a LEXIS search conducted by staff at the Library of the Institute for Advanced Legal Studies of the University of London on February 10, 1994. While the data set of British cases dates from 1945, the earliest citation to the ECHR was in *Hubbard and others v. Pitt and others* (a Queen's Bench decision of November 8, 1974).

3. See table 7.1 in chapter 7 for the complete specification.

Chapter 2

1. All references to articles and sections are to the European Convention on Human Rights and Fundamental Freedoms (1953).

2. Customs and current practices of the Court, other than the formal requirements of the ECHR, were described to me during interviews I conducted in August 1990 with Marc-André Eissen, registrar (*greffier*) of the Court (who had served for twenty-two years at the time of the interview), and with Sir Vincent Evans, the judge of United Kingdom nationality then serving on the Court.

Chapter 3

1. In the case references that follow, A refers to the series A publications, which contain the judgments of the European Court of Human Rights. B refers to the series B publications, which contain the reports of the European Commission on Human Rights.

2. Pages 126–241 of the Commission's report are on the question of discrimination under Art. 14.

3. Page references are to the report of *Brannigan and McBride* in the *European Human Rights Report*.

4. This case involved six members of the Murray family. The principal applicant was Mrs. Margaret Murray. The case recently decided by the European Court on the right of silence and on the right of access to lawyers while in police custody is that of *John Murray v. United Kingdom*.

5. Page references are to the report of *Murray (Margaret) v. United Kingdom* in the *European Human Rights Report*.

6. Page references are to the report of *McCann and Others* in the *Human Rights Law Journal*.

Chapter 6

1. The most recent issue of the *European Human Rights Report* received by the author when finally updating this book was Vol. 22, Part 4 (October 1996). The most recent issue of the *Human Rights Law Journal* received was Vol. 17, nos. 3–6 (October 1996).

2. Page references are to the report of *Goodwin v. United Kingdom* in the *European Human Rights Report.*

Chapter 7

1. The data search produced 256 case references, but these included duplications and some references to cases from the Court of Justice of the European Community and from the European Court of Human Rights. Elimination of these produced a net of 169 case references. I do not suggest that this search was exhaustive of all possible references to the ECHR under English law, but the references should be sufficiently representative for an assessment of the evolution of the case law.

REFERENCES

Articles or books

Abraham, H. 1993. *The Judicial Process: An Introductory Analysis of the Courts of the United States, England and France*. 6th ed. New York: Oxford University Press.

Amnesty International. 1972. *Report of an Enquiry into Allegations of Ill Treatment in Northern Ireland*. London: Amnesty International.

Arlidge, A., and D. Eady. 1982. *The Law of Contempt*. London: Sweet and Maxwell.

Bagehot, W. 1867. *The English Constitution*. 1963 ed. Glasgow: Fontana/Collins.

Bailey, S., D. Harris, and B. Jones, eds. 1991. *Civil Liberties: Cases and Materials*. 3d ed. London: Butterworths.

Bell, J. 1993. *The Irish Troubles: A Generation of Violence*. Dublin: Gill and Macmillan.

Bernhardt, R. 1981. *Human Rights and the Individual in International Law*. Vol. 8, *Encyclopedia of Public International Law*. Amsterdam: North Holland Publishing Co.

———. 1993. "The Convention and Domestic Law." In *The European System for the Protection of Human Rights*, eds. R. St. J. Macdonald, F. Matscher, and H. Petzold, 25–40. Dordrecht: Martinus Nijhoff.

Bernhardt, R., and J. A. Jolowics, eds. 1987. *International Enforcement of Civil Rights* (Reports submitted to the Colloquium of the International Association of Legal Science). Berlin: Springer-Verlag.

Bevan, V. 1986. *The Development of British Immigration Law*. London: Croom Helm.

Bingham, T. 1993. "The European Convention on Human Rights: Time to Incorporate," *Law Quarterly Review* 109: 390–400.

Blackburn, R. 1990. "Legal and Political Arguments for a United Kingdom Bill of Rights." In *Human Rights for the 1990s: Legal, Political and Ethical Issues*, eds. R. Blackburn and J. Taylor, 109–20. London: Mansell.

Blackburn, R., and J. Taylor, eds. 1990. *Human Rights for the 1990s: Legal, Political and Ethical Issues*. London: Mansell.

Bossuyt, V., and Y. Vanden Bosch. 1985. "Judges and Judgments: 25 Years of Judicial Activity of the Court of Strasbourg." *Revue belge de droit international* 18 (1984–85): 695–712.

Boyle, K., and T. Hadden. 1994. *Northern Ireland: The Choice*. Harmondsworth, United Kingdom: Penguin Books.

Boyle, K., T. Hadden, and P. Hillyard. 1975. *Law and State: The Case of Northern Ireland*. London: Martin Robertson.

————. 1980. *Ten Years in Northern Ireland: The Legal Control of Political Violence.* London: Cobden Trust.

Bradley, A. 1991. "The United Kingdom Before the Strasbourg Court, 1975–1990." In *Edinburgh Essays in Public Law,* eds. W. Finnie, C. Himsworth, and N. Walker, 185–214. Edinburgh: Edinburgh University Press.

Brewer-Carías, A. 1989. *Judicial Review in Comparative Law.* Cambridge: Cambridge University Press.

Brown, C. 1985. *Black and White Britain: The Third PSI Survey.* Aldershot, United Kingdom: Gower.

Brownlie, I., ed. 1992. *Basic Documents on Human Rights.* 3d ed. Oxford: Clarendon Press.

Carillo-Salcedo, J. 1993. "The Place of the European Convention in International Law." In *The European System for the Protection of Human Rights,* eds. R. St. J. Macdonald, F. Matscher, and H. Petzold, 15–24. Dordrecht: Martinus Nijhoff Publishers.

Castles, S., and G. Kosack. 1985. *Immigrant Workers and Class Structure in Western Europe.* 2d. ed. Oxford: Oxford University Press.

Charter 88. 1994. "A Flawed Democracy." In *Democracy in Britain: A Reader,* eds. J. Lively and A. Lively, 31–33. Oxford: Blackwell.

Churchill, R., and J. Young. 1991. "Compliance with Judgments of the European Court of Human Rights and Decisions of the Committee of Ministers: The Experience of the United Kingdom." *The British Yearbook of International Law, 1991* 62: 183–346.

Clutterbuck, R. 1973. *Protest and the Urban Guerilla.* London: Cassell.

————. 1977. *Guerrillas and Terrorists.* London: Faber and Faber.

Cohen, G. 1989. *The European Convention on Human Rights.* Paris: Economica.

Cohen, S., and L. Taylor. 1978. *Prison Secrets.* London: National Council for Civil Liberties and Radical Alternatives to Prison.

Commission on Racial Equality. 1985. *Immigration Control: Report of a Formal Investigation.* London: Commission on Racial Equality.

Council of Europe. 1990. *European Court of Human Rights: Survey of Activities, 1959–89.* Strasbourg: Council of Europe.

Council of Europe. (annual eds.). *Yearbook of the European Convention on Human Rights.* The Hague: Martinus Nijhoff.

Curtis, L., and M. Jempson. 1993. *Interference on the Airwaves: Ireland, the Media and the Broadcasting Ban.* London: Campaign for Press and Broadcasting Freedom.

Cvetic, G. 1987. "Immigration Cases in Strasbourg: The Right to Family Life under Article 8 of the European Convention." *International and Comparative Law Quarterly* 36: 647–55.

Davis, K. 1971. *Discretionary Justice: A Preliminary Inquiry.* Urbana: University of Illinois Press.

Davis, K., et al. 1976. *Discretionary Justice in Europe and America.* Urbana: University of Illinois Press.

Dembitz, N. 1945. "Racial Discrimination and the Military Judgment: The Supreme Court's Korematsu and Endo Decisions." *Columbia Law Review* 45: 175–239.

Dickson, B. 1989. "The Prevention of Terrorism (Temporary Provisions) Act 1989." *Northern Ireland Law Quarterly* 40: 250–67.

Dilulio, J., Jr. 1990. "Conclusion: What Judges Can Do to Improve Prisons and Jails." In *Courts, Corrections and the Constitution,* ed. J. Dilulio, Jr., 287–322. New York: Oxford University Press.

———, ed. 1990. *Courts, Corrections and the Constitution.* New York: Oxford University Press.

Ditchfield, J. 1990. *Control in Prison: A Review of the Literature* (Home Office Research Study 118). London: Her Majesty's Stationery Office.

Douglas, G., and S. Jones. 1983. "Prisoners and the European Convention on Human Rights." In *The Effect on English Domestic Law of Membership of the European Communities and the Ratification of the European Convention on Human Rights,* eds. M. Furmston, R. Kerridge, and B. Sufrin, 352–86. The Hague: Martinus Nijhoff.

Drzemczewski, A. 1995. "Ensuring Compatibility of Domestic Law with the European Convention on Human Rights Prior to Ratification: The Hungarian Model." *Human Rights Law Journal* 16, no. 7–9: 247–60.

Drzemczewski, A., and J. Meyer-Ladewig. 1994. "Principal Characteristics of the New ECHR Control Mechanism as Established by Protocol No. 11, Signed on 11 May 1994." *Human Rights Law Journal* 15, no. 3: 81–86.

Dummett, A., and A. Nicol. 1990. *Subjects, Citizens, Aliens and Others.* London: Weidenfeld and Nicolson.

Dworkin, R. 1990. *A Bill of Rights for Britain* (Chatto CounterBlasts No. 16). London: Chatto & Windus.

Eissen, M. 1986. "La Cour européenne des droits de l'homme," *Revue du droit public et de la science politique en France et à l'étranger* 102: 1539–1783.

———. 1989. "L'Interaction des jurisprudences constitutionnelles nationales et de la jurisprudence de la cour européenne des droits de l'homme." In *Conseil constitutionnel et cour européenne des droits de l'homme,* eds. D. Rousseau and F. Sudre. Paris: Editions Sth.

Eklund-Olson, S., and S. Martin. 1990. "*Ruiz:* A Struggle over Legitimacy." In *Courts, Corrections and the Constitution,* ed. J. Dilulio, Jr., 73–93. New York: Oxford University Press.

European Human Rights Law Review. 1995. "Editorial" (Launch Issue 1995).

———. 1995. "Special Case Note: McCann and Others v. United Kingdom." (Launch Issue 1995).

Ewing, K. D., and C. A. Gearty. 1990. *Freedom under Thatcher: Civil Liberties in Modern Britain.* Oxford: Clarendon Press.

Ewing, W. 1976. "Human Rights in Northern Ireland." In *Case Studies in Human Rights and Fundamental Freedoms,* ed. W. Veerhaven, 35–68. The Hague: Martinus Nijhoff.

Farrell, M. 1976. *Northern Ireland: The Orange State.* London: Pluto Press.

Faulkner, B. 1978. *Memoirs of a Statesman.* London: Weidenfeld and Nicolson.

Fawcett, Sir J. 1985. "Applications of the European Convention on Human Rights." In

Accountability and Prisons: Opening Up a Closed World, ed. M. Maguire, J. Vagg, and R. Morgan, 61–77. London: Tavistock.

———. 1987. *The Application of the European Convention on Human Rights.* 2d ed. Oxford: Clarendon Press.

Feeley, M., and R. Hanson. 1990. "The Impact of Judicial Intervention on Prisons and Jails: A Framework for Analysis and a Review of the Literature." In *Courts, Corrections and the Constitution,* ed. J. Dilulio, Jr., 12–46. New York: Oxford University Press.

Feldman, D. 1993. *Civil Liberties and Human Rights in England and Wales.* Oxford: Clarendon Press.

Finnie, W. 1982. "Rights of Persons Detained under the Anti-Terrorist Legislation." *Modern Law Review* 45: 215–20.

———. 1989. "The Prevention of Terrorism Act and the European Convention on Human Rights." *Modern Law Review* 52: 703–10.

———. 1991. "Anti-Terrorist Legislation and the European Convention on Human Rights." *Modern Law Review* 54: 288–93.

Forsythe, D. 1991. *The Internationalization of Human Rights.* Lexington, Mass.: Lexington Books.

Fransman, L. 1989. *British Nationality Law.* London: Fourmat Publishing.

Freiburgh, E., and M. Villiger. 1993. "The European Commission of Human Rights." In *The European System for the Protection of Human Rights,* eds. R. St. J. Macdonald, F. Matscher, and H. Petzold, 605–20. Dordrecht: Martinus Nijhoff.

Furmston, M., R. Kerridge, and B. Sufin, eds. 1983. *The Effect on English Domestic Law of Membership of the European Communities and of Ratification of the European Convention on Human Rights.* The Hague: Martinus Nijhoff.

Galligan, D. 1986. *Discretionary Powers: A Legal Study of Official Discretion.* Oxford: Clarendon Press.

Gardner, J. 1994. "Freedom of Expression." In *Individual Rights and the Law in Britain,* eds. C. McCrudden and G. Chambers, 209–38. Oxford: Clarendon Press.

Gearty, C. 1990. "The Media Ban, The European Convention and English Judges." *Cambridge Law Journal* 49: 187–89.

———. 1993. "The European Court of Human Rights and the Protection of Civil Liberties: An Overview." *Cambridge Law Journal* 52: 89–127.

Girdner, A., and A. Loftis. 1969. *The Great Betrayal: The Evacuation of Japanese-Americans During World War II.* New York: Macmillan.

Gordon, P. 1985. *Policing Immigration: Britain's Internal Controls.* London: Pluto Press.

Gray, C. 1987. *Judicial Remedies in International Law.* Oxford: Clarendon Press.

Guelke, A. 1988. *Northern Ireland: The International Perspective.* Dublin: Gill and Macmillan.

Hampson, F. 1990. "The United Kingdom Before the European Court of Human Rights." In *Yearbook of European Law, 1989,* eds. A. Barav and D. A. Wyatt, 121–73. Oxford: Clarendon Press.

———. 1993. "Children in Care and the European Convention on Human Rights." In *Aspects of Incorporation of the European Convention on Human Rights into Domestic Law,* 77–86. London: British Institute of International and Comparative Law and British Institute of Human Rights.

Hartman, J. 1981. "Derogation from Human Rights Treaties in Public Emergencies: A Critique of Implementation by the European Commission and Court of Human Rights and the Human Rights Committee of the United Nations." *Harvard International Law Journal* 22: 1–52.

Hawkins, K., ed. 1992. *The Uses of Discretion.* Oxford: Clarendon Press.

Helsinki Watch. 1992. *Prison Conditions in Northern Ireland.* New York: Human Rights Watch.

———. 1993. "Northern Ireland: Human Rights Abuses by All Sides." *Helsinki Watch* 5, no. 6 (May 1993).

Heuston, R. F. V. 1970. "*Liversidge v. Anderson* in Retrospect." *Law Quarterly Review* 86: 33–68.

———. 1971. "*Liversidge v. Anderson:* Two Footnotes." *Law Quarterly Review* 87: 161–66.

Higgens, R. 1985. "The European Convention on Human Rights." In *Human Rights in International Law: Legal and Policy Issues,* ed. T. Meron. Oxford: Clarendon Press.

Hogan, G., and C. Walker. 1989. *Political Violence and the Law in Northern Ireland.* Manchester: Manchester University Press.

Hondius, E. 1988. "De Hoge Raad en buitenlands hoogste gerechten," in *De Hoge Raad der Nederlanden, 1938–88: En portret.* Zwolle, Netherlands: Tjeenk Willink.

Hudson, M. 1944. *International Tribunals: Past and Future.* Washington: Brookings Institution.

Human Rights Watch. 1991. *Human Rights in Northern Ireland.* New York: Human Rights Watch.

Hunter, B. 1993. *The Statesman's Yearbook,* 1993–94. New York: St. Martin's Press.

Jackson, D. 1992. *Even the Children of Strangers: Equality Under the U.S. Constitution.* Lawrence: University Press of Kansas.

———. 1994. "Judging Human Rights: The Formative Years of the European Court of Human Rights, 1959–89." *Windsor Yearbook of Access to Justice,* 217–36.

Jacobs, F. 1975. *The European Convention on Human Rights.* Oxford: Clarendon Press.

Jacobson, H. 1984. *Networks of Interdependence: International Organizations and the Global Political System.* New York: Alfred Knopf.

Jancovic, B. 1983. *Public International Law.* Dobbs Ferry, N.Y.: Transnational Publishers.

Kerridge, R. 1983. "Incorporation of the European Convention on Human Rights into United Kingdom." In *The Effect on English Domestic Law of Membership of the European Communities and of Ratification of the European Convention on Human Rights,* eds. M. Furmston, R. Kerridge, and B. E. Sufin, 247–82. The Hague: Martinus Nijhoff.

Kidd, C. 1987. "Disciplinary Proceedings and the Right to a Fair Criminal Trial Under the European Convention on Human Rights." *International and Comparative Law Quarterly* 36: 856–72.

King, R., and K. McDermott. 1989. "British Prisons 1970–1987: The Ever Deepening Crisis." *British Journal of Criminology* 29: 107–28.

King, R., and R. Morgan. 1980. *The Future of the Prison System.* Westmead, United Kingdom: Gower Publishing Co.

Kitson, F. 1971. *Low Intensity Operations: Subversion, Insurgency, Peace-Keeping.* London: Faber and Faber.

Lacey, N. 1992. "The Jurisprudence of Discretion: Escaping the Legal Paradigm." In *The Uses of Discretion*, ed. K. Hawkins, 361–88. Oxford: Clarendon Press.

Lalumière, C. 1993. "Human Rights in Europe: Challenges for the Next Millennium." In *The European System for the Protection of Human Rights,* eds. R. St. J. Macdonald, F. Matscher, and H. Petzold, xv-xx. Dordrecht: Martinus Nijhoff.

Lasok, D., and J. W. Bridge. 1987. *Law and Institutions of the European Community.* London: Butterworths.

Layton-Henry, Z. 1992. *The Politics of Immigration: Immigration, "Race" and "Race" Relations in Post-War Britain.* Oxford: Blackwell.

Lempert, R. 1992. "Discretion in a Behavioral Perspective: The Case of a Public Housing Eviction Board." In *The Uses of Discretion,* ed. K. Hawkins, 185–230. Oxford: Clarendon Press.

Lester, A. 1984. "Fundamental Human Rights: The United Kingdom Isolated." *Public Law,* 1984: 46–72.

———. 1993. "Freedom of Expression." In *The European System for the Protection of Human Rights,* eds. R. St. J. Macdonald, F. Matscher, and H. Petzold, 465–91. Dordrecht: Martinus Nijhoff.

Lively, J., and A. Lively, eds. 1994. *Democracy in Britain: A Reader.* Oxford: Blackwell.

Lowe, N. 1983. "The English Law of Contempt of Court and Article 10 of the European Convention on Human Rights." In *The Effect on English Domestic Law of Membership of the European Communities and of Ratification of the European Convention on Human Rights,* eds. M. Furmston, R. Kerridge, and B. Surfin, 318–51. The Hague: Martinus Nijhoff.

Lustgarten, L., and I. Leigh. 1994. *In from the Cold: National Security and Parliamentary Democracy.* Oxford: Clarendon Press.

Macdonald, R. St. J., F. Matscher, and H. Petzold, eds. 1993. *The European System for the Protection of Human Rights.* Dordrecht: Martinus Nijhoff.

Maguire, M., J. Vagg, and R. Morgan, eds. 1985. *Accountability and Prisons: Opening Up a Closed World.* London: Tavistock.

Mahoney, P., and S. Prebensen. 1993. "The European Court of Human Rights." In *The European System for the Protection of Human Rights,* eds. R. St. J. Macdonald, F. Matscher, and H. Petzold, 621–43. Dordrecht: Martinus Nijhoff.

Marston, G. 1993. "The United Kingdom's Part in the Preparation of the European Convention on Human Rights, 1950." *International and Comparative Law Quarterly* 42: 796–826.

Matscher, F. 1993. "Methods of Interpretation of the Convention." In *The European System for the Protection of Human Rights,* eds. R. St. J. Macdonald, F. Matscher, and H. Petzold, 63–81. Dordrecht: Martinus Nijhoff.

Matscher, F., and H. Petzold, eds. 1990. *Protecting Human Rights: The European Dimension—Studies in Honor of Gérard J. Wiarda.* 2d. ed. Cologne: C. Heyman.

McCrudden, C., and G. Chambers, eds. 1994. *Individual Rights and the Law in Britain.* Oxford: Clarendon Press.

Meron, T., ed. 1985. *Human Rights in International Law: Legal and Policy Issues.* Oxford: Clarendon Press.

Merrills, J. 1988. *The Development of International Law by the European Court of Human Rights.* Manchester: Manchester University Press.

———. 1993. *Human Rights in Europe: A Study of the European Convention on Human Rights.* Manchester: Manchester University Press.

Meyer-Ladewig, J. 1993. "Reform of the Control Machinery." In *The European System for the Protection of Human Rights,* eds. R. St. J. Macdonald, F. Matscher, and H. Petzold, 909–26. Dordrecht: Martinus Nijhoff.

Morgan, R., and H. Jones. 1991. "Prison Discipline: The Case of Implementing Woolf." *British Journal of Criminology* 31: 280–91.

Norton, P. 1991. *The British Polity.* 2d. ed. New York: Longman.

O'Boyle, M. 1977. "Emergency Situations and the Protection of Human Rights: A Model Derogation Provision for a Northern Ireland Bill of Rights." *Northern Ireland Law Quarterly* 28: 160–87.

Observer (London). October 17, 1993. "Top Judges: Jail Not the Answer."

Packer, H. 1968. *The Limits of the Criminal Sanction.* Palo Alto: Stanford University Press.

Powell, E. 1978. "Parliamentary Government." In *Democracy in Britain: A Reader,* 1994 ed., ed. J. Lively and A. Lively, 30–31. Oxford: Blackwell.

Prowse, R., H. Weber, and C. Wilson. 1992. "Rights and Prisons in Germany: Blueprint for Britain?" *International Journal of the Sociology of Law* 20: 111–34.

Rees, M. 1985. *Northern Ireland: A Personal Perspective.* London: Methuen.

Renteln, A. 1990. *International Human Rights: Universalism Versus Relativism.* Newbury Park, Calif.: Sage Publications.

Rogge, K. 1993. "Fact-Finding." In *The European System for the Protection of Human Rights,* eds. R. St. J. Macdonald, F. Matscher, and H. Petzold, 677–701. Dordrecht: Martinus Nijhoff.

Rose, R. 1971. *Governing Without Consensus.* London: Faber and Faber.

———. 1976. *Northern Ireland: A Time of Choice.* London: Macmillan.

Rossiter, C. 1948. *Constitutional Dictatorship: Crisis Government in the Modern Democracies.* Princeton: Princeton University Press.

Rutherford, A. 1993. *Criminal Justice and the Pursuit of Decency.* Oxford: Oxford University Press.

Ryle, M. 1981. "The Commons Today: A General Survey." In *The Commons Today,* eds. S. Walkand and M. Ryle, 11–38. Glasgow: Fontana.

Scarman, Lord. 1992. "The Need for a Written Constitution." In *Democracy in Britain: A Reader,* 1994 ed., ed. J. Lively and A. Lively, 14–15. Oxford: Blackwell.

Sherlock, A. 1991. "Anti-Terrorist Legislation and the Convention." *European Law Review* 16 (1991): 266–68.

Simpson, A. W. Brian. 1992. *In the Highest Degree Odious: Detention Without Trial in Wartime Britain.* Oxford: Clarendon Press.

Statewatch. 1993. "Northern Ireland: PTA Ruling." Vol. 3, no. 3 (May–June 1993): 9–10.

———. 1994. "ECHR Rules on Right to Silence." Vol. 4, no. 5 (September–October 1994).

————. 1995a. "Asylum Refusals Soar." Vol. 5, no. 1 (January–February 1995).

————. 1995b. "Safe Country List." Vol. 5, no. 3 (May–June 1995).

————. 1995c. "Gibraltar and Beyond." Vol. 5, no. 5 (September–October 1995).

————. 1995d. "EC Rules against Britain." Vol. 5, no. 6 (November–December 1995).

————. 1995e. "The Lilley-Howard Package." Vol. 5, no. 6 (November–December 1995).

Stern, V. 1993. *Bricks of Shame: Britain's Prisons.* 3d ed. Harmondsworth, United Kingdom: Penguin Books.

Stone, A. 1992. *The Birth of Judicial Politics in France: The Constitutional Council in Comparative Perspective.* New York: Oxford University Press.

Strossen, N. 1990. "Recent U.S. and International Judicial Protection of Individual Rights: A Comparative Legal Process Analysis and Proposed Synthesis." *Hastings Law Journal* 41: 805–904.

Sunday Times (London). January 24, 1992. "Our Thalidomide Children: A Cause for National Shame."

————. February 21, 1993. "Media Celebrate Famous Victory for Free Speech."

————. March 28, 1993. "The Case for Internment."

————. February 13, 1994. "Freedom of Speech: Worth Making a Song and Dance About."

Sunkin, M. 1992. "The Incidence and Effect of Judicial Review Procedures against Central Government in the United Kingdom." In *Comparative Judicial Review and Public Policy,* eds. D. Jackson and N. Tate, 143–56. Westport, Conn.: Greenwood Press.

Sunkin, M., L. Bridges, and G. Mészáros. 1993. *Judicial Review in Perspective: An Investigation of Trends in the Use and Operation of the Judicial Review Procedure in England and Wales.* London: The Public Law Project.

Teitgen, P.-H. 1993. "Introduction to the European Convention on Human Rights." In *The European System for the Protection of Human Rights,* eds. R. St. J. Macdonald, F. Matscher, and H. Petzold, 3–14. Dordrecht: Martinus Nijhoff.

ten Kate, J. 1989. "The Importance of Being Justice: Some Remarks about the Dutch Supreme Court and Its Members." (Unpublished paper presented at the 1989 Interim Meeting of the Research Committee on Comparative Judicial Studies of the International Political Science Association, University of Lund, Sweden).

Times (London). November 30, 1988. "European Court Ruling a Setback to Security."

————. December 7, 1988. "Law Must Be Used to Hit Cash Roots of Terror."

————. December 23, 1988. "Britain Defies European Ruling."

————. May 24, 1990. "Peers' Concern for Human Rights."

————. May 26, 1992. "Paths to Faster Justice."

————. January 19, 1994. "IRA Man Takes UK to European Court over Right to Silence."

————. January 23, 1995. "Tolstoy's European Challenge over Libel."

————. January 26, 1995. "Law Chief Backs Bill on Human Rights."

Treverton-Jones, G. 1989. *Imprisonment: The Legal Status and Rights of Prisoners.* London: Sweet and Maxwell.

United Nations High Commissioner for Refugees. 1979. *Handbook on Procedures and Criteria for Determining Refugee Status: Under the 1951 Convention and the 1967*

Protocol Relating to the Status of Refugees. Geneva: Office of the United Nations High Commissioner for Refugees.

van Dijk, P., and G. van Hoof. 1990. *Theory and Practice of the European Convention on Human Rights.* 2d ed. Deventer, Netherlands: Kluwer Law and Taxation Publishers.

Walker, C. 1992. *The Prevention of Terrorism in British Law.* Manchester: Manchester University Press.

Walkland, S., and M. Ryle. 1981. *The Commons Today.* Glasgow: Fontana.

Warbrick, C. 1990. "The European Convention of Human Rights." *Yearbook of European Law,* 548–50.

Winchester, S. 1974. *In Holy Terror: Reporting the Ulster Troubles.* London: Faber.

Yearbook of the European Convention on Human Rights. See Council of Europe, *Yearbook.*

Yonah, A., and A. O'Day, eds. 1986. *Ireland's Terrorist Dilemma.* Dordrecht: Martinus Nijhoff.

Zellick, G. 1974. "Prisoners' Rights in England." *University of Toronto Law Journal* 24: 331–46.

———. 1979. "The Case for Prisoners' Rights," in *Prisons, Past and Future,* ed. J. Freeman, 105–21. London: Heinemann.

———. 1981. "The Prison Rules and the Courts." *Criminal Law Review,* 602–16.

Cases

Abdulaziz, Cabales and Balkandali v. United Kingdom, 94 Eur. Ct. H.R. (ser. A) (1985).

Ahmad v. Inner London Education Authority, [1978] 1 All E.R. 574 (Court of Appeal).

Ahmad v. United Kingdom, 4 Eur. H.R. Rep. 126 (1981) (Commission report).

Air Canada v. United Kingdom, 316-A Eur. Ct. H.R. (ser. A) (1995).

Airey v. Ireland, 32 Eur. Ct. H.R. (ser. A) (1979).

Associated Newspapers Group Ltd. and Others v. Wade, [1979] 1 WLR 697 (Court of Appeal).

Associated Provincial Picture Houses, Ltd. v. Wednesbury Corporation [1947] 1 All E.R. 498 (King's Bench), affirmed, [1947] 2 All E.R. 680 (Court of Appeal).

Attorney-General v. Associated Newspapers Ltd. and Others [1993] 2 All E.R. 535 (Queen's Bench), [1994] 1 All E.R. 556 (House of Lords).

Attorney-General v. British Broadcasting Corporation [1980] 3 All E.R. 161 (House of Lords).

Attorney-General v. English [1982] 2 All E.R. 903 (Queen's Bench and House of Lords).

Attorney-General v. Guardian Newspapers Ltd. and Others [1987] 3 All E.R. 316 (*Spycatcher* ruling on interlocutory injunction against *The Guardian, The Observer,* and *The Sunday Times* before the Chancery Division, Court of Appeal, and House of Lords).

Attorney General v. Guardian Newspapers Ltd. and Others (No. 2) [1988] 3 All E.R. 545 (*Spycatcher* case, Chancery, Court of Appeal and House of Lords opinions on the merits, 1987–88).

Attorney-General v. London Weekend Television [1972] 3 All E.R. 1146 (thalidomide case involving television broadcast, Queen's Bench).

Attorney-General v. Newspaper Publishing plc and Others [1987] 3 All E.R. 276 (*Spycatcher* case involving *The Independent, The London Evening Standard,* and *The London Daily News* before the Chancery Division and the Court of Appeal).

Attorney General v. Observer Ltd.; re an application by Derbyshire County Council [1988] 1 All E.R. 385 (Chancery).

Attorney-General v. Times Newspapers Ltd. [1972] 3 All E.R. 1136 (thalidomide case before the Queen's Bench).

Attorney-General v. Times Newspapers Ltd. [1973] 1 All E.R. 815 (thalidomide case before the Court of Appeal).

Attorney-General v. Times Newspapers Ltd. [1973] 3 All E.R. 54 (thalidomide case before the House of Lords).

Attorney-General v. Times Newspapers Ltd. and another [1991] 2 All E.R. 398 (*Spycatcher*, contempt ruling before the House of Lords).

Autronic AG v. Switzerland, 178 Eur. Ct. H.R. (ser. A) (1990).

Baker v. Carr, 369 U.S. 186 (1962).

Barberá, Messequé and Jabardo v. Spain, 146 Eur. Ct. H.R. (ser. A) (1988).

Barfod v. Denmark, 149 Eur. Ct. H.R. (ser. A) (1989).

Barthold v. Germany, 90 Eur. Ct. H.R. (ser. A) (1985).

Becker v. Home Office [1972] 2 All E.R. 676 (Court of Appeal).

Beldjoudi v. France, 234A Eur. Ct. H.R. (ser. A) (1992).

Berrehab v. Netherlands, 138 Eur. Ct. H.R. (ser. A) (1988).

Bognor Regis Urban District Council v. Campion [1972] 2 All E.R. 61 (Queen's Bench).

Boner v. United Kingdom, 300-B Eur. Ct. H.R. (ser. A) (1994).

Bowers v. Hardwick, 478 U.S. 186 (1986).

Boyle and Rice v. United Kingdom, 131 Eur. Ct. H.R. (ser. A) (1988).

Brannigan and McBride v. United Kingdom, 258-B Eur Ct. H.R. (ser. A); 17 Eur. H.R. Rep. 539 (1993).

Brind and Others v. United Kingdom, 18 Eur. Hum. Rts. Rep. CD76 (1994).

Brogan and Others v. United Kingdom, 145-B Eur. Ct. H.R. (ser. A) (1988).

Brown v. Board of Education, 347 U.S. 483 (1954).

Brozicek v. Italy, 167 Eur. Ct. H.R. (ser. A) (1989).

Bugdaycay v. Home Secretary, [1986] 1 All E.R. 458 (Court of Appeal), [1987] 1 All E.R. 940 (House of Lords).

Byrne and Others v. United Kingdom, 51 Eur Comm'n. H.R. Dec. & Rep. 5 (1985); 1987 Y.B. Eur. Conv. on H.R. 171 (Committee of Ministers, Res. DH [87] 7).

Campbell v. United Kingdom, 233 Eur. Ct. H.R. (ser. A) (1992).

Campbell and Cosans v. United Kingdom, 48 Eur. Ct. H.R. (ser. A) (1982)

Campbell and Fell v. United Kingdom, 80 Eur. Ct. H.R. (ser. A.) (1984).

Castells v. Spain, 236 Eur. Ct. H.R. (ser. A) (1992).

Chahal Family v. United Kingdom, 20 Eur. Hum. Rts. Rep CD19 (1995)

Cheall v. Association of Professional, Executive, Clerical and Computer Staff [1982] 3 All E.R. 855 (Queen's Bench and Court of Appeal), reversed [1983] 1 All E.R. 1130 (House of Lords).

Chief Constable of the North Wales Police v. Evans [1982] 3 All E.R. 141.

Choudhury v. United Kingdom, 12 H.R.L.J. 172 (1991) (Commission report).

Chundawadra v. Immigration Appeal Tribunal, [1988] Imm. A.R. 161.

City of Chicago v. Tribune Co., 139 N.E. 86 (1923).

Colman v. United Kingdom, 258-D Eur. Ct. H.R. (ser. A) (1993).

Cossey v. United Kingdom, 184 Eur. Ct. H.R. (ser. A) (1990).

Costello-Roberts v. United Kingdom, 247-C Eur. Ct. H.R. (ser. A) (1993).

Craig v. Boren, 429 U.S. 190 (1976).

Darnell v. United Kingdom, 272 Eur. Ct. H.R. (ser. A) (1993).

Derbyshire County Council v. Times Newspapers Ltd. and Others, [1991] 4 All E.R. 795 (Queen's Bench), [1992] 3 All E.R. 65 (Court of Appeal), [1993] 1 All E.R. 1011 (House of Lords).

Djeroud v. France, 191-B Eur. Ct. H.R. (ser. A) (1991).

Dobson and Another v. Hastings and Others [1992] 2 All E.R. 94 (Chancery).

Dred Scott v. Sanford, 60 U.S. 393 (1856).

Dudgeon v. United Kingdom, 45 Eur. Ct. H.R. (ser. A) (1981).

East African Asians v. United Kingdom, 15 *Human Rights Law Journal* 215 (1973) (Commission report); 15 *Human Rights Law Journal* 232 (1977) (Committee of Ministers); 19 *European Human Rights Report* CD1 (1995) (Report of abortive friendly settlement discussions).

Edwards v. United Kingdom, 247-B Eur. Ct. H.R. (ser. A) (1992).

Endo (see *ex parte Endo*)

Ex parte Endo, 323 U.S. 283 (1944).

Ex parte Lynch, [1979–80] N.I.L.R. 1.

Ex parte Milligan, 71 U.S. (4 Wall.) 2 (1866).

F v. Wirral Metropolitan Borough Council and Another, [1991] 2 All E.R. 648 (Court of Appeal).

Farrant v. United Kingdom, 1987 Y.B. Eur. Conv. on H.R. 166 (Resolution of the Committee of Ministers); 50 Eur. Comm'n. H.R. Dec. & Rep. 5 (1985).

Fayed v. United Kingdom, 294-B Eur. Ct. H.R. (ser. A) (1994).

Fernandes v. Home Secretary, [1981] Imm. A.R. 1 (Court of Appeal).

Foley v. Connelie, 435 U.S. 291 (1978).

Fox, Campbell & Hartley v. United Kingdom, 182 Eur. Ct. H.R. (ser. A) (1990).

Frontiero v. Richardson, 411 U.S. 677 (1973).

Gaima v. Home Secretary, [1989] Imm. A.R. 205 (Court of Appeal).

Gay News Ltd. and Lemon v. United Kingdom, 5 Eur. H.R. Rep. 123 (1982) (Commission report).

Glassnap v. Germany, 104 Eur. Ct. H.R. (ser. A) (1986).

Gleaves v. Deakin and Others, [1978] 3 All E.R. 252 (Queen's Bench), [1979] 2 All E.R. 497 (House of Lords).

Golder v United Kingdom, 18 Eur. Ct. H.R. (ser. A.) (1975).

Grace v. United Kingdom, 62 Eur. Comm'n H.R. Dec. & Rep. 22 (1989).

Graham v. Richardson, 403 U.S. 365 (1971).

Granger v. United Kingdom, 172 Eur. Ct. H.R. (ser. A.) (1990).

Greene v. Secretary of State for Home Affairs, [1941] 3 All E.R. 104 (Court of Appeal), [1941] 3 All E.R. 388 (House of Lords).

Gregg v. Georgia, 428 U.S. 153 (1976).

Guardian (see *Observer and Guardian*)

Guilfoyle v. Home Office, [1981] 1 All E.R. 943 (Court of Appeal).

Guinn v. U.S., 238 U.S. 347 (1915).

Hamer v. United Kingdom, 4 Eur. H.R. Rep. 139 (1979) (Commission Report).

Haw Tua Tau v. Public Prosecutor and other appeals, [1981] 3 All E.R. 14 (Privy Council).

Herczegfalvy v. Austria, 244 Eur. Ct. H.R. (ser. A) (1992).

Hirabayashi v. U.S., 320 U.S. 81 (1943).

Home Office v. Harman, [1981] 2 All E.R. 349 (Queen's Bench and Court of Appeal), [1982] 1 All E.R. 532 (House of Lords).

Hone v. Maze Prison Board of Visitors, [1988] 1 All E.R. 321 (House of Lords).

Hubbard and Others v. Pitt and Others, [1975] 1 All E.R. 1056 (Queen's Bench), affirmed on other grounds [1975] 3 All E.R. 1 (Court of Appeal).

Hussain v. United Kingdom, 22 Eur. H.R. Rep. 1 (1996).

Informationsverein Lentia and Others v. Austria, 276 Eur. Ct. H.R. (ser. A) (1990).

Ingraham v. Wright, 430 U.S. 651 (1977).

In re McElduff, [1972] N.I.L.R. 1 (House of Lords).

Ireland v. United Kingdom, 23 Eur. Comm'n H.R. (ser. B.) (1976).

Ireland v. United Kingdom, 25 Eur. Ct. H.R. (ser. A) (1978).

Iye v. Home Secretary, [1994] Imm. A.R. 63 (Court of Appeal).

Jersild v. Denmark, 298 Eur. Ct. H.R. (ser. A) (1994).

Jones and Lee v. Miah and Miah, 24 H.L.R. 578 (1992).

K.D. (See *Re K.D.*)

Knechtl v. United Kingdom, 1970 Y.B. Eur. Conv. on H.R. (Eur. Comm'n on H.R.).

Korematsu v. U.S., 323 U.S. 214 (1944).

Kosiek v. Germany, 105 Eur. Ct. H.R. (ser. A) (1986).

Lamguindaz v. United Kingdom, 258-C Eur. Ct. H.R. (ser. A) (1993).

Leander v. Sweden, 116 Eur. Ct. H.R. (ser. A) (1987).

Lingens v. Austria, 103 Eur. Ct. H.R. (ser. A) (1986).

Liversidge v. Anderson, [1941] 2 All E.R. 612 (Court of Appeal), [1941] 3 All E.R. 338 (House of Lords).

L'Office Cherifien des Phosphates and another v. Yamashita-Shinnihon Steamship Co. Ltd. (The Boucraa), [1993] 3 All E.R. 686 (Court of Appeal), [1994] 1 All E.R. 29 (House of Lords).

Lynch, ex parte, [1980] N.I.L.R. 126 (Queen's Bench).

M v. H and Others, [1988] 3 All E.R. 5.

Malone v. Commissioner of Police of the Metropolis (No. 2), [1979] 2 All E.R. 620 (Chancery).

Malone v. United Kingdom, 82 Eur. Ct. of H.R. (ser. A) (1984).

Manchester Corporation v. Williams [1891] 1 Q.B. 94 (Queen's Bench).

Mapp v. Ohio, 367 U.S. 343 (1961).

markt intern Verlag GmbH and Klaus Beerman v. Germany, 165 Eur. Ct. H.R. (ser. A)
  (1989).

Maxwell v. United Kingdom, 300-C Eur. Ct. H.R. (ser. A) (1994).

McCallum v. United Kingdom, 183 Eur. Ct. H.R. (ser. A) (1990).

McCann and Others v. United Kingdom, 16 Hum. Rts. L.J. 260, 21 Eur. H.R. Rep. 97
  (1995).

McComb v. United Kingdom, 1986 Y.B. Eur. Conv. on H.R. 122 (Eur. Comm'n on H.R.).

McElduff (see *In re McElduff*)

McKee v. Chief Constable for Northern Ireland [1985] 1 All E.R. 1 (House of Lords).

McMichael v. United Kingdom, 307-B Eur. Ct. H.R. (ser. A) (1995).

Michael M. v. Superior Court of Sonoma County, 450 U.S. 464 (1981).

Milligan (see *Ex parte Milligan*)

Mistry v. The Entry Clearance Officer, Bombay, [1976] Imm. A.R. 54 (Immigration
  Appeal Tribunal).

Molinos v. Cyprus, 259 Eur. Ct. H.R. (ser. A) (1993).

Moore v. Secretary of State for Scotland, [1985] S.L.T. 322.

Moustaquim v. Belgium, 193 Eur. Ct. of H.R. (ser. A) (1991).

Müller and Others v. Switzerland, 133 Eur. Ct. H.R. (ser. A) (1988).

Murray (John) v. United Kingdom, 22 Eur. H.R. Rep. 29, 17 Hum. Rts. L. J. 39 (1996).

Murray (Margaret) v. United Kingdom, 19 Eur. H.R. Rep. 193; 300 Eur. Ct. H.R. (ser.
  A) (1994).

Near v. Minnesota, 283 U.S. 697 (1931).

New York Times v. U.S., 403 U.S. 713 (1971).

New York Times v. Sullivan, 376 U.S. 254 (1964).

Nielsen v. Denmark, 144 Eur. Ct. H.R. (ser. A.) (1988).

Oberschlick v. Austria, 204 Eur. Ct. H.R. (ser. A) (1991).

Observer and Guardian v. United Kingdom, 216 Eur. Ct. H.R. (ser. A) (1991) (*Spycatcher*
  case).

Open Door and Dublin Well Woman v. Ireland, 246 Eur. Ct. H.R. (ser. A) (1992).

Pan-American World Airways v. Department of Trade, [1976]1 Lloyds Rep. 257.

Pickering v. Liverpool Daily Post and Echo Newspapers plc and Others, [1991] 1 All
  E.R. 622 (House of Lords).

Piermont v. France, 314 Eur. Ct. H.R. (ser. A) (1995).

Plyler v. Doe, 457 U.S. 202 (1982).

Powell v. Alabama, 287 U.S. 45 (1932).

Powell and Rayner v. United Kingdom, 172 Eur. Ct. H.R. (ser. A) (1990)

Rantzen v. Mirror Group Newspapers (1986) Ltd., [1993] 4 All E.R. 975 (Court of
  Appeal).

Raymond v. Honey, [1981] 2 All E.R. 1084 (Queen's Bench), [1982] 1 All E.R. 756
  (House of Lords).

Reed v. United Kingdom, 25 Eur. Comm'n H.R. Dec. & Rep. 5 (1981) (Commission
  report).

R. v. Brown and other appeals, [1993] 2 All E.R. 75 (House of Lords).

R. v. Canons Park Mental Health Review Tribunal, ex parte A, [1994] 1 All E.R. 481 (Queen's Bench).

R. v. Chief Immigration Officer, Heathrow Airport and another, ex parte Salamat Bibi, [1976] 3 All E.R. 843 (Court of Appeal).

R. v. Chief Metropolitan Stipendiary Magistrate, ex parte Choudhury [1991] 1 All ER 306.

R. v. General Medical Council, ex parte Colman, [1990] 1 All E.R. 489 (Court of Appeal).

R. v. Governor of Pentonville Prison, ex parte Chinoy, [1992] 1 All E.R. 317 (Queen's Bench).

R. v. Home Secretary, ex parte Anderson, [1984] 1 All E.R. 920 (Queen's Bench).

R. v. Home Secretary and another, ex parte Bhajan Singh, [1975] 2 All E.R. 1081 (Court of Appeal).

R. v. Home Secretary, ex parte Brind, [1990] 1 All E.R. 469 (Court of Appeal); [1991] 1 All E.R. 720 (House of Lords).

R. v. Home Secretary ex parte Bugdaycay [1986], 1 All E.R. 457 (Court of Appeal).

R. v. Home Secretary, ex parte Chahal, [1993] Imm. A.R. 362 (Queen's Bench), [1995] 1 All E.R. 658 (Court of Appeal). (See also *Chahal Family v. United Kingdom*.)

R. v. Home Secretary, ex parte Jeyakumaran, [1985] Imm. A.R. 45 (Queen's Bench).

R. v. Home Secretary, ex parte K, [1990] 1 All E.R. 703 (Queen's Bench), [1990] 3 All E.R. 562 (Court of Appeal).

R. v. Home Secretary, ex parte Leech, [1993] 4 All E.R. 539 (Court of Appeal).

R. v. Home Secretary, ex parte Northumbria Police Authority, [1987] 2 All E.R. 282 (Queen's Bench), [1988] 1 All E.R. 556 (Court of Appeal).

R. v. Home Secretary, ex parte Phansopkar and Another, [1975] 3 All E.R. 497 (Court of Appeal).

R. v. Home Secretary, ex parte Sivakumaran and Others, [1988) 1 All E.R. 193 (House of Lords).

R. v. Home Secretary and Others, ex parte Tarrant and Another, [1984] 1 All E.R. 799 (Queen's Bench).

R. v. Home Secretary, ex parte Wynne, [1992], 2 All E.R. 301.

R. v. Immigration Appeal Tribunal, ex parte Chundawadra, [1987] Imm. A.R. 227 (Queen's Bench).

R. v. Lemon; R. v. Gay News Ltd., [1978] 3 All E.R. 175 (Court of Appeal), [1979] 1 All E.R. 898 (House of Lords).

R. v. McCormick and Others, [1977] N.I.L.R. 105 (Belfast City Commission).

R. v. Miah, [1974] 1 All E.R. 1110 (Court of Appeal). See also *Waddington v. Miah*, [1974] 2 All E.R. 377 (House of Lords).

R. v. Redbourne, [1993], 2 All E.R. 753.

R. v. Secretary of State for the Home Department, ex parte (name of petitioner). For purposes of brevity these are all listed here as *R. v. Home Secretary, ex parte* (alphabetical with last name of petitioner).

R. v. United Kingdom, 121 Eur. Ct. of H.R. (ser. A)(1987).

Re K D (a minor), [1988] 1 All E.R. 577 (House of Lords).

Ruiz v. Estelle, 503 F. Supp. 1265 (S.D. Tex. 1980), aff'd 679 F.2d 1115 (5th Cir. 1982, cert. denied, 460 U.S. 1042 (1983).

S v. Switzerland, 220 Eur. Ct. of H.R. (ser. A) (1991).

Salamat Bibi (see *R. v. Chief Immigration Officer and another, Heathrow Airport, ex parte Salamat Bibi*)

Schenk v. Switzerland, 140 Eur. Ct. H.R. (ser. A.) (1988).

Schering Chemicals Ltd. v. Falkman Ltd. and Others, [1981] 2 All E.R. 321 (Court of Appeal).

Schönenberger and Durmaz v. Switzerland, 137 Eur. Ct. H.R. (ser. A) (1988).

Schwabe v. Austria, 242-B Eur. Ct. H.R. (ser. A) (1993).

Shapiro v. Thompson, 394 U.S. 618 (1969).

Sibson v. United Kingdom, 258-A Eur. Ct. H.R. (ser. A) (1993)

Silver and Others v. United Kingdom, 61 Eur. Ct. H.R. (ser. A.) (1983).

Soering v. United Kingdom, 161 Eur. Ct. H.R. (ser. A) (1989).

Stanford v. United Kingdom, 282-A Eur. Ct. H.R. (ser. A) (1994).

Sunday Times v. United Kingdom, 30 Eur. Ct. H.R. (ser. A) (1979) (thalidomide case).

Sunday Times v. United Kingdom (No. 2), 217 Eur. Ct. H.R. (ser. A) (1991) (*Spycatcher* case).

T v. United Kingdom, 49 Eur. Comm'n H.R. Dec. and Rep. 5 (1986) (Commission report).

Taylor v. Co-operative Retail Services Ltd., [1982] I.C.R. 600 (Court of Appeal).

Thorgeir Thorgeirson v. Iceland, 239 Eur. Ct. H.R. (ser. A) (1993).

Thynne, Wilson and Gunnell v. United Kingdom, 190-A Eur. Ct. H.R. (ser. A) (1990).

Times Newspapers Ltd. and Others v. United Kingdom, 15 Eur. H.R. Rep. 49 (1993) (Commission report).

Times Newspapers Ltd. and Others v. United Kingdom, 8 Eur. H.R. Rep. 54 (1984) (Commission report).

Tinker v. Des Moines Independent School District, 393 U.S. 503 (1969).

Toll v. Moreno, 458 U.S. 1 (1982).

Tolstoy Miloslavsky v. United Kingdom, 316-B Eur. Ct. H.R. (ser. A) (1995).

Tyrer v. United Kingdom, 26 Eur. Ct. H.R. (ser. A) (1978).

United Kingdom Association of Professional Engineers and another v. Advisory Conciliation and Arbitration Service, [1979] 2 All E.R. 478 (Court of Appeal); [1980] 1 All E.R. 612 (House of Lords).

U.S. v. Carolene Products Co., 394 U.S. 144 (1938).

Vereinigung Demokratischer Soldaten Österreichs and Gubi v. Austria, 302 Eur. Ct. H.R. (ser. A) (1994).

Vereniging Weekblad Bluf! v. The Netherlands, 316 Eur. Ct. H.R. (ser. A) (1995).

Vilvarajah and Others v. United Kingdom, 215 Eur. Ct. H.R. (ser. A) (1991).

Vogt v. Germany, 323 Eur. Ct. H.R. (ser. A) (1995).

Weber v. Switzerland, 177 Eur. Ct. H.R. (ser. A) (1990).

Weeks v. United Kingdom, 114 Eur. Ct. H.R. (ser. A) (1987).

Welch v. United Kingdom, 307-A Eur. Ct. H.R. (ser. A) (1995).

Wheeler and Others v. Leicester City Council, [1985] 2 All E.R. 151 (Court of Appeal), [1985] 2 All E.R. 1106 (House of Lords).

Williams v. Home Office (No. 2), [1981] 1 All E.R. 1211 (Queen's Bench), dismissed on procedural grounds [1982] 2 All E.R. 564 (Court of Appeal).

Wynne v. Home Secretary, [1993], 2 All E.R. 301.

Wynne v. United Kingdom, 294-A Eur. Ct. H.R. (ser. A) (1994).

X v. United Kingdom, 46 Eur. Ct. H.R. (ser. A) (1981).

Y v. United Kingdom, 247-A Eur. Ct. H.R. (ser. A) (1992).

Yick Wo v. Hopkins, 118 U.S. 356 (1886).

Young, James and Webster v. United Kingdom, 44 Eur. Ct. H.R. (ser. A.) (1981).

Statutes, Government Documents, and Official Reports

Act for the Better Protection of Person and Property in Ireland 1881 (see Protection of Person and Property below).

Aliens Act 1905, 5 Edw. 7, ch. 13.

Aliens Act 1919 (See Aliens Restriction [Amendment] 1919).

Aliens Restriction Act 1914, 4–5 Geo. 5, ch. 12.

Aliens Restriction (Amendment) Act 1919, 31 *Halsbury's Statutes* 8 (1994 reissue).

Asylum and Immigration Appeals Act 1993, 31 *Halsbury's Statutes* 215 (1994 reissue).

Baker Report (1984). "Review of the operations of the Northern Ireland Emergency Provisions Act 1978." Cmnd. 9222.

Bennett Report (1979). "Report of a committee of inquiry into police interrogation procedures in Northern Ireland." Cmnd. 7497.

British Nationalities and Status of Aliens Act 1922, 12–13 Geo. 5, ch. 44.

British Nationality Act 1948, 31 *Halsbury's Statutes* 12 (1994 reissue).

British Nationality Act 1981, 31 *Halsbury's Statutes* 127 (1994 reissue).

Calcutt Report (1993). "Review of press self-regulation." Cmnd. 2135.

Cameron Report. (1969). "Disturbances in Northern Ireland." Belfast, Cmnd. 532.

Civil Authorities (Special Powers) Act (Northern Ireland) 1922, 12–13 Geo. 5, ch. 5 (Northern Ireland).

Civil Authorities (Special Powers) Act (Northern Ireland) 1933, 23–24 Geo. 5, ch. 12 (Northern Ireland).

Commonwealth Immigrants Act 1962, 10–11 Eliz. 2, ch. 21.

Commonwealth Immigrants Act 1968, 16–17 Eliz. 2, ch. 9.

Compton Report (1971). "Report of the enquiry into allegations against the security forces of physical brutality in Northern Ireland arising out of events on the 9th of August 1971." Cmnd. 4823.

Contempt of Court Act 1981, 11 *Halsbury's Statutes* 185 (1991 reissue).

Courts and Legal Services Act 1990, 11 *Halsbury's Statutes* 720, 1211.

Criminal Justice and Public Order Act 1994, ch. 33 (see *Halsbury's Statutes [Current Statute Service]*). Inferences from the silence of accused, secs. 34–39, Vol. 17, pp. 6–15.

Diplock Report (1972). "Report of the commission to consider legal procedures to deal with terrorist activities in Northern Ireland." Cmnd. 5185.

Drug Trafficking Offences Act 1986, 12 *Halsbury's Statutes* 994 (1994 reissue).

Education Act 1944, 15 *Halsbury's Statutes* 120 (1994 reissue).

Emergency Powers Act 1920, 48 *Halsbury's Statutes* 933 (1995 reissue).

Emergency Powers (Defence) Act 1939, 2–3 Geo. 6, ch. 62.

Emergency Powers (Defence) Act 1940, 3–4 Geo. 6, ch. 20.

Gardiner Report (1975). "Report of a committee to consider, in the context of civil liberties and human rights, measures to deal with terrorism in Northern Ireland." Cmnd. 5847.

Home Office (1971). *Legal advice to Prisoners.* Cmnd. 4846.

Immigration Act 1971, 31 *Halsbury's Statutes* 52 (1994 reissue).

Interception of Communication Act 1985, 34 *Halsbury's Statutes* 616, 45 *Halsbury's Statutes* 304 (1994 reissue).

Jellicoe Report (1983). "Review of the operation of the Prevention of Terrorism (Temporary Provisions) Acts 1974 and 1976." Cmnd. 8803.

Medical Act 1983, 31–32 Eliz. 2, ch. 54, also 38 *Halsbury's Statutes* 156.

Mental Health Act 1983, 28 *Halsbury's Statutes* 632.

Northern Ireland (Emergency Provisions) Act 1973, 31 *Halsbury's Statutes* 416 (1994 reissue).

Northern Ireland (Emergency Provisions) Act 1978, 26–27 Eliz. 2, ch. 5.

Northern Ireland (Emergency Provisions) Act 1991, 31 *Halsbury's Statutes* 719 (1994 reissue).

Northern Ireland (Emergency Provisions) (Amendment) Act 1975, 31 *Halsbury's Statutes* 482 (1994 reissue).

Northern Ireland (Temporary Provisions) Act 1972, 31 *Halsbury's Statutes* 345 (1994 reissue).

Official Secrets Act 1911, 12 *Halsbury's Statutes* 171 (1994 reissue).

Official Secrets Act 1920, 12 *Halsbury's Statutes* 185 (1994 reissue).

Official Secrets Act 1939, 12 *Halsbury's Statutes* 215 (1994 reissue).

Official Secrets Act 1989, 12 *Halsbury's Statutes* 1388 (1994 reissue).

Parker Report (1972). "Report of a committee to consider authorized procedures for the interrogation of persons suspected of terrorism." Cmnd. 4901.

Phillimore Report (1972). "Report of the Phillimore Committee on Contempt of Court." (1974) Cmnd. 5794.

Prevention of Terrorism (Temporary Provisions) Act 1974, 1974, ch. 55.

Prevention of Terrorism (Temporary Provisions) Act 1976, 1976, ch. 8.

Prevention of Terrorism (Temporary Provisions) Act 1984, 1984, ch. 8.

Prevention of Terrorism (Temporary Provisions) Act 1989, 12 *Halsbury's Statutes* 1317 (1994 reissue).

Prisons (Scotland) Act 1952, 15–16 Geo. 6 and 1 Eliz. 2, ch. 61.

Protection of Life and Property (Ireland) Act 1871, 34 Vict. ch. 35.

Protection of Person and Property (Ireland) Act 1881, 44 Vict. ch. 4.

Restoration of Order in Ireland Act 1920, 10–11 Geo. 5, ch. 31.

Scarman Report (1972). "Report on violence and civil disturbance in Northern Ireland in 1969." Belfast, Cmnd. 566.

Shackleton Report (1978). "Review of the operation of the Prevention of Terrorism (Temporary Provisions) Acts 1974 and 1976." Cmnd. 7324.

Standing Advisory Commission on Human Rights (1977). "The protection of human rights by law in Northern Ireland." Cmnd. 7009.

Woolf Report (1991). "Prison disturbances April 1990: Report of an inquiry by the Rt. Hon. Lord Justice Woolf and His Honour Judge Stephen Tumin." Cmnd. 1456.

INDEX

Abdulaziz, Cabales and Balkandali v. United Kingdom (1985), 89–93; family rights in, 91–92

Abdulaziz, Mrs. Nargis, 89, 91

Access to justice, 80, 151, 167; under common law, 76; delays in, 15–16; in immigration cases, 93; for political refugees, 98–99; poverty and, 20; for prisoners, 67–68, 71, 128–29, 132; in *Silver* case, 72; in *Vilvarajah and Others*, 97. *See also* Judicial system, British

Accountability: in British human rights, 3–4; of British judges, 166–67, 172–73; and freedom of the press, 170, 173; of officials, 3–4, 163–71; to Parliament, 164–65, 170–71; under Wednesbury principles, 166–67. *See also* Discretion, administrative

Ackner, Lord, 81, 162

Act for the Better Protection of Person and Property in Ireland, 46

Ahmad v. Inner London Education Authority (1977), 139–40

Airey v. Ireland (1979), 20

Albany Prison disturbances, 73, 75

Aldershot bombing (1972), 33–34

Alienage, in U.S. constitutional law, 161–62

Aliens: collective expulsion of, 179; political activity of, 178; regulation by home secretary, 83, 100, 133, 135, 138–39. *See also* Immigration; National security

Aliens Act 1905, 82–83

Aliens Restriction Act 1914, 83

Amnesty International, 97, 104

Arrest, 175–76; under Civil Authorities Act, 35; under Northern Ireland (Temporary Provisions) Act, 39; under Prevention of Terrorism Act, 48–49; prompt review of,

53–54; reasonable grounds for, 168. *See also* Detention

Article 1 (ECHR), 174. *See also* Securing of Rights

Article 2 (ECHR), 174–75; violations of, 31, 56. *See also* Deprivation of life

Article 3 (ECHR), 175; in immigration cases, 88–89, 98; violations of, 40–41. *See also* Degrading treatment; Torture

Article 4 (ECHR), 175. *See also* Compulsory labor; Slavery

Article 5 (ECHR), 175–76; in *Brogan and Others*, 49–50; case references to, 126–28; violations of, 20, 41, 42. *See also* Deprivation of liberty; Detention; Promptness of trial; Security of person

Article 6 (ECHR), 176; case references to, 128–32; in *John Murray v. United Kingdom*, 31, 130; in prisoners' rights cases, 67, 69; violations of, 18–19, 20, 21, table 2.2. *See also* Access to justice; Due process; Promptness of trial; Right to counsel; Right to silence

Article 7 (ECHR), 176–77; case references to, 132–33

Article 8 (ECHR), 177; case references to, 133–39; in family life cases, 91–92; in gender discrimination cases, 92–93; in immigration cases, 89; in prisoners' rights cases, 177; violations of, 18, 21. *See also* Gender discrimination; Family rights; National security; Privacy rights

Article 9 (ECHR), 177; case references to, 139–41. *See also* Freedom of religion

Article 10 (ECHR), 106–7, 177; case references to, 141–45; violations of, 18. *See also* Freedom of conscience; Freedom of

Article 10—*continued*
    expression; Freedom of religion; National
    security
Article 11 (ECHR), 177–78; case references to,
    145–48. *See also* Freedom of association
Article 13 (ECHR), 93, 178; and judicial
    review, 98–99. *See also* Access to justice
Article 14 (ECHR), 43, 178; in gender
    discrimination cases, 92–93; in immigration
    cases, 89; violations of, 19–20. *See also*
    Discrimination, freedom from; Gender
    discrimination
Article 15 (ECHR), 42, 178. *See also*
    Derogation, right of
Article 17 (ECHR), 178
Article 18 (ECHR), 178
Associated Newspapers Group v. Wade
    (1979), 142, 151
Associated Provincial Picture Houses, Ltd. v.
    Wednesbury Corp. (1947), 167. *See also*
    Wednesbury principles
Asylum, political, 2; and administrative
    discretion, 94–104; in ECHR, 98, 105; in *ex*
    parte Chahal, 102; judicial review of, 103;
    objective test for, 94–95; in torture cases,
    102. *See also* Refugees, Tamil
Asylum and Immigration Appeals Act 1993,
    103
Atkin, Lord, 47–48
Attorney-client privilege. *See* Right to counsel
Attorney-General v. Associated Newspapers
    (1994), 122–23
Attorney-General v. British Broadcasting
    Corp. (1980), 121, 143
Attorney-General v. English (1982), 113–14
Austria, violations of ECHR, 19, 107

Bagehot, Walter, 5
Baker, Sir George, 52–53
Baker v. Carr (1962), 160
Balkandali, Mrs. Sohair, 89, 91, 93
Barberà et al. v. Spain (1988), 22
Barthold v. Germany (1985), 106
Belgium, violations of ECHR, 1, 136
Bell, J. Bowyer, 37
Berrehab v. Netherlands (1988), 136
Bigi, Judge, 119

A Bill of Rights for Britain (Dworkin), 3, 172
Bill of Rights (United States), 2, 11;
    application to public policy, 8; in World
    War II, 159
Bindschedler-Robert, Judge Denise, 26; career
    of, 25; dissents by, 22, 24
Birdi v. Secretary of State for Home Affairs,
    100
"Birmingham Six," 128, 135
Black, Justice, 159
"Bloody Sunday" (1974), 38
Bognor Regis Urban District Council v.
    Campion (1992), 120
Boner v. United Kingdom (1994), 17
Bookbinder, David, 119
Bowers v. Hardwick (1986), 30, 156
Boyle, K., 33
Boyle and Rice v. United Kingdom (1988),
    76–77
Brandon, Lord, 116–17
Brannigan and McBride v. United Kingdom
    (1993), 18; derogation in, 54–55, 60
Brennan, Justice, 161
Bricks of Shame (Stern), 64, 80, 81
Bridge, Lord, 101, 102, 103; on applicability of
    ECHR, 150; on freedom of speech, 117, 119
"Bridlington principles," 146, 147
British Broadcasting Corp., 143; restraints on,
    121, 122
British Dependent Territory, citizens of, 90
British intelligence services, 2, 38, 83
British Nationality Acts: of 1914, 83; of 1918,
    83; of 1948, 86, 87; of 1964, 88; of 1981, 85–
    86, 90
British Overseas citizens, 90
British Protected Persons (BPPs), 86, 89
British Refugee Council, 97
British Security Service (MI5), 83; in
    Spycatcher cases, 107–8, 114–18
Broadcasting, restraints on, 121–22
Brogan and Others v. United Kingdom
    (1988), 48–52; derogation in, 18, 49, 51, 54,
    59; judicial review in, 54
Browne-Wilkinson, Vice Chancellor, 114, 143
Brown v. Board of Education (1954), 7, 157
Broziek v. Italy (1989), 14
Bugdaycay v. Home Secretary (1987), 101

Burger, Warren, 161

Byrne and Others v. United Kingdom (1987), 75–76

Cabales, Mrs. Arcely, 89, 91

Calcutt, Sir David, 60, 124

Callaghan, James, 34

Cameron Commission Report (1969), 32

Campaign for Social Justice (1964), 32

Campbell, Marie, 52

Campbell, Sean, 73, 74, 75

Campbell, Thomas, 77–78

Campbell and Cosans v. United Kingdom (1982), 153, 156

Campbell and Fell v. United Kingdom (1984), 73–75, 76; European Court on, 130; prior ventilation in, 74–75

Campbell v. United Kingdom (1992), 17, 77–79; dissent in, 78, 129

Canadian Charter of Rights and Human Freedoms (1982), 11

Capital punishment, 156

Cassin, René, 27, 28

Catch 22 (Heller), 98

Catholics, of Northern Ireland, 32–33; in "Troubles," 34

Censorship. *See* Freedom of expression; Freedom of the press

Chahal Family v. United Kingdom (1995), 103, 104

Chahal (immigrant), 102, 103, 104

Charter 88 movement, 3

Cheall v. Association of Professional, Executive, Clerical and Computer Staff (1981), 146

Chief Constable of the North Wales Police v. Evans (1982), 103

Choudhury v. United Kingdom (1991), 141, 142

Churchill, Winston, 11

Citizenship, 153; in United Kingdom-and-Colonies, 84–93. *See also* Aliens; Immigration; Nationality

City of Chicago v. Tribune Co. (1923), 120

Civil Authorities (Special Powers) Act (Northern Ireland, 1922), 34, 35, 45, 46

Civil Service, British, 6–7

Civil War, American, 158

Clutterbuck, Richard, 33

Cohen, Stan, 69–70, 79

Common law, English, ix; access to courts under, 76, 93, 129, 151; applicability of ECHR to, 61–62, 105, 108–9, 124, 126, 148–52, 156, 157; Discretion and Emergency Powers under, 43; effect of American constitutional law on, 120; emergency powers under, 45–58; and freedom of association, 151; freedom of expression in, 106–7, 120, 123, 129, 143, 145, 151; human rights in, 9–10, 151, 157; incorporation of ECHR into, 9, 10, 18, 62, 98–99, 171–73; prior restraint in, 121, 125, 151; and prisoners' rights, 72; right to counsel under, 151. *See also* Judicial review, British; Judicial system, British; Law lords

Commonwealth Immigrants Act 1962, 83, 87; gender discrimination in, 89

Commonwealth Immigrants Act 1968, 84, 86, 87; racial discrimination in, 88

Compton, Sir Edmund, 37

Compton Report, 37, 40

Compulsory labor, 39

Confidentiality: and freedom of the press, 2, 144; in second *Sunday Times* case, 115–16; in *Spycatcher* cases, 118; and terrorism, 53, 54–55

Conseil constitutionnel (Stone), 29

Constitution (United States): amendments to, 2; First Amendment, 162; Fourteenth Amendment, 19, 157, 160, 161

Contempt of Court Act 1981, 113

Contractual obligations, 178

Convention Relating to the Status of Refugees (1954), 94

Correspondence, prisoners', 71–73, 74, 153; in *Campbell v. the United Kingdom*, 77–79, 129; in *Farrant v. United Kingdom*, 76

Costello v. United Kingdom (1985), 77

Council of Europe, 11, 174; committee of ministers, 12, 13

Counterintelligence, 83

Court of Justice, International, 12, 27

Court of Justice of the European Community, 29, 60, 132

Courts: constitutional, 29; delays in, 1; discretion in, 10. *See also* Judicial system, British

Courts and Legal Services Act 1990, 122

Coyle (detainee), 49

Craig v. Boren (1976), 92

Credos (criminal justice), 64–65; confrontations between, 79–81

Cremona, Judge, 22

Crime control, and due process, 64

Criminal Evidence (Northern Ireland) Order 1988, 58, 61, 129

Criminal Justice and Public Order Act 1994, 60

Criminal Justice and the Pursuit of Decency (Rutherford), 64–65, 80

Cross, Lord, 112

Crown, British: executive power of, 3–4

Cruelty. *See* Degrading treatment

CUKCs (citizens of United Kingdom-and-Colonies), 86–89; spouses of, 89–93

Daily Mail, 110

Daily News, 114

Darnell v. United Kingdom (1993), 17

Davis, Kenneth Culp, 10, 99, 163–64, 165, 166

Death penalty, 180

Defence of the Realm Act, 46, 100

Degrading treatment, 30; in *East African Asians* case, 88–89; in *Ireland v. United Kingdom*, 41–42

Delays. *See* Access to justice; Promptness of trial

De Meyer, Judge, 55, 119

Denning, Lord, 151; on applicability of ECHR, 149; on European Commission, 128; on *ex parte Bhajan Singh*, 100, 148–49; on freedom of association, 145–48; on freedom of religion, 139–40, 142; on freedom of the press, 111, 120, 121; on *Guilfoyle v. Home Office*, 78–79, 128, 135; on immigration, 133–34, 136; on national security, 168–69; on prisoners' rights, 65

Deportation, 135, 136

Deprivation of liberty, 20; in *Ireland v. United Kingdom*, 40; in *McCann and Others*, 56

Deprivation of life, 38, 174

Derbyshire County Council v. Times

Newspapers (1993), 106, 108, 109, 119, 145; citation of ECHR in, 124, 129, 157; prior restraint in, 151; U.S. constitutional law in, 162

Derogation, 178; in *Brannigan and McBride*, 54–55, 60; in *Brogan and Others*, 49, 51, 54, 59; in *Ireland v. United Kingdom*, 18, 38, 40, 41, 42, 44, 48; margin of appreciation in, 55; from Protocols, 180; right of, 8–9, 59

Detention, 175; and availability of habeas corpus writ, 49–50; under Civil Authorities Act, 35; in *Fox, Campbell & Hartley*, 52; incommunicado, 55; in *Ireland v. United Kingdom*, 42; lawfulness of, 20; under Northern Ireland (Temporary Provisions) Act, 39; under Prevention of Terrorism Act, 48–49; of Tamils, 96; in "Troubles," 34; during World War II, 45, 46–48. *See also* Arrest

Detention of Terrorists Order (1972), 35, 39

Dilhorne, Viscount, 143

Diplock, Lord, 129; on freedom of association, 147; on libel, 142–43

Diplock Commission report, 36, 40

Diplock Courts, 31, 36

Discretion, administrative, 3–4, 82, 94–95, 99, 163–71; checks on, 170, 171; in European Court, 30; of home secretary, 6–7, 82, 100, 163–71; judicial review of, 164–65, 168; in judicial system, 10; and Parliamentary Opposition, 170; in political asylum, 94–104; proposals for constraint on, 169. *See also* Accountability

Discretionary Justice (Davis), 10, 163–64

Discretionary Powers (Galligan), 169–70

Discrimination, freedom from, 19–20; dissent in European Court, 21; in *Ireland v. United Kingdom*, 38, 40, 43–44. *See also* Gender discrimination; Racial discrimination

Dissent: in *Campbell v. United Kingdom*, 78, 129; on due process, 21; in European Court, 15, 20–26, tables 2.3–2.5; on family rights, 21; on freedom from discrimination, 21; on freedom of expression, 25, 119; by Lord Scarman, 130, 152; in *Vilvarajah and Others*, 103

Djeroud v. France (1991), 136

Dobson v. Hastings (1991), 144
Domestic courts, European, 28
Domestic law. *See* Common law, English
Domestic remedy. *See* Access to justice
Donnelly and Others (1972), 30
Dred Scott v. Sanford (1856), 158
Drug Trafficking Offences Act 1986, 132
Dudgeon case (1981), 30, 153
Due process, 176; in American prison system,
 160–61; and crime control, 64; Diplock
 Commission on, 36; dissent in European
 Court, 21; in national security, 158; in
 United States, 156; violations of ECHR in,
 18–19, 20, 126. *See also* Access to justice;
 Promptness of trial; Right to counsel
Dummett, A., 82, 83, 87–88
Dutch Supreme Court, 27
Dworkin, Ronald, 3, 171–72

East African Asians, immigration to U.K., 84
East African Asians v. United Kingdom
 (1973), 86–89, 93
Easter riots (1969), 33
Easter Rising (Dublin, 1916), 32, 33, 46
ECHR. *See* European Convention on Human
 Rights
École Nationale de la Magistrature, 28
Education, right to, 178
Education Act 1944, 139–40
Eissen, Marc-André, 12
Emergency Powers Act 1973, 36, 43
Emergency Powers (Defence) Act 1939, 45
Endo, Mitsue, 159
The English Constitution (Bagehot), 5
English Intelligence Centre, 38
Entrenchment, Parliamentary, 172
Equal protection, 19
European Commission on Human Rights: on
 Brind case, 122; on *Brogan and Others*, 49;
 on *Campbell and Fell*, 74; case volume of,
 15; creation of, 12; delays under, 15–16; on
 East African Asians v. United Kingdom,
 86–89; election to, 12; on *Farrant v. United
 Kingdom*, 76; on first *Sunday Times* case,
 111; on "five techniques," 37, 38, 41; on
 Fox, Campbell & Hartley, 52; on freedom
 of expression, 114; on freedom of religion,
 140; on *Golder* case, 69; on *Guilfoyle v.*

Home Office, 135; on immigration, 88–89;
 individual petition to, 13, 57, 61; on *Ireland
 v. United Kingdom,* 40–41, 59; on *Knechtl
 v. United Kingdom,* 67–68; Lord Denning
 on, 128; procedures of, 13–14; proportionality principle of, 167; on religious
 freedom, 140; scholarship on, 11; status of
 proceedings, 78; on "Troubles," 34–35; on
 Vilvarajah and Others, 97, 98
European Convention on Human Rights, ix;
 applicability to common law, 61–62, 105,
 108–9, 124, 126, 148–52, 156, 157; asylum
 in, 95; and British judicial review, 99–104;
 citation in British courts, 10, 100, 101, 102,
 126–52, 182, table 7.1; enabling legislation
 for, 9, 10; enforceability of, 9, 28; establishment of, 11, 126; in *ex parte Brind,* 100,
 101, 102, 127, 144, 150; on family rights,
 18, 19, 20, 89, 90–92, 133–34; freedom of
 expression in, 25, 106–10, 119, 141–45, 167;
 immigration in, 88, 126, 133–39, 148–49;
 incorporation into common law, 9, 10, 18,
 62, 98–99, 171–73; interpretation of, 29–30;
 in *Ireland v. United Kingdom,* 38, 39–44;
 nonderogable violations of, 59; political
 asylum in, 98; privacy rights under, 10, 30,
 176; proportionality in, 167; ratification by
 United Kingdom, 60; security of person in,
 25, 126–29; system breaches of, 110, 119;
 on terrorism, 30; violations by type, 109–
 10, 153; violations by United Kingdom, ix,
 1–2, 16–20, 154–56, 163, table 8.1;
 Yearbook of, 12, 67. *See also* Articles;
 Protocols
European Court of Human Rights, ix; British
 freedom of expression cases before, 107–10;
 on British judicial review, 101–2; and
 British prison system, 65–69; on *Brogan
 and Others,* 51–52; on *Campbell and Fell,*
 75; case volume of, 15–16; claims decided
 by, table 2.2; creation of, 12; decision-
 making processes of, 29–30; delays under,
 15–16; dissent in, 15, 20–26; election to,
 12–13, 15; evidence before, 14; on first
 Sunday Times case, 112–13; on "five
 techniques," 41–42; on *Fox, Campbell &
 Hartley,* 52–53; on freedom of expression,
 107; on freedom of the press, 118–19;

ECHR—*continued*
  history (1959-1989), 16; on *Ireland v. United Kingdom*, 41–45, 48; judicial review by, x; Lord Denning on, 128; on *Margaret Murray* case, 55–56; on margin of appreciation, 43, 54; national composition of, 12; precedents of, 11; on prior restraint, 118, 119; procedures of, 13–15; qualifications for, 28–29; referrals by member states to, 109; registrar of, 14–15; on second *Sunday Times* case, 116; state defendants, table 2.1; use of discretion, 30; use of proportionality principle, 167; on *Vilvarajah and Others*, 97, 98. *See also* Judges, of European Court
European Human Rights Reports, 107
European Union, 60; membership of, 11
Evans, Judge Vincent, 25, 29; on *Fox, Campbell & Hartley*, 53; on *Iye v. Home Secretary*, 139
The Evening Standard, 114
Ewing, K. D., 105, 171, 172
Ewing, W., 33
Ex parte Endo (1944), 158, 159–60
Ex parte Lynch (1980), 50–51, 168

Family rights, 153, 177, 178; in *Abdulaziz, Cabales and Balkandali v. United Kingdom*, 90–92; access to children in, 136; case references to ECHR in, 133–34; dissent in European Court, 21; and immigration, 89, 105; under Magna Carta, 151; termination by state, 130–31; violations of ECHR in, 18, 19, 20, 89
Farquharson, Lord Justice, 81
Farrant, David, 76
Farrant v. United Kingdom (1987), 76–77
Farrell, Mairead, 56
Farrell, Michael, 33
Faulkner, Brian, 34
Federal Republic of Germany, 19; administrative review system of, 165; *Bundesgerichtshof*, 27
Feldman, David, 100
Fell, Father Patrick, 73, 74, 75
Fernandes v. Home secretary (1980), 135–36
Fitzmaurice, Judge Gerald, 44–45
"Five techniques," 36–37, 39; abandonment

of, 58; European Court on, 41–45. *See also* Torture
Foighel, Judge, 119
Foley v. Connelie (1978), 161
Food and water, deprivation of, 37, 44
Fox, Bernard, 52
Fox, Campbell and Hartley v. United Kingdom (1990), 17, 52–54, 60; dissent in, 53; and *Margaret Murray* case, 55–56
France: administrative courts of, 28; Civil Code, 133; constitutional adjudication in, 29; *Cour de cassation*, 27; violations of ECHR, 19, 136
Franchise, British, 3
Freedom of association, 20, 176; under common law, 151; Lord Denning on, 145–46, 147–48
Freedom of conscience, 20; in Universal Declaration of Human Rights, 143
Freedom of expression, 1, 2, 126, 153, 177; in *Brind* case, 167; British cases before European Court, 107–10; case references in ECHR, 141–45; in common law, 106–7, 120, 123, 129, 143, 145, 151; dissent in ECHR cases, 25, 119; European Commission on, 114; Lord Scarman on, 130; margin of appreciation in, 112–13, 117; for prisoners, 75; in *Spycatcher* cases, 114–19; in thalidomide controversy, 110–11; in theater, 124
Freedom of religion, 20, 144–45, 178; European Commission on, 140
Freedom of the press, 2, 153; and administrative accountability, 170, 173; and British contempt cases, 107, 113, 121, 122; and confidentiality, 2, 144; law lords on, 111, 162; and national security, 118; in U.S. constitutional law, 162–63
Freedom of thought, 20
Freeland, Sir John, 78, 79
Frontiero v. Richardson (1973), 91, 92
F v. Wirral Metropolitan Borough Council (1991), 131, 137

Gaima v. Home Secretary (1989), 101
Galligan, D. J., 169–70
Gardiner, Lord, 37, 58
Gardiner Commission (1975), 39

Gardner, John, 106
Gay News Ltd. and Lemon v. United Kingdom (1982), 140–41
Gearty, C. A., 105, 171, 172
Gender discrimination: in immigration, 89–93; Supreme Court on, 92
General Medical Council, 144
Gibraltar, IRA in, 56–57, 63
Gibson, Lord Justice, 144
Gleaves v. Deakin (1979), 142
Goff, Lord, 124
Gölcüklü, Judge: career of, 25; dissents by, 22
Golder, Sidney, 68
Golder v. United Kingdom (1975), 9, 68–70, 126; home secretary on, 132; Lord Bridge on, 129; in Prison Act of 1952, 75, 80
Grace v. United Kingdom (1977), 77
Graham v. Richardson (1971), 161, 162
Grandfather clauses, in immigration, 86
Granger v. United Kingdom (1990), 17
Great Britain, countries comprising, ix
Greene, Ben, 46, 47
Green v. Secretary of State for Home Affairs (1941), 46–47, 167
Gregg v. Georgia (1976), 156
Griffith, J. A. G., 172
Guardian case. *See The Observer and Guardian v. United Kingdom* (1991)
Guernsey, ix
Guilfoyle, Patrick, 128
Guilfoyle v. Home Office (1980), 78–79, 128
Guinn v. U.S. (1915), 86

Habeas corpus, writ of: availability for detainees, 49–50; in *Brannigan and McBride*, 55; under Civil Authorities Act, 36; in *Fox, Campbell & Hartley*, 52; judicial review through, 42, 43, 50–51; purpose of, 7; suspension of, 9, 45–46
Habeas Corpus Suspension Acts (1866-67), 45–46
Hadden, T., 33
Hague Peace Conference (1899), 27
Halisham, Lord, 165
Hampson, François, 16–17, 108–10, 123–24
Handbook on Procedures and Criteria for Determining Refugees Status, 101
Hartley (detainee), 52

Hawkins, Keith, 169
Haw Tua Tau v. Public Prosecutor (1981), 129
Heath, Edward, 38, 58
Heseltine, Michael, 57
Hirabayashi v. U.S. (1943), 158–59
Hogg, Quintin, 66
Homeless Citizens League (1963), 32
Home Office v. Harman (1982), 130, 143
Home secretary: on access to courts, 80; in asylum cases, 103; in *Brogan and Others*, 51–52; discretion of, 6–7, 82, 100, 163–71; in *ex parte Chahal*, 102; in *Fernandes* case, 135; in *Golder* case, 68–69, 70; judicial review of, 99, 101, 105, 167; in *Knechtl v. United Kingdom*, 66–67, 68; and Prevention of Terrorism Act, 49; and prisoners' rights, 131; regulation of aliens, 83, 100, 133, 135, 138–39; in *Silver* case, 72; in *Sivakumaran* case, 94–95; on Tamil refugees, 98; use of emergency powers, 45; in *Vilvarajah and Others*, 95–96; in World War II, 45, 47–48
Homosexuals: consenting, 30, 137–38, 153; newspapers for, 140–41
Hone v. Maze Prison Board of Visitors (1988), 130, 151
Hooding, 37, 44
House of Commons: influence of, 3; leadership in, 6
House of Lords Appellate Committee. *See* Law lords
Housing Act 1988, 132
Howard, Michael, 104
Howe, Sir Geoffrey, 57
Hubbard and Others v. Pitt and Others (1974), 124
Human rights: attitude of British judges to, 109, 123–24; judicial enforcement of, 1; and national sovereignty, 8; politics of adjudication, 28–29; principles of, x; transnational, 28, 108; in the United States, 7–8, 163; universal principles of, 8–9; Western discourse on, 8
Human rights, British: accountability in, 3–4; in common law, 9–10, 151, 157; effect of secrecy on, 163–64
Husbands, nonpatrial, 90, 93
Hussain v. United Kingdom (1996), 153

Hutchinson, Lord, 62

Immigration, 153; case references to ECHR in, 126, 133–39, 148–49; of East African Asians, 84; European Commission on, 88–89; family rights in, 89; gender discrimination in, 89–93; judicial review for, 91, 105, 166; and poverty, 83; racial discrimination in, 85, 86, 88, 93; regulation of, 82–86; rights in, 1, 2, 82; societal impact of, 82; and unemployment, 90–91, 92, 93. *See also* Aliens; Nationality

Immigration Act 1971, 84–85, 86, 89; in *Vilvarajah* case, 96

Immigration Appeal Tribunal, 149

Imperialism, British, 82, 83

The Independent, 114

Independent Broadcasting Authority (IBA), restraints on, 121, 122

Indian Peacekeeping Force (IPKF, Sri Lanka), 96, 97

In from the Cold (Lustgarten and Leigh), 168

Ingraham v. Wright (1977), 156

Interception of Communications Act (1985), 134–35

Interlocutory injunctions, 115, 116, 118

International Court of Justice, 12, 27

International Political Science Association, x

International Sikh Youth Federation, 102

Internment: under Civil Authorities Act, 35; in *Ireland v. United Kingdom*, 39, 42; *Times* on, 62, 63; in World War II, 59. *See also* Detention

Interrogation: under Civil Authorities Act, 35; under Emergency Powers Act, 36; in *Ireland v. United Kingdom*, 42; of Tamils, 96

In the Highest Degree Odious (Simpson), 45

Ireland v. United Kingdom (1978), 31–45, 58; articles of ECHR cited in, 38, 39–45; derogation in, 18, 38, 40, 41, 42, 44, 48; dissent in, 44–45; European Court on, 41–45, 48; United Kingdom's response to, 18, 38, 40, 41, 42. *See also* Northern Ireland

Irish Free State, 32

Irish Republican Army (IRA): discrimination of political opinion against, 40; European Court on, 43; in Gibralter, 56–57, 63; under

Prevention of Terrorism Act, 48; Provisional wing of, 33–34; *Times* on, 63

Isle of Man, ix

Italy, violations of ECHR, 1, 19

Iye v. Home Secretary (1994), 138–39

Jackson, Justice, 159

Japanese Americans, 158–59

John Murray v. United Kingdom (1996), 18; article 6 under, 31, 130; right to silence in, 57–58, 60–61, 181n4

Jones and Lee v. Miah and Miah (1992), 132

Jowett (Lord Chancellor), 61

Judges, British: accountability of, 166–67, 172–73; attitude toward human rights, 109, 123–24; deference to executive branch, 168–69; judicial review by, 28. *See also* Law lords

Judges, of European Court, 1; age of, 26; background characteristics of, 26–28; dissent by, 22–26, tables 2.3–2.5; election of, 12–13, 15; gender of, 26; qualifications of, 28–29

Judicial Politics since 1920 (Griffith), 172

Judicial review: and domestic remedy, 98–99; by European Court, x

Judicial review, American, 2, 157–63, 165; by Supreme Court, 59

Judicial review, British, 2–3, 28; of asylum rights, 95; in *Brind*, 103, 121; in *Brogan and Others* (1988), 54; in common law, 28, 48; decision-making procedure under, 168; of discretionary powers, 164–71; and ECHR, 99–104, 173; through habeas corpus, 42, 43, 50–51; of home secretary, 99, 101, 105, 121; of housing cases, 166; in immigration cases, 91, 105, 166; of political asylum, 103; reasonable grounds for, 167; of *Vilvarajah* case, 96. *See also* Common law, English; Wednesbury principles

Judicial system, British: contempt powers of, 107, 113, 121, 122, 123; references to ECHR in, 10, 100, 101, 102, 126–52, table 7.1. *See also* Access to justice; Judges, British; Judicial review, British; Law lords

Justice, William, 160

Keith, Lord, 106, 119, 120

Kenya, citizenship in, 87
Kerridge, Robert, 172
Knechtl, Gyula, 65–66
Knechtl v. United Kingdom (1970), 65–68
Korematsu v. U.S. (1944), 158, 159

Lacey, Nicola, 169
Lamguindaz v. United Kingdom (1993), 136
Law: ex post facto, 132, 151, 176–77;
 international, 28
Law lords, 108, 109; on contempt, 123;
 definition of, 3; in first *Sunday Times* case,
 24, 111, 113; on freedom of association,
 146; on freedom of expression, 106; on
 freedom of the press, 162; in *Hone v. Maze
 Prison Board*, 130; on *Spycatcher* cases,
 115, 116–18, 121; during World War II, 47;
 in *Wynne v. Home Secretary*, 131–32
Legal aid, for prisoners, 66
Leicester City Council, 143
Leigh, I., 168
Lester, Anthony, 87, 170
Lewis, Anthony, 108
Libel: blasphemous, 140–41, 145; civil actions
 for, 119–20; in common law, 106; damages
 in, 122; defamatory, 142–43, 145; in
 Derbyshire County Council case, 145; in
 first *Sunday Times* case, 108; legal counsel
 on, 70; malicious, 141
Liberty of movement, 179; and immigration,
 88. *See also* Deprivation of liberty
Lilley, Peter, 104
Lingens v. Austria (1986), 107
Litigation, press coverage of, 110–14
Liversidge, Robert W., 46
Liversidge v. Anderson (1941), 47–48, 167
Local governments, British, 6
Lustgarten, L., 168
Lynch, Martin Henry, 50

Magna Carta, 2; family rights under, 151;
 Lord Scarman on, 133; violation of, 131
The Mail on Sunday, 122–23
Major, John, 170
Makarczyk, Judge, 55
*Malone v. Commission of Police of the
 Metropolis (no. 2)* (1979), 134
Malone v. United Kingdom (1984), 134–35

Manchester Corporation v. Williams (1891),
 119–20
Mapp v. Ohio, 7–8, 160
Margaret Murray v. United Kingdom (1994),
 54, 55–56, 60
Margin of appreciation: in *Brannigan and
 McBride*, 54; in *Brind* case, 122; in
 derogation cases, 55; in freedom of
 expression, 112–13, 117; in *Ireland v.
 United Kingdom*, 43
Marshall, Justice John, 59
Marxists, in IRA, 33
Matscher, Judge: career of, 25; dissents by, 22,
 24; on ECHR, 29–30
Maugham, Viscount, 47, 48
"Maxwell, the Musical," 124
Maxwell v. United Kingdom (1995), 17
McBride (plaintiff), 54
McCallum v. the United Kingdom (1990), 77
McCann, Danny, 56, 57
McCann and Others v. United Kingdom
 (1995), 18, 31, 56–57
McComb v. United Kingdom (1986), 78
*McKee v. Chief Constable for Northern
 Ireland* (1984), 51, 53, 168
McMichael v. United Kingdom (1995), 17
McNair, Lord, 27
McNeil, Hector, 60
Megarry, Vice Chancellor, 134
Mental Health Acts, 127
*Michael M. v. Superior Court of Sonoma
 County* (1981), 92
*Mistry v. The Entry Clearance Officer,
 Bombay* (1975), 133–34, 149
Moustaquim v. Belgium (1991), 136–37
Murray, Anthony, 129–30
Murray, John, 18
Murray, Margaret, 54, 55–56, 181n4
Mustill, Lord, 135, 137, 138
M v. H and Others (1988), 137

National Council on Civil Liberties, 69
Nationality, 1, 2, 82–86, 126; in ECHR, 88;
 gender discrimination in, 90; in U.S.
 constitutional law, 161–62. *See also* British
 Nationality Act; Immigration
National security, 2, 176, 177; in *Chahal
 Family v. United Kingdom*, 103, 168; and

National security—*continued*
   freedom of the press, 118; in *Ireland v.
   United Kingdom,* 43; Lord Denning on,
   168–69; and Supreme Court, 158–59; and
   terrorism, 158; in World War II, 60
National Union of Journalists, 122
Near v. Minnesota (1931), 118, 121, 162
Neill, Lord Justice, 122
Newspapers, British: coverage of litigation,
   110–14; for homosexuals, 140–41;
   prisoners' access to, 75; on *Spycatcher,* 114.
   See also Freedom of the press
New York Times v. Sullivan (1964), 120, 162
New York Times v. U.S. (1971), 118, 162
Nicol, A., 82, 83, 87
Nielsen v. Denmark (1988), 25
Noise, torture by, 37, 44
Nonpatrials, 84, 85; in *East African Asians v.
   United Kingdom,* 86; spouses of, 89–93,
   133
Northern Ireland, ix; British rule in, 35, 39,
   42; class conflict in, 33; peace talks in, 62–
   63; prevention of terrorism in, 1, 31–45,
   48–49, 50, 51, 153, 158, 163; religious
   conflict in, 32, 33; restraint of broadcasting
   on, 122. *See also Ireland v. United
   Kingdom*
Northern Ireland: The Choice (Boyle and
   Hadden), 33
Northern Ireland cases, 30; derogation in, 55
Northern Ireland Civil Rights Association
   (NICRA), 30, 33
Northern Ireland (Emergency Provisions) Act
   1978, 51; Baker report on, 52–53
Northern Ireland (Emergency Provisions)
   Amendment 1975, 39, 40; habeas corpus
   under, 50
Northern Ireland (Temporary Provisions)
   Acts: of 1972, 39; of 1987, 53–54, 58

*The Observer and Guardian v. United
   Kingdom* (1991), 17, 114–19, 144;
   interlocutory injunctions in, 118. *See also
   Spycatcher* cases
*L'Office Cherifien des Phosphates v.
   Yamashita-Shinnihon Steamship Co.*
   (1993), 132–33, 151
Official Secrets Act, 83

Operation Demetrius (1971), 36–37, 60
Oyston, Owen, 119

Packer, Herbert, 64–65
Paisley, Ian, 33
Palm, Judge Elizabeth, 26
*Pan-American World Airways v. Department
   of Trade* (1975), 149
Parachute Regiment (Great Britain), 33
Parental rights. *See* Family rights
Parker Report, 37–38, 40, 58
Parliament, ix; accountability of government
   to, 164–65, 170–71; delegation of power, 7;
   ombudsman office, 165; Opposition in, 170;
   power structure of, 3–6; sovereignty
   tradition of, 172
Patrials: in British Nationality Act, 85–86, 89;
   definition of, 84–85
Peaceful enjoyment of possessions, 20, 179
Pederson, Judge Inger Helga, 26
Pekkanen, Judge Raimo, 26
Penal codes: conflicts among, 79; *credos* of,
   64–65, 79–81; justice in, 80, 81; of Soviet
   Union, 34
Pentagon Papers case, 118, 162
Permanent Court of Arbitration, 27
Pettiti, Judge Louis-Edmund: career of, 25, 28;
   on derogation, 55; dissents by, 22, 26, 119
Phillimore Committee on Contempt of Court,
   113
*Pickering v. Liverpool Daily Post and Echo
   Newspapers plc and Others* (1991), 127
Pinheiro Farinha, Judge, 22
Plyler v. Doe (1982), 161
Political correctness, 143–44
Political parties, British: evolution of, 3–4,
   165; patronage in, 4–5
The Politics of the Judiciary (Griffith), 172
Pollock, Sir Frederick, 47
Potts, Judge, 102, 103, 168
Powell, Enoch, 5, 6, 84
Powell v. Alabama (1932), 7
Press Complaints Commission, 124
Presumption of innocence, 129
Prevention of Terrorism Acts, 100
Prevention of Terrorism (Temporary
   Provisions) Acts: of 1976, 50; of 1984, 48–
   49, 51; of 1989, 39

Prior restraint, 118; in common law, 121, 125, 151; Supreme Court's use of, 7, 118

Prior ventilation (of prisoners' complaints), 69–70, 71, 171; in *Campbell and Fell*, 74–75; unlawfulness of, 76

Prison Act of 1952, 75

Prison Department: change in, 80–81; secrecy in, 79, 80, 81

Prisoners: disciplinary proceedings against, 73; freedom of expression for, 75

Prisoners' rights, 1–2, 9, 64, 109, 126, 153; access to justice as, 67–68; administrative discretion in, 164; under common law, 72; to correspondence, 71–73, 74, 76, 77–79, 129, 153; to counsel, 66, 69–72; before European Commission and Court, 9, 65–79; home secretary on, 131; to privacy, 78, 79. *See also* Right to counsel

Prison riots, 73, 75, 81

Prison Rules (1964), 66

Prisons (Scotland) Act 1952, 77

Prison system, American: due process in, 160–61

Privacy rights: of consenting homosexuals, 30, 137–38, 153; dissent in European Court, 21; under ECHR, 10, 30, 176; for prisoners, 78, 79; and public policy, 151; violations of ECHR in, 18, 19; wiretapping and, 134, 137

Promptness of trial, 20, 176; in *Brogan and Others*, 49

Proportionality, in ECHR, 167

Proposition 187 (California), 161

Protection of Life and Property (Ireland) Act 1871, 46

Protestants, of Northern Ireland, 32, 33–34

Protocol No. 1 (ECHR), 20, 179

Protocol No. 4 (ECHR), 179; ratification of, 91. *See also* Liberty of movement

Protocol No. 11 (ECHR), 16

Protocol Relating to the Status of Refugees (1966), 94

Provos (Provisional IRA), 33–34

"Queen's peace," enforcement of, 7

R. v. Brown and other appeals (1993), 132, 137, 151

R. v. Canons Park Mental Health Review Tribunal, ex parte A (1993), 127

R. v. Chief Immigration Officer, Heathrow Airport, ex parte Salamat Bibi (1980), 134, 136, 149, 152

R. v. Chief Metropolitan Stipendiary Magistrate, ex parte Choudhury (1990), 141, 142, 145

R. v. Gay News Ltd. (1978), 140, 141

R. v. General Medical Council, ex parte Colman (1989), 144

R. v. Governor of Pentonville Prison, ex parte Chinoy (1990), 137

R. v. Home Secretary, ex parte Anderson (1983), 75, 76

R. v. Home Secretary, ex parte Bhajan Singh (1975), 100, 148–49

R. v. Home Secretary, ex parte Brind (1991), 157; European Commission on, 122; judicial review in, 103, 121, 167; reference to ECHR in, 100, 101, 102, 127, 131, 144, 150

R. v. Home Secretary, ex parte Chahal (1993), 102, 168

R. v. Home Secretary, ex parte Jeyakumaran (1985), 101

R. v. Home Secretary, ex parte K (1990), 127

R. v. Home Secretary, ex parte Phansopkar and Others (1975), 84–85, 149, 151

R. v. Home Secretary, ex parte Sivakumaran et al. (1988), 94–95, 96

R. v. Home Secretary, ex parte Tarrant (1983), 73, 129

R. v. Immigration Appeal Tribunal, ex parte Chundawadra (1987), 136, 137, 149

R. v. Lemon (1978), 140, 141

R. v. Preston and Others (1993), 135

R. v. Redbourne (1992), 132

R. v. United Kingdom (1987), 130–31, 137

Race Relations Bill 1968, 84

Racial discrimination, 178; and immigration, 85, 86, 88, 93

Radical Alternatives to Prison (RAP), 69–70

Rantzen v. Mirror Group of Newspapers (1993), 122, 145, 151

Raymond v. Honey (1983), 76, 128–29, 151

Reading, Lord, 168

Reed, John Michael, 70–71

Reed v. United Kingdom (1981), 70–71, 75

Reform Act of 1832, 3

Refugees: expulsion of, 102; U.N. procedures on, 94–95, 97, 101. *See also* Aliens; Immigration

Refugees, Tamil, 94–97, 103; home secretary on, 98

Reid, Lord, 111

Re K D (1988), 131, 137

Renteln, A., 8

Representation of People Act 1884, 3

Republic of Ireland, ix. *See also Ireland v. United Kingdom*

Restoration of Order in Ireland Act 1920, 46

Rights, derogable, 8–9

Right to counsel: in *Campbell v. United Kingdom*, 78–79, 129; in common law, 151; in *Guilfoyle v. Home Office*, 128; in *John Murray v. United Kingdom*, 57, 58, 181n4; for prisoners, 66, 68, 69–72, 129; in United States, 7

Right to liberty. *See* Deprivation of liberty

Right to life, 31, 174

Right to silence: in *John Murray v. United Kingdom*, 57–58, 60–61, 181n4; limitations on, 129

Roosevelt, Eleanor, 28

Rose, Richard, 33

Roskill, Lord Justice, 51, 134, 149

Rossiter, Clinton, 47

"Royal prerogative" (of home secretary), 7

Royal Ulster Constabulary (RUC), 33, 34, 42; arrests by, 35

Ruiz v. Estelle (1986), 160

Rushdie, Salman, 141, 142, 145

Russo, Judge, 119

Rutherford, Andrew, 64–65, 80

Ryssdal, Judge Rolv, 13, 26

Satanic verses (Rushdie), 141, 142

Savage, Sean, 56, 57

Scarman, Lord: advocacy of constitution, 171; on applicability of ECHR, 149; dissents by, 130, 152; on first *Sunday Times* case, 120–21; on freedom of expression, 141–42; on freedom of religion, 139, 140; on *Gleaves v. Deakin*, 130; on immigration, 133

Schenk v. Switzerland (1988), 25

Schering Chemicals Ltd. v. Falkman Ltd. (1981), 121, 143

Scotland: legal system of, ix; Prisons Act, 77

Secrecy: in British government, 3, 6, 60, 83, 163; and control of immigration, 83; effect on human rights, 163–64; in Prison Department, 79, 80, 81

Securing of rights, in *Ireland v. United Kingdom*, 38

Security of person, 175; dissent in ECHR cases, 25; ECHR references to, 126–29

Segregation: challenges to, 86; legal constitution of, 157

Servitude, in *Ireland v. United Kingdom*, 39

Shapiro v. Thompson (1969), 160

"Shuttlecocking" (of immigrants), 88

Silver and Others v. United Kingdom (1983), 71–73, 74, 80; citations to, 75; correspondence rules in, 76

Simpson, Brian, 45

Simultaneous ventilation (of prisoners' complaints), 71, 72, 171; in *Campbell and Fell*, 74; in *Grace v. United Kingdom*, 77; as violation of ECHR, 75–76

Singapore, criminal procedure in, 129

Singh, Bhajan, 100, 148

Sinhalese, of Sri Lanka, 95, 97

Slavery, 86, 175; in *Ireland v. United Kingdom*, 39

Sleep deprivation, 37, 44

Slynn, Lord, 137, 138

Soering case (1989), 156

Soviet Union: demise of, 123; penal code of, 34

Spain, violations of ECHR, 19, 22

Special Air Service, 56

Spielman, Judge: career of, 25; dissents by, 22, 26

Spotlight (BBC program), 57

Spycatcher cases, 144; and British Security Service, 107–8, 114–18; confidentiality in, 118; freedom of expression in, 114–19; House of Lords on, 115, 116–18, 121; Lord Bridge on, 117; and U.S. constitutional law, 162

Sri Lanka: refugees from, 94–97, 104; Tamil conflict in, 97–98

Staughton, Lord Justice, 103, 131

Stern, Vivien, 64, 80, 81

Stone, Alec, 29

Strangeways Prison rights, 81

Strossen, Nadine, 30

The Sunday Times v. United Kingdom (No. 1) (1979), 108, 110–14, 141; dissent in, 24; European Commission on, 111; prior restraint in, 118

The Sunday Times v. United Kingdom (No. 2) (1991), 17, 107–8, 114–19, 144. *See also* *Spycatcher* cases

Sunkin, Maurice, 166, 169

Supreme Court, U.S.: on capital punishment, 156; civil rights in, 157; in *ex parte Milligan*, 158; on gender discrimination, 92; human rights issues in, 7–8, 30; judicial review by, 59; law clerks in, 15; nationality in, 161; on national security, 158–59; on prior restraints, 7, 118; privacy rights in, 156; qualification for, 28, 29; segregation cases before, 86

Suspicion, reasonable, 53, 55–56, 60

Switzerland, violations of ECHR, 19

Tamil liberation groups, 97, 104

Taylor, Justice, 149

Taylor, Laurie, 69–70, 79

Taylor v. Co-operative Retail Services Ltd. (1982), 147–48

Teitgen, Pierre-Henri, 28

Templeman, Lord, 101, 137

ten Kate, Jan, 27–28

Terrorism: cases before ECHR, 18, 31–45, 126; and confidentiality, 53, 54–55; definition under Emergency Provisions Act, 52; in *Ireland v. United Kingdom*, 32; by Loyalists, 43; objectivity in, 53; Sikh, 102; and threats to national security, 158

Thalidomide controversy, 107, 110–11, 113, 141

Thatcher, Margaret, 165

Theater, censorship of, 124

Thynne, Wilson and Gunnell v. United Kingdom (1990), 17

The Times, on internment, 62, 63

Times Newspaper Group, 106, 113

Times Newspapers Ltd. and Others v. United Kingdom (1984), 114

Tinker v. Des Moines (1969), 160

Toll v. Moreno (1982), 161

Tolstoy Miloslavsky v. United Kingdom (1995), 17, 107, 122; damages in, 123

Torture, 175; European Court on, 42; political asylum from, 98; U.N. convention against, 102; universal prohibitions against, 8. *See also* "Five techniques"

Trades Union Congress, 146, 147

Trial by jury, Diplock Commission on, 36

"Troubles" (Northern Ireland), 32–34; British army in, 34; emergency regulations during, 34–37; Phase I of, 33–36, 39; Phase II-II of, 39

Turpin, Colin, 170

T v. United Kingdom (1986), 74

Tyrer case, 153

Ulster Volunteer Forces, 33

United Kingdom: accountability of officials, 3–4, 163–71; account of Gibraltar killings, 57; adherence to ECHR, 8; asylum in, 2; attitude toward human rights, 109; bill of rights for, 3, 10, 156, 157, 165, 171–73; common law tradition of, ix; complaints of Ireland against, 38, 39–40; constitutional issues in, 3, 108, 171–73; countries comprising, ix; derogation in *Brannigan and McBride*, 54–55, 60; derogation in *Brogan and Others*, 49, 51, 54, 59; derogation in *Ireland v. United Kingdom*, 18, 38, 40, 41, 42, 44, 48; discretion of officials in, 3–4, 82, 94–95, 99, 163–71; franchise in, 59; human rights record of, 7, 163; liberal traditions of, 153; ministers of state, 6; racial discrimination in, 85, 86, 88; ratification of ECHR, 60; and ratification of Fourth Protocol, 91; response to *Ireland v. United Kingdom*, 18, 38, 40, 41, 42; right of entry into, 85–86; secrecy in government of, 3, 6, 60, 83, 163; self-restraint of officials in, 3; Standing Advisory Commission on Human Rights, 62; use of emergency powers, 34–37, 39, 40, 43, 45–58, 59; use of "five techniques," 37, 38, 39,

United Kingdom—*continued*
   41, 58; violations of ECHR, ix, 1–2, 16–20,
   154–56, 163, table 8.1. *See also* Common
   law, English; Judicial review, British;
   Judicial system, British
United Kingdom-and-Colonies, rights of
   citizens in, 84, 85–89. *See also* CUKCs
*United Kingdom Association of Professional
   Engineers v. Advisory Conciliation and
   Arbitration Service* (1979), 145–46, 151
United Nations: Convention against Torture,
   102; High Commission for Refugees, 94–
   95, 97, 101
United States: alienage laws in, 161–62; due
   process in, 156; human rights in, 7–8, 163.
   See also Bill of Rights; Constitution;
   Judicial review, American; Prison system,
   American; Supreme Court, U.S.
United States v. Carolene Products Co.
   (1938), 7, 113
Universal Declaration of Human Rights
   (1948), 1, 27, 28; in ECHR, 174; formula-
   tion of, 61; freedom of conscience in, 143;
   ratification of, 8
The Uses of Discretion (Keith), 169

Ventilation. *See* Prior ventilation; Simulta-
   neous ventilation
Vilhjálmsson, Judge, 22
Vilvarajah, Nadarajah, 95–97, 98
Vilvarajah and Others v. United Kingdom
   (1991), 95–99, 101, 104; dissent in, 103

Waller, Lord Justice, 135

Wall-standing, 37, 44
Walsh, Judge, 55
Watkins, Lord Justice, 136
Wednesbury principles, 99, 135, 157; on
   immigration, 138–39; judicial accountabil-
   ity under, 166–67; judicial assertiveness
   under, 169; and restrain of broadcasting,
   122; in *Vilvarajah* case, 103. *See also*
   Judicial review, British
Welch v. United Kingdom (1995), 17
Welfare policy, American, 160
Wheeler v. Leicester City Council (1985), 143,
   151
Wickham, David, 79–80
Wilberforce, Lord, 129
Wilson, Harold, 108
Wiretapping, 134, 137
Witnesses, intimidation of, 38
Wives, nonpatrial, 90, 94, 133
Woolf, Lord Justice, 81
World War II: due process during, 158;
   emergency powers during, 45, 59; national
   security during, 60, 158–60
Wright, Peter, 107–8. *See also Spycatcher*
   cases
Wynne v. Home Secretary (1993), 131–32

X v. United Kingdom (1981), 126–28

Yick Wo v. Hopkins (1886), 161
Young, James and Webster v. United Kingdom
   (1981), 20, 146
Younger, Kenneth, 61

Donald W. Jackson is Herman Brown Professor of Political Science at Texas Christian University and author of a number of books, most recently *Even the Children of Strangers: Equality under the U.S. Constitution* (1992) and *Presidential Leadership and Civil Rights Policy* (coedited with James W. Riddlesperger, Jr., 1995).